THE STRONGMAN

A TRUE LIFE
PICTORIAL AUTOBIOGRAPHY OF
THE HERCULES OF THE SCREEN
JOE BONOMO

352 THRILLING PAGES AND OVER **750** ACTION PHOTOS

THE BOOK TO TOP ALL BOOKS ABOUT THE MOVIES!

CREDITS

Editor-in-Chief & Design Supervisor
SAMUEL M. SHERMAN

Story Editor
EUGENE CONRAD

Art Director
TONY GARCIA

Special Photography
TONY BRUNO (Bruno of Hollywood)

Color Cover Design
TED ESHBAUGH

Editorial Consultant
RUTH RIVA SHERMAN

Stunt Research
HARVEY PARRY

Studio Research
CLINTON MARTIN

Production Secretary
B. HOMEWOOD

This book illustrated from the extensive photo library of Bonomo Studios Inc.

Additional Acknowledgments—Universal Pictures Co. Inc., Paramount Pictures Corp., New York Daily News, New York Public Library, Alan G. Barbour, Paul Malvern.

Type— MARTIN CO.   Veloxes— SCREEN-O-MATIC DOTS
Photo Services— ADAMS PHOTOPRINT CO. INC.

PRINTED IN THE UNITED STATES OF AMERICA By J.W. CLEMENT CO.
Special Color Jackets by GENERAL OFFSET PRINTING

Copyright © MCMLXVIII JOE BONOMO   Published by BONOMO STUDIOS INC.
1841 Broadway New York, New York 10023

Dedication

To my old friends and comrades of those early days in New York and Hollywood—to the great strongmen, boxing and wrestling champions of the world, who shared their secrets with me and taught me the rules and values of clean living—to such men as Charles Atlas and Earl Lederman, Jack Dempsey, George Bothner, the late Bernarr Macfadden and Warren Lincoln Travis, who gave me both their counsel and their friendship—to Carl Laemmle, Cecil B. De Mille and the many other studio heads, publicity men, producers and directors whose belief in me and invaluable advice and help made success possible—to those unsung heroes whose names appear more often on obituary lists than on screen; those intrepid souls who risk life and limb to provide the thrills for moviegoers, the stuntmen, past and present—and finally to the multitudes of movie fans without whose support my career would have died aborning—to all of these this book is devotedly dedicated.

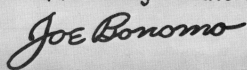

Joe Bonomo

CONTENTS

CONTENTS

Chapter #1

Joe Bonomo TAKE #1

LIKE A LOT OF PEOPLE, all my life I've wanted to write a book, but I never intended it should be about **me.** Now that I'm faced with that prospect it's slightly frightening, for the story of my life is going to make such a crazy, mixed up, impossible sounding affair that you either won't believe it and catalogue me as a congenital liar—or you **will** believe it and recommend me for psychiatric treatment. However, it's too late now, I'm committed to it, so move up to the edge of your chair, get a firm grip on your nervous system and hold onto your hat.

Of course, this tome may never see the light of day for I have one great advantage over most book writers. When it's completed, if I don't like it, I can always wrap it in a telephone directory and tear it into confetti with my bare hands.

I think very few of us ever achieve our childhood ambitions. In this uncertain world the "road of growing up" is too filled with unexpected detours and compromises for a girl or boy to follow a direct line to that distant star to which they have hitched their wagon. And it may be all for the best or we'd surely have an oversupply of trained nurses, airline stewardesses, policemen, firemen and United States' presidents. I guess I could have had a more laudible ambition, but the important thing is that I eventually achieved the goal that, as a small boy, I had set my heart on—to someday be known as the strongest man in the world—which, you will admit, with some three billion humans cluttering up the earth, was taking on fairly long odds.

I don't flatter myself that the realization of my early ambitions was evidence of any exceptional talent. As you will soon learn I was far from being a child prodigy and even today my I.Q. will not stand too close inspection. But I knew what I wanted, I had "the will to win,"

and I was willing to pay the price in hard work and self denial. So armed, there are few doors that will not open to you . . . and if you pursue your goal relentlessly, no matter how far out of reach it may seem, if it is at all within the realm of possibility, you can attain it.

As so often happens, the achieving of my original goal was merely a beginning that led me into a many faceted career fraught with thrills, danger and accomplishments far beyond my early imaginings. It eventually led me into an acting career in motion pictures, but on the way up I spent several years in what is perhaps the world's most dangerous profession . . . that of a motion picture stuntman.

As I look back to the countless times I have, of my own volition, teetered on the slippery Brink of Eternity, the thirty seven bones I've had broken, the weary months I've spent in hospital beds, the hairbreadth brushes I've had with certain death . . . I wonder if a more apt title for this story might not be "The Memoirs of a Blooming Idiot." For in retrospect it seems that no one, in his right mind, would pursue such a profession. By actual count I've had my right arm broken in eleven different places and my right leg broken four times. However, my luck wasn't ALL bad—my left arm was broken only twice and my left leg just once. I had eleven foot bones broken, sixteen cracked or broken ribs, seven fingers broken, one broken hip and seven dislocated spinal discs. Yet I know, with full knowledge of all the hazards, I'd do it all over again.

In good conscience I can't recommend such a career to those of you who want to be good insurance risks or wish to some day bask in the benificence of Social Security . . . but until you have made mortal danger your constant companion . . . until you have walked into the Jaws of Death, to leap out just as they snapped shut behind you, you haven't lived life to the fullest or felt the glorious thrill of merely being alive.

But to take a step backward, it was the reputation I built as a strongman that made everything that followed possible. Even before I had reached full maturity I had bested all competition and was being hailed as the strongest man in the world. Like "The Village Blacksmith" the muscles in my brawny arms stood out like iron bands,

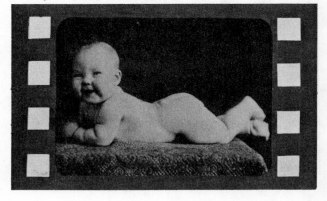

Age: 3 months

only I went that famed blacksmith one better and used to **wind** iron bands around them like so much Scotch tape. I would twist iron pipe into the letters of the alphabet and, with one good grunt, straighten out a horse-shoe, bend a railroad spike double and crush a large raw potato in one hand. (Just try that one sometime.)

With a harness lift I could easily pick up full size automobiles, weighing between two and three thousand pounds, and then repeat the lift when they were filled with passengers. In a support lift I would raise steel bars over my head with three large men suspended from each end . . . and perform dozens of other feats of strength that left my audiences gasping in unbelief and amazement.

But when you have such enormous strength, such things are not amazing to YOU. There is little thrill in repeatedly doing what you know you CAN do, even though others may find it vastly beyond them. Once you know you can drive a steel spike through a two inch plank with one blow of your fist, it seems a bit silly not to use a sledge-hammer. It would be a lot easier on the hands. Also, like "the fastest gun in the West," you have to keep proving your prowess to every pseudo strongman whose home-town rooters have told him he was the greatest . . . and that gets monotonous, too.

I used to think how tired a side-show giant must get of BEING a giant. It could have been fun growing up, but once he's up there, he spends the rest of his life just being gawked at and

Age: 3 years

trying to find clothes and beds that fit him.

Well, you can get just as tired of being the strongest man in the world. It's wonderfully satisfying at first, but with my temperament, when the novelty has worn off, you start longing for new thrills, something dangerously exciting, that will send your blood racing through your veins.

Where's the connection between this and the tightrope of danger I was eventually destined to walk? Perhaps I'd best start at the very beginning where perhaps I should have started in the first place.

I wish I could say that I was born on Mount Olympus, the abode of the gods. The infant who was someday to be proclaimed as "The Modern Apollo" should have had a godlike background. But either the Stork who brought me had never read ancient history or he had a twisted sense of humor, for he dropped me off at, of all places, Coney Island. (Somehow you never think of anyone being BORN in Coney Island.)

Of course there's a reason for everything, and Coney Island got into the act by way of Istanbul, Turkey. My sainted father, Albert J. Bonomo, a Spanish Turk, heard the siren call of America and migrated here. I've always said that in passing the Statue of Liberty he mistook Miss Liberty's torch for an ice cream cone and figured that must be the national industry, for he headed straight for Coney Island and went into the business. It wasn't long before Bonomo's Ice Cream and Ice Cream Cones were known far and wide, eventually becoming a part of the Coney Island tradition.

7

Then one day he met a little French girl, Esther Judka, and from the first moment he couldn't get her out of his mind. He kept telling himself he was building a new business in a strange land, that he had no time for foolishness such as love, but her great dark eyes and enchanting smile kept haunting him. He learned that she and her father had a little candy factory where they made a superior type of French candy, so one day he dropped by to sample the product . . . and the next day . . . and the next. I think Fate then decided that between his ice cream and her candy they had a common mission to add poundage to the human form divine, for soon they joined hands and forces to add to the caloric output. They took two days off . . . one for their wedding and one for their honeymoon . . . and then went back to work again. No two people were ever busier but I doubt that any couple were ever happier. Eventually my brother Victor came along and three years later, on Christmas day 1901, during a raging blizzard, the Stork staggered in with little Joe.

While I am discussing my family background, there is an angle of heredity that may have had some bearing on my later abnormal physical development. My great uncle, on my father's side, was Yousiff Hussane, famous around the turn of the century as "The Terrible Turk" of wrestling. His story is a tragic one but I recount it for the moral lesson involved.

Uncle Yousiff was a champion wrestler and a man of enormous strength. He made big money in the wrestling profession, but for reasons known only to himself, he trusted neither people nor banks. He always insisted on being paid off in gold pieces which he carried about with him in a money belt strapped around his middle . . . a belt that never left his person. He figured that anyone would have to overpower him to rob him and no one was strong enough to do **that**. He even wore that leather money belt while wrestling, sleeping, even in the bathtub. Being such a huge and powerful man he seemed not to notice its increasing weight as he gradually assumed the status of a miniature Fort Knox.

But ironically, his love for gold, coupled with his mistrust of his fellow man, became his undoing. He had the misfortune of being on the S.S. La Bourgoyne when, during a violent storm, it foundered and went down in the Atlantic. Seeing there were more passengers than there were lifeboats to accommodate them, he gallantly went over the side of the sinking ship. He was a powerful swimmer and rescue was close at hand, but his moneybelt, with its fortune in gold pieces, was like an anchor dragging him down. He merely had to discard it and his rescue would have been assured, but rather than part with his precious gold he chose to go with it to a watery grave. I think I learned a great lesson from that, for to me, the accumulation of money has always been a secondary consideration.

Chapter #2

"MAMA WAS A WONDERFUL COOK"

THE MAN WHO WROTE "There is No Place Like Home" never knew the Bonomos, but he SHOULD have . . . for assuredly there was never a place like OUR home. We had a large three-story house with an ice cream and candy factory on the first floor, the Bonomo domicile on the second floor and a dormitory that housed thirty odd workers on the third floor. During the Coney Island summer season the place was a veritable beehive of industry. Papa was an indefatigable worker and set a furious pace that all of us had to match. We worked early and late and seven days a week. Though still small boys, Victor and I had to lend a hand and Mama, who did all the cooking, seemed to turn out about 120 meals every day.

But with the end of summer the crowds of pleasure seekers dwindled to a handful and Coney Island pulled a blanket of sand over its gaudy head and went into hibernation until the following Spring. Fortunately, by this time, Papa had always made enough money to live comfortably and leisurely for the rest of the year.

With little to do in the off season, Papa, who incidentally spoke seven languages, became a "joiner," belonging to all the clubs and societies he could find. He joined the Masons, the Elks, the Italian-American Club, the Greek-American Club and a half dozen others. And I'll never know how he rationalized it but he belonged to four different churches. Papa really spread himself around.

Mama and Papa also loved to entertain and an evening at the Bonomo home resembled a meeting of the United Nations, for good friends were welcome regardless of faith or nationality. The Bonomo way of life included a philosophy which respected the right of every man to worship his God in his own way. A man's good character was his passport and his religious beliefs or politics were never questioned. But had a stranger dropped in while conversation was at full volume he might well have wondered if he had blundered into a modern Tower of Babel, for Papa seemed to be able to carry on conversations in several languages at once, without a moment's slowdown to shift linguistic gears.

But as conversational as Papa was he disapproved too much conversation from us children and he had his own way of making a point. Once when he thought I was talking too much he took me by the arm and marched me up to a mirror saying "When you look at yourself what do you see?" Before I had a chance to answer he said "You see two ears and two eyes but only one mouth. Your Creator wanted you to hear a lot and see a lot. If He had wanted you to talk a lot. He'd have given you a second mouth, too." And if there IS such a thing as a dual personality Papa had it. Socially there wasn't a more popular or better liked man in Coney Island, but when it came to business he was a relentless driver and a hard man to tangle with.

By way of contrast, Mama was a soft-spoken gentle woman who lived for her husband, her children and her home—and had her wonderful cooking to keep her busy. Our workers were Turks, Spaniards, Italians and Greeks and Mama had her own system for making them feel at home and keeping them happy. She would have Turkish meals one day, Spanish meals the next, then Italian, then Greek. If there was ever any dissatisfaction in the heart of a worker, it was forgotten after one of her wonderful dinners. Other ice cream and candy makers at Coney Island may have had labor troubles, but not the Bonomos. We always got the pick of the men and kept them all season long. Mama was a wonderful cook!

The scene was the ocean off Coney Island, on a late midsummer afternoon, when I was just eight years old. With my canoe tied to my waist, I was swimming out to sea . . . away from the noise of the merry-go-rounds and the rides and the other kids and their fun. To heck with 'em, I thought. They don't like me and I don't like them, so to heck with 'em. I'd like to see any of 'em swim like this. "Toothpicks," huh? Well, maybe I **am** skinny, but one thing I can do is swim . . . better'n any of 'em . . . better even than my brother Victor. To heck with Victor, too. To heck with everybody. Me and Babe we'll stick together and they can all go fly a kite!

Mama, Papa, Victor and "little Joe."

I glanced over my shoulder to see Babe, my beachcomber pup, paddling valiantly along behind me. I wish I could drown, I thought. They wouldn't make fun of me THEN. Maybe tomorrow I'll leave the canoe on the beach and just keep swimming out until—then I heard a whimpering behind me. No, I couldn't do that to Babe. He didn't laugh at me . . . he was my friend. But as for the rest of 'em . . . they could all go fly a kite.

I pulled the canoe up and climbed in, dragging Babe in after me. He shook himself, then sat down quivering, tuckered out, trying to catch his breath. I looked at him a moment—a wet, bedraggled, panting little mongrel . . . too tired even to wag his tail . . . a sorry caricature of a dog. Me and Babe. What a pair!

What's wrong with this picture? The little boy who would someday become famous as "The Man Who Knows No Fear" . . . was already so afraid of life he almost didn't want to go on.

Fear is a devastating emotion that can paralyze both the body and the mind. I am sure all of us have, at some time, experienced it in one form or another. The fear of physical danger is common to all creatures, from the largest mastodon to the smallest of insects. In man, the reaction to this type of fear is unmistakable. The blood leaves the face, the muscles tense and grow taut, the perspiration glands work overtime, the pulse quickens and oft-times movement is impossible, which accounts for the expression "scared stiff." Fear must even generate an odor, for animals can sense the slightest feeling of fear in a human, as any lion tamer will attest. I have known jungle cats to turn on their trainer and tear him to pieces when, for just a split second, his courage failed him and fear crept in.

My fears were not of physical danger, but they were none the less real and poignant. To a little boy the fear of ridicule and derision from other children, for physical deficiencies over which he seemingly has no control, is soul chilling . . . and when I took stock of myself I realized, with sinking heart, that every laugh and jibe was justified. I know it's customary with professional strongmen, (even though they were so husky at birth the doctor almost hesitated to give them that first slap; and even though they started growing up as veritable butterballs) to claim they were skinny, puny living skeletons until the magic of physical culture came into their lives. Well, I wasn't exactly a living skeleton, but if you'd grown hair on me I could have passed for one of those spider monkeys you see in the zoo. My arms and legs were so thin you'd wonder they didn't break off. I wasn't called "Toothpicks" for nothing.

In consequence I became over-sensitive, self-conscious and withdrawn. My constant and abiding fear was of being openly ridiculed, shunted aside and laughed at by my fellows . . . and unfortunately children are often thoughtlessly, even though unintentionally, cruel. Small wonder that by the time I had reached my eighth birthday I had a well developed inferiority complex and a deep-seated, burning resentment toward other children and the world in general.

Like all little boys I wanted the companionship and the admiration of others and yet I was afraid to assert myself in any situation . . . afraid I would fail and be laughed at still more. I'd look at the other kids, including my brother Victor, and they were all bigger, stronger and more assured than I felt I could ever hope to be. They knew what to do . . . what to say. I would sit and listen and maybe think of something important, but be afraid to say it for fear they'd laugh—or think of something funny but be afraid to say **that** for fear they **wouldn't** laugh. I seldom joined in their games because I was seldom invited . . . and when I wasn't invited I was too proud and hurt to ask.

You'll admit this was a pretty tough situation for a little kid to try to work himself out of and hardly a propitious start along the road to fame and fortune.

But never underestimate a boy—or a girl, either, for that matter. Those little heads that on occasion seem so vacuous, may contain the seeds of genius. All the great names of history were once just little guys or gals, not too different from all the other little guys and gals in the world. But somewhere along the way of growing up, something triggered the intricate mechanism of their minds and they went on to scale the heights. I was never touched by the Magic Wand of Genius, but Fate gave me a nudge or two that jolted me out of my inhibitions, or rather, jolted my inhibitions out of ME.

In order to properly explain this I must tell you about my work . . . for even at the tender age of eight I was already quite a shrewd little businessman. Every day I would patrol the Coney Island beach with a basket of Bonomo's Salt-Water Taffy, hawking my wares in a high, shrill voice. I had never heard the word "blackmail," but I soon learned that if I lingered long enough in the vicinity of love-smitten young couples, who were trying to whisper sweet nothings into one-another's ears . . . and if I kept my voice at a sufficiently ear-piercing pitch . . . they'd quickly buy my taffy to be rid of me.

Soon, encouraged by the success of this "hush-money" angle, I conceived an even bolder scheme. I had noticed that many couples, when evening came, settled down on the darkened Coney Island beach for a little unobserved "smootching." So I cut up some large squares of newspaper, loaded my basket with jumbo size Hershey Almond Bars and, armed with a flash-light, started making my rounds. I'd wait until a couple of young lovers got nicely settled, then I'd shine my flash-light in their faces and say, "Jumbo Hershey Almond Bar, only a quarter." (The regular price was only ten cents but I figured the extra fifteen was cheap enough for an evening of privacy.) If they bought the bar I'd place it beside them on one of the squares of newspaper saying, "This will show me you're customers so I won't have to bother you again." Most of the time they'd just leave the bar on the paper so I'd be sure to stay away. If they didn't buy I'd be around again about every ten minutes, flashing a beam of light on them. After my second or third visitation they usually got the idea and gave in.

Mama and Papa, who knew nothing of the high pressure methods I had evolved, marveled at my success and wondered how I did it, but they weren't going to find out from ME. Papa was straight-laced about business and I had a feeling that if he found out I'd be the youngest retired business man in America.

I also observed that at many of the boardwalk refreshment stands, excursionists, clutching a couple of hot dogs or sandwiches in one hand while juggling ice cream or soda pop in the other, quite frequently dropped their change, some of which disappeared through the cracks of said boardwalk. I immediately started sifting the sand under these vantage points and as coin after coin came into view, I suddenly felt the thrill of the Klondike "sourdough" panning for gold. Then I became a bit smarter and spread newspapers under the boardwalk, which caught the coins as they fell, so all I had to do was scoop them up . . . which proved to be quite a labor-saving device.

As a little money-maker I was doing all right; but the praise I received from Mama and Papa was small comfort, for the kids still rejected me. I was an eight year old pariah . . . an outcast . . . and I used to cry myself to sleep wondering what I'd ever be able to do about it.

Coney Island's famed Luna Park, long gone from the scene. A great amusement center that has left many with treasured memories.

Chapter #3
The PAPERWEIGHT KID'S FIRST FIGHT—

CONEY ISLAND in those days was a tough place . . . the spawning ground of some of New York's worst hoodlums . . . and some of the kids were tough from the moment they could toddle. I was to learn that the hard way.

It happened during the same Summer I've just been talking about. With a full basket of taffy I started down the beach on my daily rounds when, just before reaching the more populated section, I passed a bunch of kids playing Johnny-On-A-Pony. I had never seen them before and I didn't like their looks, so I tried to hurry past them as though I hadn't noticed them. As I did, the largest boy in the group, a mean looking kid, snatched a handful of taffy from my basket.

"Thanks, pal," he said, giving me an evil grin, "charge this to my account."

The others began to crowd around and I felt there was going to be trouble, but this kind of trouble didn't scare me.

"You put that taffy back or pay for it," I said firmly.

"Sure I'll pay for it, pal . . . just send me a bill to my office." Then with a smirk he grabbed another handful and started passing it around to the others. I put my basket down and squared off, doubling up my skinny little fists.

"You just touch another piece if you dare," I said grimly, waving my fists in the air threateningly.

Even though he was larger and much heavier than I was, I wasn't afraid. I was to learn, later in life, that physical fear wasn't in my make up. Perhaps it should have been. It would have kept me out of a lot of subsequent trouble.

The bully leered at me in evident amusement as I continued to wave my fists about, trying to assume a pugilistic pose.

"We'd better be careful, guys," he said, "this may be John L. Sullivan, Junior." With that he gave me a surprise push and I went sprawling over another of the kids who had sneaked around and knelt down behind me. At that, another of them picked up my basket and emptied it in the sand.

At this a loud guffaw went up from the others and I suddenly saw red—I was being laughed at again. I jumped up and, swinging wildly, I went for the bully. I was going to see how tough he really **was**. As you have probably guessed it didn't take me long to find out.

When I finally picked up my basket and went home, crying more from humiliation than from the beating I had received, I had a bloody nose, two black eyes and hardly a spot on my body that didn't hurt. That big kid had punched me around until he was arm weary. As I stumbled into my mother's waiting arms I wondered if I'd ever be able to defend myself against the bullies of the world.

But that night I didn't cry myself to sleep. I lay in the darkness for at least an hour, with my little fists clenched again, trying to figure out a solution. When I finally fell asleep, I met that big kid again in my dreams and gave him the greatest beating of his life!

The following Fall found me back in school and marked the first turning point in my life. One day our entire class was taken on an educational tour of one of New York's great museums. We looked at things in glass cases and things hanging on the walls—and then we looked at more things in glass cases and more things hanging on the walls. Well . . . you know how museums are. After two or three hours of this, most of the kids had enough. So somebody started some "horse-play" and someone got hurt a little and started to cry. That was when our teacher, Miss Kennedy, and four guys from the museum who came out of the corners, all said "SH-H-H!" at the same time. And we all wondered what was the use of museums if you couldn't enjoy yourself in them.

Well anyway . . . after we'd been through about twenty big rooms, all of a sudden we came to a big statue.

"And this is a reproduction of the famous Apollo Belvedere," Miss Kennedy was saying. Then she talked about the statue for a while, but no one was paying attention so I guess they weren't much impressed. That is . . . nobody but me. Even now it is hard for me to explain what I felt as I looked up at that huge, perfectly proportioned figure. The promise of such strength beneath those rippling muscles . . . the poise . . . the grace . . . it almost took my breath away. I didn't hear what Miss Kennedy was saying any more. I just gaped in wonderment at that great statue . . . the most beautiful thing I had ever seen.

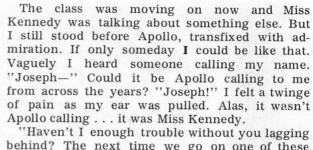

The class was moving on now and Miss Kennedy was talking about something else. But I still stood before Apollo, transfixed with admiration. If only someday **I** could be like that. Vaguely I heard someone calling my name. "Joseph—" Could it be Apollo calling to me from across the years? "Joseph!" I felt a twinge of pain as my ear was pulled. Alas, it wasn't Apollo calling . . . it was Miss Kennedy.

"Haven't I enough trouble without you lagging behind? The next time we go on one of these trips you'll be **left** behind!" She was pushing me ahead of her now and the class was laughing. Their laughter echoed and bounced back at me from all sides. I could feel my face flush with humiliation and the fear of further ridicule. I wanted to run away . . . to hide in one of those suits of armor I'd seen there.

The laughter finally stopped and Miss Kennedy was again droning on about something or other. The class moved along and I found myself at the tail end again. As they moved into the next room I turned and walked the other way. A moment later I was again before the statue of Apollo. I stood there for a long time, just marveling at his utter perfection, trying not to make a mental comparison between my scrawny little body and his wonderful physique. As I finally turned away hopelessly, there was Miss Kennedy, standing in the doorway, watching me curiously. I hurried over to her.

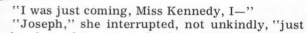

"I was just coming, Miss Kennedy, I—"

"Joseph," she interrupted, not unkindly, "just why does that statue fascinate you so?" Then without waiting for me to answer—"You'd like to be like Apollo when you grow up. Isn't that it?"

I didn't answer . . . I knew the thought was too ridiculous. I wasn't going to have Miss Kennedy laughing at me, too.

She put her hand on my shoulder and started walking me down the corridor.

"I have news for you, Joseph. Someday you CAN be like Apollo if you want to badly enough. We can be almost anything we want to be in life if we just try hard enough and are willing to pay the price. Never forget that, Joseph."

"No ma'am," I said. I thought Miss Kennedy was just trying to be kind . . . and probably she was . . . but her words stayed in my mind and I caught myself saying them over and over again. And I guess if you repeat something often enough you start to believe it. At first it glimmered as just a vague hope, but in time it crystallized into determination. I didn't know how, but impossible as it might seem, some day I WOULD be like Apollo.

Someone should erect a statue to the Miss Kennedys of the world . . . those forgotten women who have influenced so many lives for good and planted a seed of hope in so many faltering little hearts.

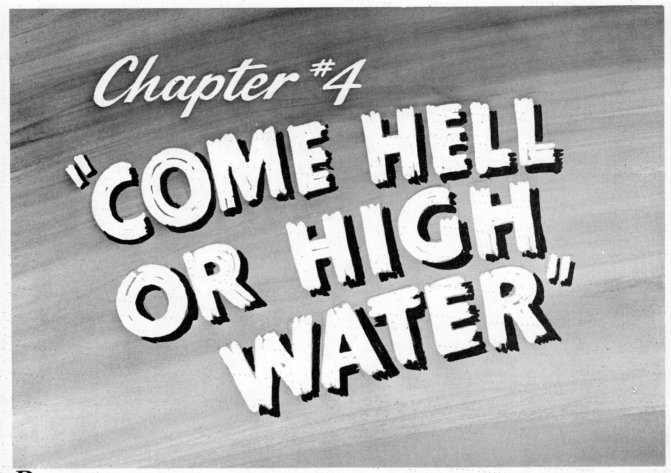

Chapter #4
"COME HELL OR HIGH WATER"

RESOLVE, I WAS TO LEARN, is half the battle. Much of the other half is will power. Determining what you want to do in life is difficult; but once that is established, the next step is an unshakeable resolve to DO it "come hell or high water." Then, assuming you are mentally and physically sound and possessed of normal intelligence, if you will faithfully hew to the line, there is no goal, within reason, that you cannot attain. It is my belief that the great majority of us are naturally endowed and equipped to achieve success IF we are willing to pay the price in "blood, sweat and tears," for the ascent to the pinnacle requires courage, fortitude, sacrifice and plenty of hard work.

Right now let's correct a popular fallacy. As my own case attests, you don't have to be a natural born superman to become a champion in sports or a world famous strongman. This has also been proven to me, hundreds of times, by men and women I have personally helped to develop. If you could have seen them when they started you would have shaken your head in dismay . . . yet some of these same men and women fought their way up to championship stature and today their names are part of the history of the sports world.

By the same rule you don't have to be born with that high an I.Q. to become a leader in the world of business, the arts or politics. Many of our outstanding business tycoons are not exceptionally brilliant . . . some of our most suc-

cessful actors, artists and literary figures are not over-burdened with brains . . . and many of our top political greats are hardly mental giants. Even many of our presidents were far from being in the genius category . . . few were voted "The boy most likely to succeed," in high-school or college.

What is it then that lifts a favored few, head and shoulders above the crowd? It is that they all have certain things in common—the resolve to succeed, the will to carry it through, the courage and stamina to face and overcome adversity and the willingness to pay the price of success . . . for only with these attributes can man hope to "emulate the gods."

Which brings us back, not only to a scared, skinny little guy named Bonomo, but to all the scared, skinny little guys in the world. They're not ALL wishing they were like Apollo . . . many of them never heard of Apollo and perhaps never will. Nor are they all wishing that someday they may be famous tycoons, actors or presidents . . . but I'll bet there's not one who doesn't secretly want to be big and strong and straight and fearless. And he can be ALL these things if he'll just make up his mind and then WORK at it.

I had made up my mind, but who could tell how to accomplish it or even where or how to begin. In those days there weren't the same opportunities for ambitious kids that there are today. There were no physical culture schools or even courses sold by mail. It would be years

Can you name these famous muscle men?

What fools these Mortals be!

Puck

THE COMIC WEEKLY

Little did I realize, as a youthful weakling, that many years later the Hearst organization would feature me as one of the greatest strongmen of the modern age, along with Sandow (center) and Louis Cyr (right).

before the famous Earl E. Lederman, Charles Atlas and others who came after them, would conceive the idea of body building schools and courses—and the renowned Vic Tanny was still a boy, destined to become a mathematics teacher long before he decided to devote his talents to developing HUMAN figures rather than figures on blackboards.

The strongmen of the world were all in circuses and carnivals, jealous of their powers and unwilling to reveal their secrets. I had the resolve and the will power, but you can't THINK yourself into muscles.

For a couple of months, not knowing WHAT to do, I spent most of my time just wishing. Then, as so often happens if you wish HARD enough and long enough, an unsuspected door suddenly opened.

It was a Saturday afternoon and I was selling some of Papa's taffy at the Coney Island side shows. But I didn't sell much taffy. Instead, I spent practically the entire day watching Ladislaw the Strongman. As is the way with these shows, his act went on about every ninety minutes and I wasn't missing a single performance . . . I didn't even go home for supper.

During his last intermission I went back to the circus wagon that was his dressing room. My basket of taffy on my arm, I climbed up the three steps at the back of the wagon, pushed open the door and peered timidly in.

Ladislaw was sprawled on a long couch, resting. He was wearing only a pair of trunks and some strange looking slippers. He was a huge Pole, a veritable giant of a man, fully six feet seven or eight, with a hairy body that seemed to be made up of nothing but bulging muscles that rippled and billowed with his every movement. He couldn't speak very good English but, luckily for me, he made up for that in a great good nature. If he had scowled at my intrusion, instead of grinning, despite my newformed resolutions I'm sure I should have taken off on the run. He reminded me of a huge bear. Gathering my courage I stepped inside.

"Want some taffy?" I asked in a slightly shaky voice.

"Sure t'ing, boy —Ladislaw like taffy."

His voice was an amiable rumble that seemed to come from deep down in his massive chest. I took a couple of faltering steps toward him and he reached into a battered tin box that was on a stand. From this he produced a coin which almost disappeared in the palm of the great hairy paw he stretched out to me . . . but I ignored this gesture.

"I don't want your money," I said . . . and reaching into my basket I dropped a large handfull of taffy into his still outstretched hand. Then I sat down on the edge of an oversized chair across from him and awaited developments. He slowly sat up, stripped the paper off a piece of the taffy and popped it into his mouth. He chomped on it noisily for about thirty seconds while he eyed me curiously. I was getting pretty uncomfortable. He suddenly swallowed with a loud gulp and pointed an oversized finger at me.

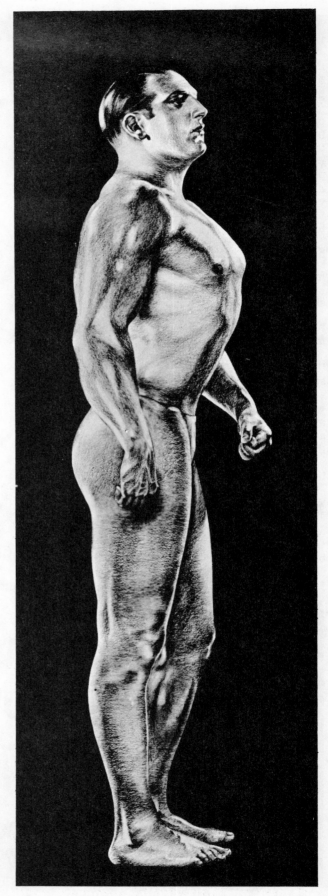

I dreamed of having the strength of Apollo.

"I see you 'round all day, boy," he said, "you no just vant to give Ladislaw taffy. Vot you vant, huh?"

"I want to be strong," I said. "I want to be like Apollo."

Ladislaw's shaggy brows came together in a puzzled frown.

"Apollo?" He seemed to be searching his memory. "This fella must be **new** strongman . . . but he not so strong like Ladislaw I betcha. Vere this fella come from?"

"Greece," I said. "He was the world's most perfect man."

"Jah?" Ladislaw was starting to bristle. "Dot's vot **he** t'inks."

He suddenly brought his fist down on the stand beside him and the whole wagon shook.

"If I get my hands on dis Greek I make him holler for help, I betcha."

The interview was getting out of hand and I hastened to explain.

"You don't understand . . . Apollo is only a statue . . . he isn't alive any more."

"That lucky for **him**," growled Ladislaw, flexing his muscles ominously. "Ladislaw most perfect man . . . strongest man in vorld."

"That's why I came here," I said earnestly. "Please, Mr. Ladislaw, tell me how I can be strong like you."

He stared at me a moment and suddenly roared with laughter. Then he reached over and pinched my little arms and roared again. It was like "Jack-and-the-Beanstalk" and he was the giant. But like little Jack, I stood my ground.

"I mean it," I said, "how can I get strong like you?"

"Vell—," he observed me for a moment, trying to conceal his amusement, then he shook his shaggy head. "You got to vait long time, boy— and vile you vait, eat like hell."

I suddenly snatched at the taffy in his hand but just as suddenly found my wrist in a vise-like grip.

"Vot you do, boy? You mad for me?"

"Well . . . if you won't tell me, I want my taffy back."

He chuckled, then suddenly sobered.

"You sure you vant be strong like Ladislaw?"

"More than anything in the world."

"Okay, boy." He picked me up without warning and threw me down on the couch. I didn't know what was going to happen but I'd asked for it and I wasn't going to "chicken out." His great fingers pinched my shoulders and arms.

"You see dot?" he was saying, "Liddle . . . like sticks. You got to make dem go like **diss**." He began to whip my arms back and forth.

"Oop—down. Oop—down—so."

Next my legs . . . then he flopped me over on my stomach and started bending me backwards and forwards, twisting me around in different directions, almost breaking me in pieces with his clumsy strength, showing me many exercises.

When he finally finished I felt as though I'd been trampled by a herd of wild buffalo . . . every bone in my body ached . . . but I had begun to get the idea.

I thanked him, gave him all the taffy in my basket and climbed painfully down the steps of the wagon. He followed me to the door.

"An' don't forget, boy," he shouted after me . . . "eat like hell!"

For the next year I ate as though the world's food supply was about to run out . . . and all my spare time was spent on the exercises he had shown me . . . so when the Carnival again arrived in Coney Island I rushed over to show Ladislaw the progress I had made, but there was another strongman working in his place.

"Gone back to Poland," the Fat Lady told me. "Made a barrel of money he did. Bought himself a castle in Warsaw."

I hoped he was happy. I owed him a lot.

An image a little closer to the real me: the kid everyone called "Toothpicks".

Chapter #5

"THE GREAT SANDOW"

I ALSO OWE MUCH to a man I never saw until many years later . . . one of the strongest men who ever lived . . . the great SANDOW. Perhaps a brief retelling of his story here may inspire other boys, as it once inspired **me**. Apollo was a mythical figure but Sandow was REAL— living proof that if I tried hard enough I could someday attain my goal.

Eugen Sandow was born in 1867, the son of a Prussian army captain. According to his memoirs he was also a "weak and puny" little boy. This festered within him, as it did in little Joe Bonomo, an unquenchable desire for strength. His practical father wanted him to learn a trade but Eugen was too engrossed in flexing his muscles and working out a system of body building that was to eventually turn him into a phenomenon of muscular power. As a result, at the age of 20 he claimed to have 18½ inch biceps, a 56 inch chest and believed himself to be the strongest man alive. However, few people had heard of him and nobody seemed to care. He realized what he needed was publicity.

At that time, in Amsterdam, the cafe owners used to have those "Test Your Strength" machines set up outside . . . the same type machine that we see, even today, in our Penny Arcades.

One morning one of the machines was found broken . . . the next morning another . . . and the following morning a third. Figuring some hoodlums must be responsible, the next evening the police set up a "stakeout" on the machines.

It wasn't long before a huskily built young fellow came strolling along, seized the handle of one of the undamaged machines and with apparently no effort smashed the machine into a tangled mass of wires, springs and broken wood. He was promptly arrested and admitted he was responsible for breaking all the machines.

"But," he said, "the sign said 'Test Your Strength' and that's all I was doing. Can I help it if I'm stronger than the machines are?" They released him with a lecture, but Sandow had made his point. The newspapers picked up the story and he got his publicity.

He now started wrestling, taking on all comers, even touring France and Italy, but no one could match his tremendous strength. Eventually he was taking on three wrestlers at a time and still winning every match. He was so strong he had to hold himself back, for he could break another wrestler's ribs with a single bear hug.

It was while wrestling in Italy that he heard of two "strength artists" who called themselves Samson and Cyclops. They were appearing in England and offering $5,000 to anyone who could match their feats of strength. Within a week, Sandow was in the front row of the theatre where they were playing. When they made their challenge he stepped up on the stage dressed in evening clothes.

The audience thought it was a prank until he stripped to the waist and his mountainous muscles came into view. Then he proceeded to duplicate every feat Samson and Cyclops had performed, except what they did with **two** hands he did with **one**. He then broke huge iron bars over his calf, arms and neck and easily snapped a half inch thick chain by merely expanding his massive chest. He topped this off by standing on two chairs and lifting a 700 pound weight with just his middle finger.

But Sandow's greatest feat that night was getting Samson and Cyclops to part with the forfeit they had lost to him. They locked themselves in their dressing room and refused to come out until, with one blow of his mighty fist, Sandow splintered the door into kindling wood. He got the money and along with it, theatrical bookings all over the world that continued throughout his entire life.

Among other features which he later added to his act were, while stripped to the waist, wrestling a full grown African lion in its cage . . . supporting an 800 pound bridge on his chest, over which rode a horse and chariot containing two charioteers; a total weight of more than 3,000 pounds . . . and a grand finale where he walked off the stage holding a platform above his head, the platform containing a grand piano with a man seated at it playing the national anthem.

So you see, when I aspired to be the world's strongest man I really had my work cut out for me! Someday I was to duplicate many of Sandow's feats and add a few of my own. Regrettably this amazing man died at the comparatively early age of 58, from a brain hemorrhage brought on when he picked up his automobile and lifted it out of a ditch.

The question has arisen many times—was I quite as strong as Sandow . . . or was I perhaps stronger? Unfortunately, we were too far apart in years to ever settle it, but one thing I'm sure of—when we were both in our prime we'd have made a wonderful pair of book-ends for the New York Athletic Club!

But to get back to little Joe, using the exercises

At age 16 I started developing my strongman's pose, with the help of my good friend Charles Atlas, who was then 24.

Ladislaw had shown me I was now working a full half hour before breakfast, before supper and before going to bed . . . and I gradually began inventing and adding other exercises. Enlisting my brother Victor's aid, I put up exercise bars in my room, fastened ropes, (on pulleys with weights on the end), to the walls and added other equipment as fast as I could afford it. Within a year the room looked like one they turn bats loose in to see if they can fly around without bumping into things. Mama screamed but Papa said it was my room and I could do anything I wanted short of setting fire to it.

breath. Once while stunting, I fell out of a tree and broke my right arm. Mama fainted . . . but Papa just grinned at me . . . and despite the pain, I grinned back. It was a happy transition from "Toothpicks" to splints.

The following Fall, Papa took us all to Europe. We were mostly in France and Turkey and, despite the language barrier, I made friends easily with the foreign kids, for I was now properly adjusted. No matter where we were I continued faithfully with my daily exercises and I found the foreign boys even more interested in developing their bodies than the boys in this country

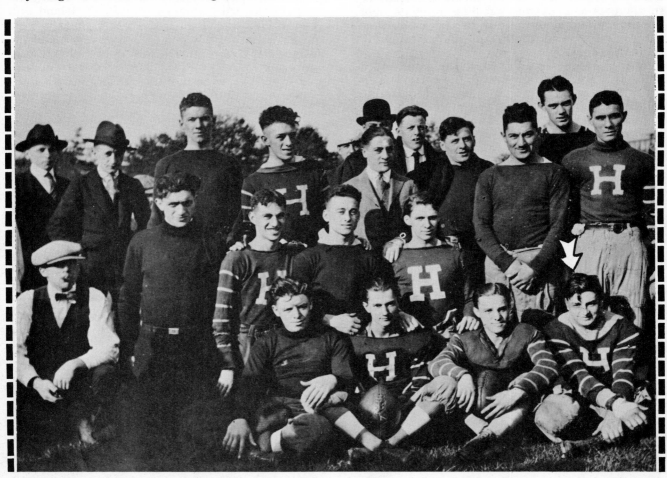

I (lower right) went big for rough and tumble sports in 1917, when I played with The Hiltons, Coney Island's first professional football team.

Soon my whole nature began to change for, as I saw the muscles developing, my self confidence grew in proportion. And, as wise old Ladislaw had advised, I continued to "eat like hell."

Incidentally, unless your doctor advises that your child is a special case, don't credit that nonsense about candy not being good for children. If a child is normal, active and otherwise eating properly, a reasonable amount of candy is "good medicine." I should know . . . I was raised on it.

I was now holding my own in sports and no one laughed at me any more. I was constantly learning new tricks of strength and trying daring stunts while my long suffering parents held their

. . . and among them were many wonderful young gymnasts and acrobats. I also saw to it that while they were learning a little from me, I was learning a lot from **them**.

When we arrived back in the United States few would have recognized, in the budding young athlete who came running happily down the gangplank, the underdeveloped little kid who, not so long before, had been the laughing stock of his schoolmates. One thing was certain . . . none of them would laugh at him NOW . . . not if they knew what was good for them!

By the time I was fourteen I had played on every athletic team in grammar school and could out-fight and out-wrestle any boy in the neighborhood. And I had done almost every daredevil stunt I could think of, in emulation of my boyhood movie idol, the great Eddie Polo, serial star and stuntman for Universal Studios. (Little did I dream then than one day, upon his retirement, I would be filling his shoes.) I had also developed into a rather phenomenal tumbler and acrobat and when I started competing in track events I applied this skill to the running high jump.

Now I never expect to leave my mark in world history or make the Hall of Fame, but at least I claim one small distinction. It was because of me that the AAU changed the rules on high jumping. I had developed a jump which I called "the porpoise dive" that made me a practically invincible competitor. I would approach the bar at full speed, head on, then leaping into the air, I would throw myself headfirst over it landing on the other side on my hands and shoulders, letting a front somersault bring me back to a standing position. It was not only a spectacular thing to see but I had no difficulty clearing the bar at well over six feet. Unfortunately many others who tried it met with such dire results that the AAU barred the porpoise dive from accepted athletic competition and ruled that a regulation high jump must be done in such a manner that the head and feet cleared the bar at approximately the same time.

With the coming of Summer the already renowned Charles Atlas came to Coney Island with an exhibition of feats of strength that was to make him world famous. We formed a friendship then that I still cherish today. By that time I was big and strong and eager to learn . . . and

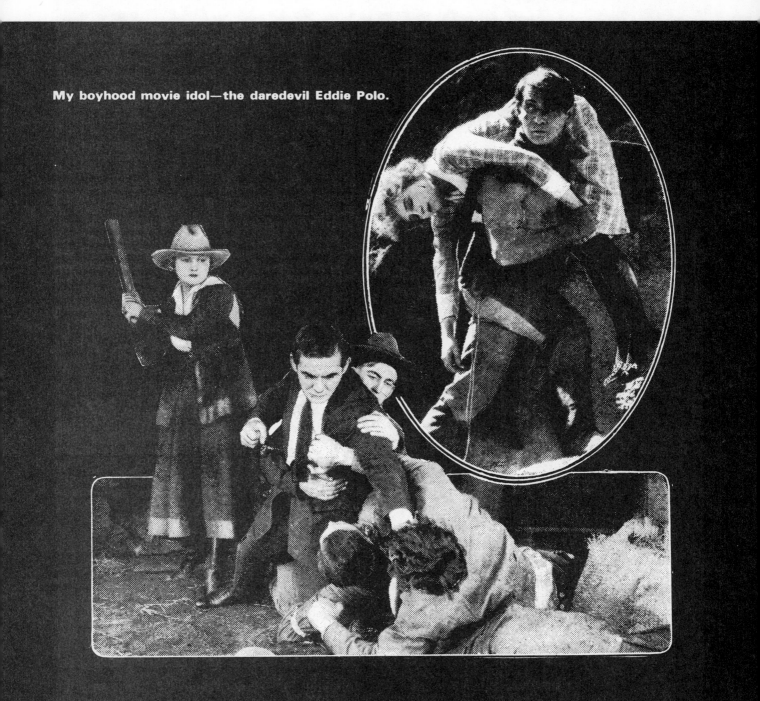

My boyhood movie idol—the daredevil Eddie Polo.

During the days when I was attending New York Military Academy I balanced my schedules with football, guard duty and even posing in one of Charles Atlas' outfits, which was to bring me good luck later on.

Working out in my own backyard gym in Coney Island. I was allowed to train with Warren Lincoln Travis' own heavy equipment, including his 1600 pound harness lift, in return for storing this material for him during the winter.

he was a natural born teacher, eager to teach ... just one of the admirable traits which have won him so many friends through the years. What I learned from Charles Atlas was invaluable. We'll hear more about him as our story unfolds.

When the Fall school term rolled around I entered Commercial High in Brooklyn. I played football and at the end of the season was picked for the mythical All-Greater New York team—the first time in the history of the school a freshman had been named. Perhaps I should mention here that Mama and Papa were inclined to frown on my athletic endeavors. Physical development was fine as a diversion but not as a career for their son. They were foreign born—they couldn't comprehend the major role athletics and sporting events play in this country and besides—look what happened to Uncle Yousiff!

So the next year I was sent to New York Military Academy, on the Hudson just a few miles from West Point, where Papa felt I would be kept under more rigid control and really have to hit the books. As I was leaving he said "From now on we forget this athlete nonsense, Joe—you already got the muscles developed so now we develop the mind." That year I won six letters ... football, basketball, swimming, wrestling, hockey and track. What could they do with me!

So they took me out of the Academy and the following September found me in Erasmus Hall High. Papa said if I was determined to get my fool neck broken, at least he wasn't going to pay for it. At Erasmus it was the same thing all over again. Mama and Papa pretended to suffer some more, but Victor told me that secretly they were beginning to feel pretty proud of me.

It was at the end of my third High School year that I decided to quit school. Although I was never a really brilliant scholar, athletics leaving me little time for study, my grades, surprisingly, were not bad.

Clowning around in my backyard in Coney Island, on Thanksgiving vacation from the New York Military Academy.

Chapter # 6
The BIRDLING TRIES HIS WINGS

THAT SUMMER I worked for Papa again, keeping in condition by heaving big bags of sugar and huge ice cream tubs around . . . and carrying two cakes of ice at a time, weighing 300 pounds each. But with the first breath of Autumn I packed my bag and took a room in New York. The overgrown birdling had flown the nest! At last I was on my way. I was going to try my wings or bust.

It may sound like a strange combination, but once in the big city I divided my efforts between playing professional football and ballroom dancing. Whereas one might have expected me to be musclebound, my exercises had kept me so supple I was as graceful on a dance floor as a South African gazelle in its natural habitat and I had the endurance of a Marathon runner. Woe be to the unfortunate girl who got me as a dancing partner . . . she was tangling with a veritable buzz-saw of Terpsichore. I never took my dancing too seriously but it was fun, good exercise, and collecting those silver loving cups and cash prizes proved to be both a pleasant and a profitable hobby.

In those days ballroom dance contests were quite the vogue and among my competitors were Arthur Murray, George Raft and a spectacular dancer named Jack Krantz who later became the famed screen star, Ricardo Cortez. (Years later I danced a Tango in a famous Hollywood musical and both staged and danced "The Champagne Hour" feature in Paul Whiteman's first

big picture for Universal—but as I look back on it I wonder if the proverbial bull in the China Shop was any more out of his natural element than Joe Bonomo tripping the light fantastic.) Then professional football came along and I took that up.

When I was playing pro football, I doubt that even the most imaginative visionaries ever pictured the extent to which the sport would grow, with millions of enthusiastic fans following the game on a national league basis and crowding huge stadia where they contribute millions of dollars a year to pay fabulously high salaries to top athletes.

Many of my teammates were the equal of any of the famous football pros of today . . . just as fast, as powerful and resourceful . . . and the game was equally bruising and dangerous, if not more so, as our protective equipment was inferior to that worn by the players of today. For all this the monetary rewards were practically negligible. When we played on our home grounds our personal take was a matter of dividing up the day's paid admissions. If the weather was good and the crowd fairly large we did all right. If it rained or snowed and the crowd was consequently sparse we played for the sport of it. However, the visiting team had to make their expenses which were paid by "passing the hat" —i.e. taking up a collection in the stands between halves. If they were making a good showing and pleasing the crowd the contributions were

25

often quite generous, but unfortunately when the spectators were **not** pleased this system hit a snag.

I recall one Saturday in particular. I was captaining the home team, the Van Sicklens, and our opponents were a highly touted aggregation from out of town known as the Stapletons. The game had been widely publicized and a goodly crowd gathered to see what promised to be a well played and thrilling contest. I shall never know exactly what was wrong . . . either we were at our peak or the Stapletons had an off-day. . . but we romped through and around them at will and the first half score looked more like the tally of a basketball game, with all the points on our side.

Between halves, the fellows who tried to take up the collection were chased out of the stands and at the end of the game the badly beaten Stapleton players had to flee for their lives amid a shower of stones, tin cans and pop bottles. Just as in the days of the old Roman gladiators, to survive in professional athletic competition, you've got to be a "crowd pleaser" . . . and when I was playing pro football, in the days of the uncontrolled fans, you had to win or defend yourself!

Many young fellows have asked me if I would recommend professional football as a career. The answer depends upon the individual. If you're good enough to become a star player you can command important money for a few years, sometimes enough to set you up for life if you save it and invest it wisely. Even if you don't, your future possibilities for a good life are greatly enhanced. Becoming nationally known, after you have discarded the shoulder pads and plastic helmet, you may well receive lucrative offers from advertising agencies, stock and bond houses, insurance firms etc. who consider your name an asset to their business. But if you are only average I would strongly advise spending those precious, vital years getting a firm foothold in your chosen profession. After six or eight years in this bruising, enervating sport, the average player is burned out and then it is often too late to build a successful career in other fields.

In the early days of football I would not have advised anyone to make a career of it unless they loved peanuts—for that was about what we played for! The game offered nothing in the way of a future. One of the greatest players I ever tangled with, a superb athlete known to his worshipping fans as Pueblo, found himself forgotten almost overnight, once he had hung up his cleated shoes.

You may have noticed that, although pro football is perhaps, with the possible exception of professional prize-fighting, the roughest and most bruising sport in the world, I have made no mention of the hazards involved. Surprisingly, with modern protective equipment and precautionary safety rules, there are practically no fatalities or instances of permanent injury. Most such unfortunate occurances are confined to high-school and college players who have not yet reached their full physical development. The perfectly developed body can absorb and withstand an almost unbelievable amount of punishment . . . as you will see in the ensuing pages.

My first few months in the Big City weren't very flattering to my ego. Between my football and dancing I was scraping together enough to live on, but I certainly wasn't setting the world on fire and no agents with lucrative offers were beating a path to the door of my furnished room. I did a little wrestling, I even sold vacuum clean-

George Raft was always tough competition on the ballroom floor.

ers. Like young fellows everywhere I was trying many doors, hoping one would open the way to a future for me.

It was around my nineteenth birthday that my years of faithful adherence to exercise and training really began to pay off. I learned about an open contest that was being held to determine the perfect strongman of the day. I entered it and won, being awarded the coveted gold medal. At that time my measurements were as follows:

Height—5-11½	
Weight—186	Ankle—8¾
Wrist—7½	Neck—16½
Forearm—13½	Chest normal—41
Biceps normal—14½	Chest expanded—45
Biceps expanded—16½	Waist—32
Thigh—23	Reach—72
Calf—16¼	Foot—10

Shortly after this and as a natural follow-up, I entered a tournament that was being held to decide the amateur wrestling championship. I had good reason to believe I could win and in the preliminary bouts I had no difficulty besting all opponents. It then came to the finale and all that stood between me and the championship was a powerfully built young fellow who had beaten the cream of the crop in amateur wrestling and had also won all his bouts in the tournament. I sized him up and figured I could take him—and I almost did—but after a terrific battle he finally succeeded in pinning me for the championship. When he had me down I should have gotten

Ricardo Cortez was a standout dancer long before he became a top motion picture star.

As a dancer I could hold my own with the best of them.

his autograph, for he not only became U.S. Olympic champion but eventually turned out to be the famous Nat Pendleton of motion picture fame, known to cinema fans the world over.

I now added fencing and ice hockey to my other athletic accomplishments. Not knowing in exactly which direction I was headed, I decided to have as many strings to my bow as possible.

Then one day someone told me that Bothner's Gym, on Forty Second Street, might be a good place for me to make a few connections. A lot of professional wrestlers frequented it and I might get a break. So I showed up there the next afternoon and started doing calisthenics, working out by myself. I had been trained in wrestling at the Military Academy by Tom Jenkins, an ex world champion, who was also the wrestling coach at West Point and one of the best mat instructors in the country. I had seldom been defeated in a match—I had almost won the amateur championship—and I figured I was pretty good.

It wasn't long before a heavily muscled man in gym clothes sauntered over.

"You're well put together, kid. Ever wrestle?"

"A little," I said cagily. "Did you?"

"A little," he grinned, "let's try a few holds."

George Bothner, in his prime, the undefeated lightweight wrestling champion of the world.

I said to myself, "Here's where you get a surprise, mister," and I lost no time in tangling with him. But **I** was the one who seemed to be getting the surprise. He just stayed on the defensive but what a defense! I tried every hold I had ever learned but I might as well have tried to throw the Rock of Gibraltar. I was both baffled and puzzled. Those holds had always worked before. But no matter what I did, he broke away easily. A fairly good-sized crowd had gathered and I was getting embarrassed. Then suddenly my opponent went on the offensive and I was reminded of my session with Ladislaw. He could have thrown me at any given moment but instead, he elected to just toss me around. I fought back as best I could, but I was glad when he finally slapped me down with a body slam and pinned me.

As I lay there dazed I felt him pat me roughly on the shoulder.

"You're all right, kid. You got a lotta promise." And he walked away.

A few minutes later I was in the shower room recuperating. There were several fellows around who had followed me in.

"That guy's pretty good," I said to one of them. "You ever wrestle with him?"

"What're you, nuts?" he asked. "I'd sooner wrestle an octupus than the Strangler."

I had been wrestling with the world champion, Strangler Lewis, famed for his murderous head-locks! And everybody in the gym knew ... but ME.

Bothner's Gym was one of my regular hangouts for the next two years, working many hours every day, perfecting my tumbling and wrestling. It was America's wrestling headquarters. All the top men were there, constantly training and experimenting. Even the greatest—perhaps the greatest more than the rest; that's why they were great—trained long and hard. Bothner's was, in effect, both clubhouse and a school for wrestlers, acrobats, tumblers, jugglers and that sort.

Run by George Bothner, undefeated lightweight wrestling champion of the world, the gym afforded wrestlers opportunities that few American gyms ever have. George himself was a superb conditioner. He had spent a lifetime wrestling, dedicating himself to the sport and to the ideals of body conditioning, becoming a top physical culture man in addition to a fine wrestling coach.

Nat Pendleton, the Olympic wrestling champion who became a famous screen comedian.

Among the men who have made Bothner's famous was George Hackenschmidt, the famed Russian Lion. Hackenschmidt was a not-too-tall man of almost superhuman strength. On one occasion, he was in the ring with an opponent who was so terrified of the Lion that he clamped his hands on one of the ropes and refused to let go. Hackenschmidt angrily grabbed this opponent around the waist, and pulling with all his strenth, pulled the very ring posts down!

The great Jim Londos was another who often wrestled at Bothner's. Others included Ed "Strangler" Lewis, Joe Stecker, the "Scissors King", Bull Montana, Dick Shikert, Hans Steinke, Cyclone Reese, Martin Ludecke, world's middleweight champ, and every other top wrestler of any importance.

In such illustrious company I was at that time, away beyond my depth . . . but because I was willing to take advice and they were willing to give it, like the girl in the song who said "I learned more from Willie, on the day we played hookey, than the teacher could have taught me in a week." . . . I learned more from those sea-

Me, ready to take on "Strangler Lewis".

Hans Steinke, the "untitled" champion of his day.

soned veterans in a year or two than I could have gleaned from other sources in a lifetime.

At no time were those men out of condition —they lived by the hard and fast rules of the training table—no tobacoo—no alcohol—never break the dietary rules—get plenty of sleep. The example they set impressed me. I must confess I have slipped up occasionally in the dietary department, especially when I visited Mama... (I never **could** resist her cooking) ... but I never let a day go by without a thorough workout.

More than once, as you will learn shortly, this "fine conditioning" saved my life.

Right here I want to stress a point for all you budding "muscle men." You don't get to be a skilled athlete or a strongman overnight... and once you've reached the heights, through arduous effort and self denial, you've got to work as hard to stay there as you did to get there. Success always has a price tag and it comes C.O.D., but it's well worth what it costs and much, much more.

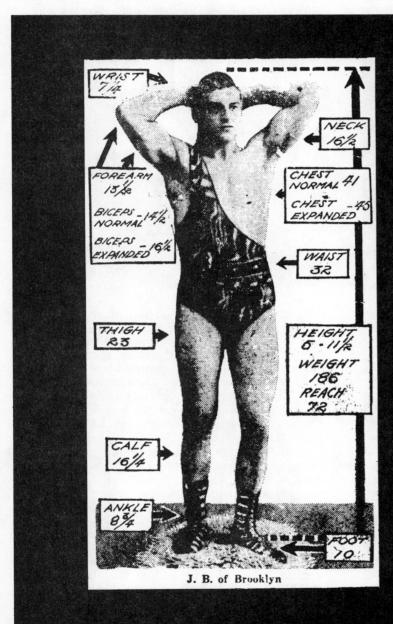

J. B. of Brooklyn

The photo that won the "Modern Apollo" contest for me, which was the forerunner of all the later "Mr. America" competitions.

ONLY NINETEEN BUT HAS ALMOST PERFECT FIGURE

(Other picture on page 1)

The Modern Apollo has been found!

He is Joseph Bonomo. He lives at 308 Sea Breeze Avenue, Coney Island, and is nineteen years of age.

Just out of school, he will now start on his career in the motion picture world in the company of which Hope Hampton, First National star, is the guiding light.

Out of more than five thousand entrants—all of whom aspired to meet the requirements in THE NEWS search for the perfect man —the committee of judges chose Bonomo as the man whose physique measured nearest to those of the Apollo, whose statue now in the Vatican in Rome, is perhaps the noblest presentation of the human form.

Camera tests also showed that Bonomo's features would photograph excellently.

The decision of the judges was based on both the physique and the features.

Chapter #7

THE MODERN APOLLO

I THINK MOST YOUNG MEN of nineteen spend considerable time wondering how they'll ever be able to take that Giant Step that leads from what they are to what they hope to be. I know I did . . . every morning . . . as I poured over the help wanted ads in the New York Times, searching for what might sound like a golden opportunity for me.

On this particular morning my search, as usual, was in vain, but as I skimmed through the rest of the paper a local news item caught my eye. The New York police were running a campaign to try and curb the dangerous habit of jaywalking, which not only cluttered up traffic but had caused many serious accidents and, in numerous instances, resulted in loss of life. The police department had issued warnings, made threats and in a few cases had made arrests, but nothing seemed to impress the hurry-mad Manhattanites or deter them from risking life and limb to save those few precious seconds that would have been lost had they waited for the signal to change.

As I read the article I suddenly got a wild idea for staging a publicity stunt that might break in the papers and perhaps bring me to the attention of Hollywood.

I knew I'd never get an okay from the police for my drastic solution to their problem, so I decided to take the bull by the horns and risk it on my own.

I phoned the newspapers to make sure some photographers would be on hand, then stationed myself at a busy intersection, during the rush hour, and awaited their arrival. When they got me in camera focus I approached the harrassed traffic officer who was vainly trying to stem the jaywalking tide of humanity who were blithely ignoring his commands and remonstrances.

I said "Pardon me, but I'm Joe Bonomo and if you'll let me take over for a moment I'd like to demonstrate a new system that will discourage jaywalking permanently."

Before he had a chance to reply, the signal changed to permit crosstown traffic to go through, and as usual several jaywalkers, (men in on the publicity stunt with me,) ignoring both the signal and his police whistle, came scurrying across regardless. As the first one started to pass us, without a word I picked him up bodily and tossed him back on the curb—and before the onlookers could comprehend what was happening, I had likewise picked the others up and tossed them back like so many loaves of bread. Then, before the astonished officer could decide what to do about it, I faded back into the crowd and disappeared.

But the cameras had caught it and I had my publicity. The afternoon edition of every paper in town carried my picture with a full account of my escapade. It hit the public funnybone and I was quite a hero.

I didn't get any wires from Hollywood producers, but I DID get a phone call from Papa telling me I'd better come home before I wound

My method of discouraging jaywalking was not a permanent solution to the problem, but it did get me a bit of publicity.

up in a strait jacket in some Daffy House.

I'll admit my solution was a bit drastic and unorthodox, but I still contend that if the police had adopted my method, in a short time jaywalkers would have been as extinct as the Dodo bird.

The professional football season was now over and even that small source of income being cut off I realized what little I had saved would be no match for my appetite. "Eating like hell" cost money. I could have touched Mama and Papa for almost any amount, but I wasn't going to play the Prodigal Son. I'd go it alone if I starved—and it was starting to look as though I had a good start in that direction!

It was then that I got an offer to pose for some art classes in Greenwich Village. I felt a bit silly doing it . . . and I hoped my family and friends would never find out . . . but I needed steaks and chops and no one was giving out free samples. My first assignment was posing as "The Thinker" and, as I sat there, minus nine tenths of my clothes, with a cold draft blowing on me, it's just as well the class didn't know **what** I was thinking! But it paid well and I didn't get pneumonia.

At just this time the New York Daily News launched a nation-wide contest to find "The Modern Apollo" and, without my knowledge, some of the art students sent in a sketch of me posing as some kind of Greek god, enclosing with it my name and address. It was probably done as a gag, but a couple of days later I recieved a letter from the contest editor. It stated that a sketch was not sufficient . . . they must have several recent photographs.

The letter was headed for the waste basket when an old memory stayed my hand—the memory of a tortured little boy before the statue of Apollo, pleading, "Why can't I be like you!" Well, here was my chance to find out how close I had come. I decided to enter the contest.

The first thing I did was. to hunt up my old friend Charles Atlas. He laughed and said he had been tempted to enter himself. I asked him why he didn't. He said because it sounded to him like the world's first male beauty contest and he was a strongman—not a beauty. I said **I** was no Adonis, but that wasn't going to keep **me** out of it. When he saw I was serious, he said he'd help me all he could, and we went to work. Wearing his leopard-skin leotard and strongman sandals, I was photographed from all angles. And it was Charlie who posed me, to show off my body to its best advantage. We then selected the best shots and sent them in to the contest editor.

The Judges were Herman Bernolet-Moens, Carton Moorepark and Robert Chanler—all well known artists and international authorities on health and human beauty. They culled through more than 5,000 entries, finally narrowing it down to twelve, of which I was **one**. We were notified to report on October 30th, at which time we would be judged "in the flesh" and "The Modern Apollo" would be selected.

Needless to say, on October 30th I was the first one there, leopard-skin, sandals and all.

And guess who won? For if I hadn't, it's a sure bet this chapter would have never been written! Yes, from among 5,000 applicants from all over America, I was adjudged the one whose physique most closely duplicated that of the great god Apollo. So you see dreams CAN come true . . . if you'll only help 'em along a little.

As "the winnah" I received a thousand dollars and a ten week movie contract, at a hundred a week, to star with Hope Hampton in the First National picture A LIGHT IN THE DARK. To star with Hope Hampton! Before I could catch my breath I was rushed to all the best known spots in New York and photographed with the beautiful star in all sorts of publicity shots. Joe Bonomo had arrived! At nineteen the world was my oyster. How wrong can a kid **be**?

Before long the picture went into production and I got my first taste of movie work. Clarence Brown was directing, E.K. Lincoln played opposite Miss Hampton and Lon Chaney was the villain. Me? Oh I was in it all right—in **lots** of parts. Although I didn't know it **then**, the Apollo contest had just been a clever publicity stunt to advertise the picture. Now it had left First National with young Bonomo on their payroll for ten weeks, and they figured they might as well use him. And use him they did!

First they told me to play a cop, chasing a jewel thief down the street. So I put on a cop's uniform and chased him. Then they told me **I** was to be the jewel thief, jumping in the river. So I made like a jewel thief and jumped. It didn't seem to make sense but Mr. Brown said "Just do as you're told, Joe . . . it'll all come out all right." So I played a guy jumping out a window . . . another guy jumping from a moving train . . . a guy getting punched in the jaw by the hero . . . and a lot of other guys . . . each in a different costume and make-up. Say, this picture was mainly about **ME!** I wondered what kind of billing they'd give me and how large my name would be on the theatre marquees.

Finally the picture was completed and released. When it opened in New York I took Mama, Papa,

Hope Hampton taught me about screen makeup and introduced me to the glamour of the movies in my first film appearance.

Apollo Finds Work as Film Actor With Hope Hampton

He was much interested in the movie camera (above, left) and in the huge arc lamp used for lighting effects. Miss Hampton explained it all.

They found just time enough to snatch a bite.

Victor and about fifty of my friends. What the heck . . . I was a celebrity. And I could scarcely wait for the picture to start. The audience had a surprise coming—they were about to see young Joe Bonomo, the most versatile actor in the world. But when the titles came on I didn't see my name and for about twenty minutes there was practically no one on the screen but Miss Hampton, Mr. Lincoln and Mr. Chaney. I couldn't understand it.

"That's me, the Jewel Thief!" I finally shouted, as I saw myself running down the street.

"Where?" asked Mama. Then they showed a closeup of the thief, but it was somebody else.

"Where's Joe?" asked Papa.

A policeman in the distance spotted the thief.

"There, Papa . . . I'm the **cop**!"

The policeman drew his gun, shouted, jumped a fence and ran toward the camera.

"Stop fooling," said Mama. It was somebody else.

"They made a mistake. You'll see, **now** I'm jumping in the river and swimming across." (All this being shown in a long shot . . . at a distance.)

"Now I'm climbing out of the water and you'll see a closeup of me." But again it was somebody else.

"Where's Joe?" asked Victor.

Somebody went sailing through a break-away window.

"There!" I pointed. Then seen from outside the building, the figure gets up and runs past the camera in a close shot. It's Lon Chaney.

And that was the way the whole picture went. When Chaney jumped off a fire-escape it was

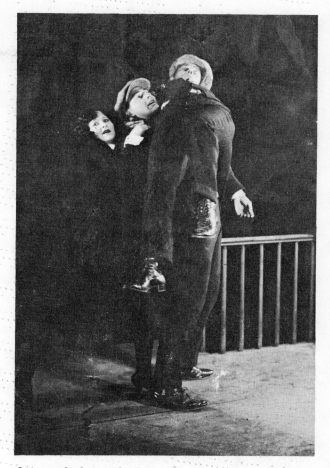

A tangled confusion of Hampton, Chaney and Bonomo.

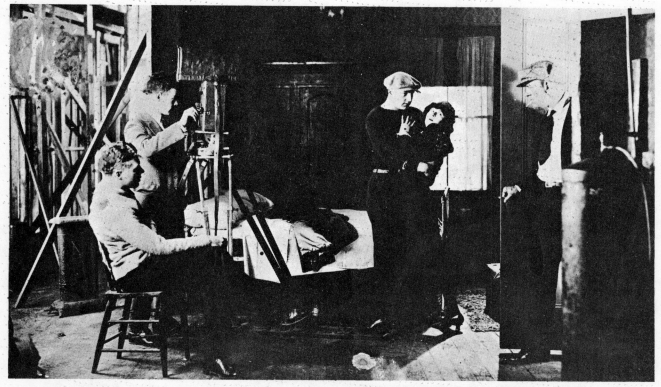

A LIGHT IN THE DARK, directed by Clarence Brown (extreme left), was a crude, early production made in the days before Lon Chaney (right) became the screen's "Master of Makeup".

ME. When he jumped off a moving train it was me **again**. That was me getting socked on the jaw, only it was never me in the closeups. That was me again, falling through a trap door . . . only the closeup showed it was Mr. Lincoln. I played more than twenty different parts, but nobody saw Joe Bonomo.

Naturally, Mama and Papa didn't understand and kept stealing sly glances at me, wondering if I had suddenly gone daft. Victor and my friends were openly sympathetic, altho secretly amused. As for me . . . I was completely stunned. I finally realized what had happened. I had been used as one of the great unsung heroes of the movie industry, who "take the cash and let the credit go," a movie stuntman.

There were some ways, though, in which my experiences in A LIGHT IN THE DARK were to help me. Lon Chaney, the great master of disguise, had taken a liking to me, and showed me many tricks of makeup which I later was to use to great advantage. And a few people, in the trade, had spotted my talent for athletics and stunts.

A few weeks later a man looked me up. He said his name was Nathan Hirsh, president of the Aywon Film Corp. He had seen me in the picture and wanted to give me a screen test.

I was flattered and impressed. It was my first visit from the president of a film company. I was to be given a screen **stunt** test and the film shown to the exhibitors after which Mr. Hirsh and I would be sold as a serial team . . . he, as the producer, and I, as a new serial star. It sure sounded great! No, there wasn't any money in it just yet, but all that would come later. So off we went to make the test. And me . . . without a cent of insurance! Mr. Hirsh had a cameraman an all around assistant, and Bonomo—a car, a camera and a towel to wipe the perspiring Bonomo brow.

In the next two days I did everything but go over Niagara Falls in a Dixie Cup, and I'm sure that was only because we were too far from Niagara Falls, there wasn't a Dixie Cup handy, and Mr. Hirsh didn't THINK of it. I never met anyone so careless with another man's life.

We drove into the country where I jumped off barns and silos, fell down a well, went around on an old mill-wheel, wrestled a live bull, swam a river and jumped off a cliff. Then we found a farmer with an old beat-up plow horse and Mr. Hirsh gave him five dollars for the use of it for a half hour. Riding bareback, as fast as that old plug could go, I stood up on his back and jumped into a tree. Then the horse galloped back and I jumped back on him and miraculously kept my balance. We finally came to a bridge with a six-foot high railing. Seeing a stream below, I vaulted the rail and went crashing down twenty feet into two feet of water, which was concealing a cluster of jagged rocks. It's a wonder I wasn't killed.

From there we drove to some harbor in Jersey and found a ship. The arrangements made, I did rope slides of all kinds, topping this off with

My athletic abilities were put to full use.

One of my first screen "stunts".

Unaware of the evil Chaney glance cast upon us.

a dive from the ninety-foot mast into the water below . . . the CHILLY water below . . . it was February.

Seeing I was still alive, which must have puzzled him a little, Mr. Hirsh then rented a motorcycle and hunted up a Bascule bridge. I had never been on a motorcycle, but **he** had, and he showed me how to run it. We waited until the bridge was raising to let a ship through . . . then I rode the motorcycle up the bridge as it got steeper in the air. Finally the angle was too much for me and I slid back down; part of the way on the motorcycle but the rest of the way with the motorcycle on ME.

Well . . after a couple of days of this sort of thing, Mr. Hirsh was a happy man.

"My boy," he said, "we got some dandy stunts. But we need a 'spectacular' to finish the film. We gotta sock 'em with a lulu!"

I was getting pretty tired but I wouldn't let on.

"How about if I jump off another bridge? A higher one . . . with more water."

Mr. Hirsh shook his head. "Not spectacular enough."

"How about off a moving train?"

"Not bad, but not quite IT."

Then the cameraman came up with an idea. "How about **from** a train, **off** a bridge, while the train is speeding **across** the bridge?"

"Now **that's** a **good** idea," said Mr. Hirsh.

I was willing, but where could we find a train and a bridge? The cameraman remembered a place up in Harlem, where freight trains crossed a

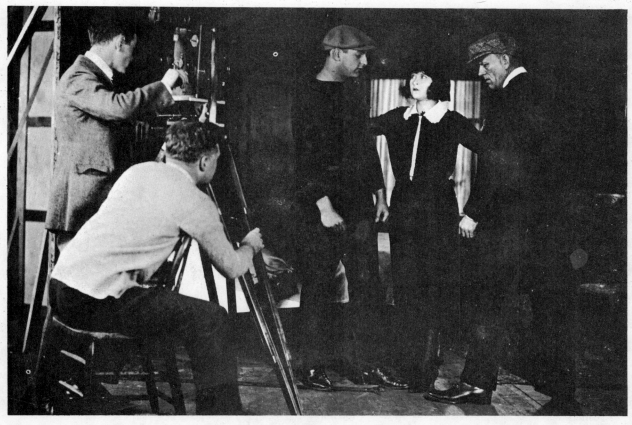

This first film proved quite an education in silent screen acting and proper movement in front of the camera.

bridge over the Harlem River. We drove up there to investigate.

We watched a train go over the bridge. There were steel girders, about six feet apart, that I would have to jump between and there were the huge bastions, upon which the bridge was supported that I would have to miss when I hit the water. I could tell the water was deep enough by the big barges coming along quite regularly. But what if I hit one of those barges? "Of course, if you're afraid—" Mr. Hirsh was saying. That settled it.

It wasn't long before the freight came puffing along. It was doing about twenty miles an hour as I grabbed one of the hand-rails and pulled myself aboard. I looked back and saw Mr. Hirsh, the cameraman and his assistant, driving crazily to get to the camera site in time. The way they were driving, I wasn't sure they'd make it, all

My big stunt test turned out to be a rough workout.

in one piece. But then . . . I wasn't sure I'd make it **myself**.

As I stood, swaying, on top of one of the freight cars, I began to regret my decision. Any number of things could go wrong. We came to the beginning of the bridge at last and I looked to see if the others were there. The car was just pulling into position and they were jumping out and setting up the camera. Mr. Hirsh waved a white handkerchief encouragingly and I waved back, wondering if that would be my last wave.

I wish I had had a practice jump, I thought. But how do you practice jumping off a freight train, speeding over a bridge?? Practice couldn't make perfect now! This had to be perfect the first time!

Now we were ON the bridge. I looked down and could see no barges and no bastions directly below . . . but those steel girders were whizzing past   awfully fast. If my timing wasn't exactly right I would hit one when I jumped, and either be bounced back under the wheels of the train, or bounced, unconscious, into the river, to certain death. And we didn't even have a boat down there to pick up the body.

I suddenly said "What the heck!", clenched my teeth, rocked my body back and forward for a couple of seconds, timing myself with the steel girders flying by, took a deep breath, ran a few steps and jumped! As I sailed through the air I saw myself coming almost head-on into one of the girders and twisted away just in time . . . but I felt a stabbing pain in my arm as my shoulder grazed it. In another split second I was free and clear. Down I plunged, fifty feet and SPLASH! Into the freezing water I went but nothing ever felt so good.

As soon as I bobbed back up to the surface I swam for the shore as fast as I could, afraid my muscles might cramp from the cold, and climbed dripping, up the bank to the car.

"See, my boy?" exulted Mr. Hirsh. "Nothing to it, was there?" He was jubilant . . . he had some good film . . . I was later to learn that all directors were like that.

"Like taking candy from a baby," I panted through my chattering teeth, " a cinch."

I undressed quickly in the car, rubbed myself dry and climbed back into my damp clothes. Never, I vowed, never again would I do such a fool thing without every kind of safety device, emergency boats and whatever else a good stunt-man needs. I now know that no amount of precaution can assure absolute safety in stunting, but you **can** eliminate a lot of the risks.

Nothing was to come of my stunt test for the Aywon Film Corporation, although it was some time before I gave up hope. However, there were benefits. I gained experience and confidice and I had gotten a print of the film. It was this print that eventually opened to me the hard-to-crash "Gates of Hollywood."

From railroad bridges to roof tops, Nathan Hirsh kept me busy.

Chapter #8

MAKING A LIVING DODGING DEATH

WHILE WAITING FOR MR. HIRSH to sign us for that big movie deal, I returned to my slightly normal way of life. I figured it would be only a matter of two or three weeks at most before he'd be wiring me that he had closed the deal and I should rush to the west coast without delay.

I decided not to break the news to Mama and Papa until the date of my departure was definitely set, but not knowing how long I'd be gone, I felt I should spend a little time with them before leaving. So I left a forwarding address at both my rooming house and the telegraph office and headed back to the home fold.

Mama and Papa thought I was back to stay and they gave me a big welcome home party. I felt a little guilty about it but I wasn't going to spoil the surprise I had in store for them. Every time the telephone or doorbell rang I knew it must be the big news at last . . . but the call from Hollywood never came.

I finally broke down and told Papa the whole story in detail. When I had finished my recital he said, "Look Joey, in ice cream and candy you don't find romance . . . or thrills . . . or headlines in the papers—but also you don't lose your arms or legs or get your head broken. Forget this foolishness and I make you vice president and someday you'll need all your big muscles to carry your money to the bank."

A week later things were humming right along in Coney Island and the Bonomos were, as usual, working early and late in their ice cream and candy factory. That is, all the Bonomos but little Joey. I had bigger fish to fry. I was back in New York.

I continued to work out at Bothner's Gym . . . pose in the Village . . . and win many a dance competition, while still waiting for the Hollywood call. After a few weeks of dwindling hopes I realized Mr. Hirsh had failed to put us over. I decided that if I was going to be a Movie star I'd better do something about it myself . . . and quickly. After all, I was twenty years old and I wasn't getting any younger! So I took my Apollo Contest press clippings and pictures, and my high school athletic clippings, and started making the rounds of the local picture studios. In those days, many were in New York City, Long Island and the Bronx. I got nowhere fast.

But finally, I managed to get in to see George Seitz, one of the Pathe directors. I showed him my publicity.

"So what do you do?" he asked.

"Anything," I said. "I'm an actor."

"We got enough actors."

"I'm also a dancer."

"We got too many dancers."

"Well," I said desperately, "I'm also a stuntman."

"That's different," he said, "we can always use a stuntman. What's your specialty?"

"I do everything," I said with conviction.

"You ever jump off a building?"

"Dozens of 'em."

"Can you ride a horse?"

"Even standing up—bareback." (Bless dear old Mr. Hirsh)

"Ever do any motorcycle stunts?" (Bless him again!)

"Practically my specialty."

I don't think he quite believed me, but he looked as though he hoped he could. I soon learned, only too painfully, why there was always a demand for motorcycle stuntmen. They didn't last very long. Seitz scribbled an address on a piece of paper and passed it to me.

"Meet me there at nine tomorrow morning . . . and be ready to go to work."

When I left the office my feet were on the ground but my head was in the clouds—which is quite a stunt in itself.

The next morning I reported at the Hudson River Ferry landing and learned I was to be stunting for Charles Hutchison in a Pathe serial, HURRICANE HUTCH, which Seitz was directing. "Hutch", who had long been famous as a motorcycle stunt artist, had now become a star and too valuable to further risk his life doing his own stunts. It seemed strange to me that the greatest motorcyclist of his time was no longer allowed on a motorcycle. In the next few hours

I found out why.

The stunt was to be a motorcycle jump from the ferry slip onto a ferryboat, after it had left the dock. The jump was to be over about thirty feet of open water. In the finished sequence it went something like this:—The heroine was in the clutches of the villain, on the ferry. Hutch, the hero, was pursuing. He arrived at the slip just as the ferry pulled away—too late. That is, too late for the ordinary man. But Hutchison, on his trusty motorcycle, just kept going and jumped the intervening distance at full speed, landing on the ferryboat deck. Then the fight . . . and so forth.

"Well, Bonomo," said Seitz, "think you can do it?"

I wasn't at all sure I could. I hadn't had much experience on motorcycles and I might get killed. But I wanted to be with the studio and this was my chance.

"A cinch," I said with a forced grin, "let's hit it."

They had built a slight ramp at the edge of the ferry slip, to give me elevation and arc enough to make the jump. Actually, no one could be sure how far away the ferry would be. It was all a matter of timing, and this was another of those stunts you couldn't rehearse. The ferryboat

Daily road work was a must for keeping in shape.

was cleared of all cars in case I couldn't stop and had to ride the full length of the boat and go off the other end into the Hudson.

Everything was set up and I drove the cycle back up the pier a hundred yards or so. I sat there with the motor chugging under me and my heart chugging inside me. Soon the ferry started to move and I gunned the motor, poised, ready to go. I checked my padding and it was all there. I was padded up tighter than a mummy. I tugged at the strap of my crash helmet, and waited. Finally they waved me my signal. I threw the cycle into gear and down the pier I went. I picked up speed fast; I must have been doing over sixty when I hit the ramp. Up we went,

Charles "Hutch" Hutchison, a matinee idol of the silent serial.

the cycle and I, flying through the air. As I saw the ferry deck coming up to meet me, I thought I'd die. We hit . . . bounced . . . and I lost the cycle. Down the deck we both went sliding, the bike going right off the far end and into the river. I only slid about half the length of the boat, but that was enough. When they got to me I was still conscious, but wishing I wasn't. Though no bones were broken, I had been slivered like a human pin-cushion, with hundreds of little deck splinters in me. I spent the next five days in the hospital, getting the splinters pulled out. Now it was from "Toothpicks" to SPLINTERS!

But the stunt was a success. They had enough good footage to make a thrilling, credible sequence. However, they spliced in a better landing in the cutting room.

While I was in the hospital I figured out what had gone wrong. In the first place, I had landed on a spot that was greasy from the crankcase

drippings of cars. If this spot had been properly cleaned, the bike wouldn't have skidded so badly. Also, if I had let most of the air out of the tires, I wouldn't have bounced so. In addition, they had lost a perfectly good motorbike that they needn't have lost. The next time we did the stunt —oh, yes, I repeated it several times in the next few months—I had a long, free-spinning spool of strong fishing line, with a 5 inch cork ball, and had this attached to the handlebars. Then, should the cycle go in the river, the floating cork ball would mark the location, and the bike could be hauled up by a grappling hook. Each time I did the stunt again, we were completely successful, and the cycle stayed aboard. There were several other times, however, when I was called on to make a speeding motorcycle jump off a dock, with no ferry involved. Each of these times my cork and fishing line invention saved the cycle.

The day before my release from the hospital, one of the casting directors dropped in.

"Don't worry, Joe," he said, "you did fine. We're going to have plenty of work for you."

I thought of those hundreds of splinters and I didn't know whether to thank him or throttle him. But after all, I had asked for it. For better or for worse, the die was cast . . . I was a movie stuntman now.

The next day I was discharged from the hospital and they had another stunt all ready for me.

This was to be a jump from a moving Fifth Avenue double-decker bus to an elevated train structure. In the sequence, Hutch was to be pursued by a bunch of bad guys, run up to the open top deck of the bus, leap about three feet through the air and catch the structure of the El as the bus passed under it. He was then to swing himself to the platform and make his getaway.

This looks easy, I thought. So I had a talk with the bus driver and told him to slow down at that particular spot so I could make the jump safely. We got everything set and the stunt came off perfectly. Nothing to it.

Later, as I was taking off my straps and belts, the cameraman approached me. He wanted to know how I did it. The secret, I explained, was to get the bus almost momentarily stopped, so there would be almost negligible forward motion at the precise moment I made the leap.

"It's impossible to hang on if you're moving forward," I explained. "The weight of your body will all be pressed against your forearms. It'll pull your grip right off the beam." The cameraman nodded.

"I guess the other guy didn't KNOW that," he said.

"What other guy?" I asked.

"The guy that got killed yesterday," he said. "Didn't they tell you?"

I suddenly felt sick.

"No," I said, "they didn't tell me."

"Yeah," he went on, "this other guy tried it yesterday and fell on his head in the street. Smashed it like a melon. They shoulda told you."

A difficult motorcycle to plane transfer—a good example of the type of production value that made serials popular long before the "talkies".

"Yes," I said, "they shoulda told me."

I was starting to wonder if maybe I should have stayed in Papa's ice cream factory.

It was late in the winter, when Cosmopolitan was working on the Marion Davies' LITTLE OLD NEW YORK picture, that I got a hurry call from Mike Connelly the casting director. He asked me if I could dig up another stuntman . . . a good swimmer. Sure I could . . . and I went to see one of my former Coney Island swimming buddies; a character we called George the Greek.

"How would you like to be in the movies, George?" I asked him.

"Don't do me no favors," said George.

"It'll pay twenty-five bucks."

George blinked. That was a lot of money in those days.

"Twenty-five bucks? What I have to do? Jump off the Brooklyn Bridge at low tide?"

"No, George," I assured him. "This is just swimming."

"Twenty-five bucks for swimmin'? For that kind of dough I'll marry a Mermaid!"

The next morning—it was one of those raw March days—we reported for work and they gave us the lowdown. We were supposed to be a couple of fishermen, in a small boat on the Hudson. A steamboat would bear down on us and cut our boat in two. Very spectacular and nothing to worry about as a tug would be nearby to pick us up. It seemed awfully cold, but we wouldn't be in the water for more than a minute or two. We were both expert swimmers so we didn't see anything too tough about it.

Well, the stunt was set up and we rowed out and waited for the steamboat. George began to grow somewhat apprehensive but I reassured him.

"The only thing you have to remember," I said, "is to avoid the ship's propeller. And don't wait 'til that big tub hits us; when it's right on top of us, but just before it hits, you dive this way off the bow and I'll go that way off the stern. Then swim like crazy. I'll meet you after the steamboat passes.

When the steamer was about 30 feet away, George started to go.

"Not yet," I yelled, "we've got to make it close to make the shot exciting."

"This is excitin' enough for me!" said George, and over the side he went. As now it was up to me I ran to the bow and looked after him, then looked up at the steamboat bearing down on me. I scurried back and forth in apparent indecision, then just a second before the crash, I went over the stern. The steamer hit the fishing boat and smashed it to pieces.

I spotted Goerge and we swam to meet each other.

"How do you like the picture business?" I shouted.

"I'll tell you later," he said through clenched teeth. The water was freezing. "What do we do now?"

"Nothing. That tug will pick us up in a minute." I pointed to a tugboat a few hundred yards away.

We waited but the tug didn't seem to be moving. We didn't know it, but it had stalled and **couldn't** move.

"Joe," George gasped, "I can't make it. The cold—I'm freezing—"

He looked in bad shape. What the devil is the matter with those morons, I thought! It was getting colder and colder, and I was beginning to feel it now, too. George was almost blue. It seemed as though hours passed, though actually it was only a matter of a few minutes more. My clothes were heavy, and the cold was almost unbearable. I looked at George.

"Joe—" he gasped. "Joe—" and he went under. I was only a few feet away from him and I reached out and grabbed him and pulled him

up again. George was unconscious. I turned him over on his back and kept him afloat. Finally, a couple of minutes later, the tug began to bear down on us.

I was numb with the cold and all but unconscious myself as they pulled us out of the water and hauled us aboard. They carried us down into the hot engine room, where George came to and we both began to thaw out.

A few minutes later we both got sick, and George immediately passed out again. As soon as the tug pulled up to the pier we were rushed to the hospital. I was all right in a few hours, but George had pneumonia. We had been in that freezing water for twelve minutes. The doctors told us that being taken down into that hot engine room was the worst thing they could have done for us; a moderate temperature room might have fixed us up all right.

Because of my conditioning I recovered fast and was discharged that afternoon. George with his pneumonia, had a rough time of it before he began to recover. In the hospital, a few days later, when he was feeling better, I jokingly asked him again what he though of the picture business.

"Like I told you before, Joe," said George, eyeing me grimly, "Don't do me no favors. The old man's restaurant is good enough for **me!**"

George had had enough, but **I** hadn't. This picture business was the life and I was going to be a star or die trying. My readiness to tackle anything was making me popular with the directors and casting directors. Although it nearly cost me my life, many times over, it was the

under me, on the seat. Then, just before the car hit, I would arc out in a long dive. It looked more dangerous than it was. In all my years of stunting I never knew anyone to be seriously hurt in a pier-head jump. But don't try it in the family jalopy . . . unless you're an experienced stuntman. Remember, there are tricks to every trade and the life you lose will be your OWN!

During that Spring I did a lot of other stunts, but the one that was to make my reputation as top stuntman in the East, was also to make Movie stunt history. I was the first man ever to be photographed for the cinema, diving from a plane in flight . . . without a parachute.

They were going to use a dummy for this sequence, but I told George Seitz I'd like to try it.

Swimming from Coney Island to the Battery in the middle of winter, and towing a lifeboat full of men.

greatest factor in my rise to whatever success I was to achieve.

I did the motorcycle-to-ferry-boat jump twice more that Spring, repeated my spectacular Harlem River train-over-the-bridge jump, and jumped motorbikes and cars into the Hudson on several occasions. On one of these jumps I set the world's motorcycle jumping record, traveling one hundred twenty six feet, six inches, from the pier to the water.

Auto jumping was more complicated. Because of the heavy motor in the front, a couple of hundred pounds of sand had to be placed in the back. This would keep the car from tumbling forward, end over end . . . in other words, somersaulting. It assured a straight, gliding flight and also eliminated the danger of the driver getting pinned under the car as it hit the water. As I rode through the air I would get my feet up

"Anyone who'd try a fool stunt like that," said George, "would be a bigger dummy than the one I was planning on."

"That's Bonomo," I grinned.

"Don't I KNOW it!" he retorted. "A one man Suicide Club! Scat! Go play Russian Roulette . . . it's safer."

But I was adamant and he finally assigned a pilot to fly me around while I planned the stunt. I noticed that in a straight-up, climbing bank, there was a moment when the forward motion of the plane practically stopped. In that instant, just before the pilot flipped it into the bank, to keep it from stalling, I felt I could safely make the dive. I reported my conclusions to George.

"Okay," he said cheerfully, "just let us know where to send the body."

With this happy thought to spur me on, I got

all padded up . . . donned a football helmet and kidney belt, climbed into the plane and we took off again . . . this time for the cameras. We were flying about seventy miles an hour. As I looked down I thought "If I **don't** come out of this alive, at least, I'll finish where I began." For we were over the ocean just off my own Coney Island.

We were about sixty feet above the water when we started the climb. The dive would be from about a hundred feet. Up, up we went. I braced my feet on the cockpit coaming. Then I got the signal from the pilot and, with a silent prayer, I dove out into space, with nothing under me but the air and the ocean. For a split second, I seemed to hang suspended in space . . . then down I plunged. Wrong or right, it was too late **now**! I broke the water with my arms and was careful to take the blow on the helmet from the top. That's all there was to it except, I thought I'd never come up. But I surfaced in time to see the pilot finishing off his bank. He waved to me and dipped his wings in salute, by way of congratulations. I waved back to let him know I was okay.

When the speedboat picked me up I felt a sharp pain in my foot. Taking off my shoe, I was amazed to find my big toe was broken. How that happened I'll never know . . . but it was a small price to pay for the reputation I had earned through that dive.

When my family heard about it, Mama almost had a nervous breakdown . . . but Papa served free ice cream to all the kids in the neighborhood.

As my reputation grew, along with it came something that should be labeled "Handle With Care—DANGEROUS." That something was **over-confidence**. Confidence is a wonderful thing and as necessary to a stuntman as it is to a big league ball player. But in stunting you only have to be OVERconfident once—for your first mistake can very well be your last. MY overconfidence very nearly wrote "FINIS" to my career, as well as to my earthly existence.

Seitz wanted a chase where Hutch, for whom I was doubling, ran along the top edge of a large billboard atop a building, and jumped across an alley to a fire-escape, on another building, about twelve feet away.

This type of stunt calls for a safety-net; but it would take a good half hour to rig it up and time was money. My common sense told me I should insist upon a net, but the picture was behind schedule as it was, and Seitz was in a bad mood.

I sized up the situation. On top of the billboard I'd be a hundred and ten feet high, but the fire-escape was one story lower. All I really had to do was just step off, leap the twelve foot gap, grab the fire-escape railing and pull myself up. Then I'd run down to the ground and the villains would be foiled again. My sense of caution said it was risky, but my overconfidence turned a deaf ear.

"What are you stalling for, Bonomo?" snapped Seitz, "Afraid you can't make it?"

Young Bonomo on his way in the movies.

"Get the cameras ready," I said, "I could do this in my sleep!"

Well, the cameras started grinding and I jogged along the foot-wide top of the billboard and jumped. I guess I must have been a little over-anxious or something for, instead of landing **alongside** the fire-escape and wrapping my arms over the rail as I had planned, I hit the outside of it with my body . . . and I hit it with terrific force. I had jumped too hard.

I felt as though that top rail had cut me in two. It knocked the wind out of me, my head was swimming and I started to lose consciousness. Then I began to slip back . . . and down. The only thing that saved me was that, as a falling cat will automatically fasten its claws into any surface it touches, I had instinctively clamped one arm over the rail. Then, suspended by that arm, I hung there for interminable seconds, while my head cleared and my strength returned. I looked down just once and almost lost my grip. That hard, asphalt pavement, a hundred feet below, was staring up at me, together with a scattering of people who were running every which way. I wondered if they were running

for a net, or just to be out from under when the body dropped.

I finally got a good grip with my other hand and swung myself over the rail to safety . . . a bit shaken but able to finish the stunt. Seitz was awaiting me at the foot of the fire-escape as I came down. He was in good spirits.

"You put on a great act up there, Joe, though for a minute, I thought you were a goner. Put a little more of that into your work from now on. That's what we need—REALISM!"

I was suddenly outraged. I almost frothed at the mouth. "Do you realize I almost fell a hundred feet? With no safety net under me?"

"Yeah," he said, his eyes suddenly bright. "It would have been too bad, but if you **had**, boy what a shot THAT would have made!"

From that experience I learned three things. (1) Never be OVERconfident. (2) Never take an unnecessary risk. (3) Never trust a man with a celluloid heart. I'm convinced that if George Seitz had thought it would have made a better picture, he'd have used his own grandmother to make that jump . . . and **she** wouldn't have had a safety-net, **either**.

A favorite of many early directors—the spectacular car dive stunt.

Chapter #9
JOE MEETS THE CHAMP

IT WAS LATER THAT SPRING that Bernarr MacFadden held his first contest to find "The World's Most Perfectly Developed Man." Charles Atlas and I remained close friends and we both decided to enter. We trained together and, in a spirit of friendly rivalry, even made a social bet of ten dollars on the outcome. We both wanted to win for we realized what it could mean to our careers. And just for the record, by now I had my OWN leopard skin, so we were starting even.

The contest opened with a great fanfare—with entries from all over the world—many of them splendid specimens of manhood. However, when the contest had progressed through the preliminaries, Charlie and I were running neck and neck, tied for first place. We remained tied through the eliminations and the finals were set for the following Monday night. I remember that Monday all too well.

Something told me not to go to work at the studio that day, but I went anyway—and broke my leg crashing a motorcycle. As the judges refused to alter the title to "The World's Most Perfectly Developed Man with a Broken Leg," Charlie Atlas not only won the title and the cash prize, but my ten dollars as well. We still kid each other about that. I claim he won by default, but Charlie says he could have broken both **his** legs and **still** have beaten me . . . but it was all in fun. At any rate, it was a turning point in both our lives. Charlie went on to become the most famous "Male Body-Beautiful" of his time, while I went on to a career in the movies. Which all goes to prove that a broken leg can be a blessing in disguise.

I figured I'd be good as new by Fall, so I again set my sights on Hollywood. That was the major league of movie work, and if I was going to have my bones broken, it wasn't going to be in New York, in the **minor** league. They were the only bones I had and I wasn't going to sell them cheaply.

As soon as I was able to get around again, I dug out my Aywon Film Corp. stunt test, my Apollo Contest pictures, photos of me with my cups from the dance competitions, and a hat-full of assorted press clippings. I bundled them up and hied me to the New York offices of Universal Pictures. Luckily, Paul Gulick, Universal's top publicity man and Fred J. McConnell, their sales-wizard, were both in. They had heard of this reckless Bonomo guy, who would do most anything. They side-stepped my clippings and promised to do what they could for me . . . but warned me it might take a long time. I figured I was getting the "don't call us, we'll call you," brush off—thanked them—and went home to Coney Island. You couldn't feel discouraged after one of Mama's meals.

During the Summer I kept up with my body building, tumbling, swimming and dancing. Someone told me that Lincoln once said "Many an opportunity is lost by not being ready" . . . and that sure wasn't going to happen to ME.

To earn my keep I drove one of Papa's trucks again, loading and unloading heavy tubs of ice and ice cream and tossing big bags of sugar around. It kept me hard as nails.

One day I had to drive to a farm over in Jersey, with a load of unpopped waste corn for their chickens. In exchange for this they'd give us a load of hay for our horses. I knew this farm was right next to Freddie Welsh's training camp, where Jack Dempsey was training for the Carpentier fight. I didn't mention it to the family, but I took along a couple of my pictures, my gym clothes and a football helmet. I had a wild idea that I might get a job as one of the Champ's sparring partners. I hadn't heard from Hollywood and that might get me some good publicity.

It was late afternoon by the time I'd delivered the corn and loaded the hay on my truck. My duty done, I headed straight for the training camp.

I pulled up in front of the training quarters and hopped out. Dempsey's manager, Jack Kearns —(I recognized him from his newspaper pictures) —was sitting with another fellow, on the porch. This other fellow turned out to be Teddy Hayes, Dempsey's top trainer. As I approached I gave them the old Bonomo smile.

"Need any sparring partners?" I asked, trying to look like one.

"We can use a few, we kill a couple every day," said Kearns, looking toward the truck. "You got a load of 'em under that hay?"

"I got **one** right **here**," I said, tapping my chest.

Now I had done some boxing, and I could handle myself pretty well, but I was certainly no pro. And I didn't have the tell-tale scars the professional fighter has. Both Kearns and Hayes regarded me with amusement.

My friendship with champ Jack Dempsey is one of over 40 years standing.

"Sorry, Kid, but no dice," Kearns said. "You couldn't even give the Champ a workout."

At that moment, who should come out the front door but Dempsey himself. He was perhaps an inch taller than I but not so well muscled. He was rugged all right, but a bit on the lean side . . . and although not much older than I, he already had the hardened look of a fighter.

"Hi, Champ," I said, striking a pugilistic pose.

"Hello," said Dempsey. He also seemed a bit amused. "Who are **you**?"

"He's your new sparring partner," said Hayes, grinning.

Dempsey grinned, too. "You're too pretty, kid," he said, "fightin' ain't for pretty boys. You oughta be out in Hollywood."

I got kind of peeved at that. Not mad—you don't get mad at Jack Dempsey. But I **was peeved**.

"That's just where I'm going, big fella," I shot back, "but right now I'm **here** and **you** don't seem to be **scarin'** me!" I hadn't meant to say it, but it was out, and I wasn't going to back down. I wondered what I'd do if he clobbered me. I certainly wouldn't take it lying down. But it was Kearns who answered me.

"Take it easy, kid," he said. "You won't get to Hollywood or anywhere else fightin' with guys like the Champ."

"Don't be too sure," grinned Hayes, "he looks pretty ferocious to ME."

Then they started laughing . . . and then I started laughing . . . and soon we were friends. I showed them the Apollo pictures and some stunt pictures and told them a little about my life and hopes. When I said I'd wrestled a lot, Dempsey offered to wrestle me. Kearns didn't like the idea too much, but Hayes thought it would be okay as long as there was no rough stuff. Just a warmup for Jack.

"All right, go ahead," said Kearns grudgingly, "but take it easy."

We wrestled in the ring for a half hour or so, and when I felt the power in Dempsey's arms and shoulders, I was glad I **wasn't** his sparring partner. He was no match for me in wrestling, though, and it boiled down to just a playful workout for us both. They asked me to dinner, and to spend the night, which I did. When I left, the next morning, I knew a friendship had been born that was to grow through the years. One of the most savage "killers" in boxing history is, outside the ring, one of the finest gentlemen and one of the nicest guys I have ever known.

The Summer at Coney Island passed pleasantly and I was getting in the best shape of my life. I trained hard and did a lot of fancy diving and tumbling. It was a tune-up for **my** championship fight . . . my personal assault on Hollywood. I had decided that as far as Gulick and McConnell were concerned, I was the forgotten man. So Joe Bonomo was going out to the Promised Land and beat down the doors, unassisted.

I was actually packing my bags when I got a call from Gulick. Could I come in to see him in the morning? He had a contract for me to sign. I certainly could!

The following day I signed with Universal Pictures at $150 a week—the equivalent of about four hundred today. At long last my devotion to the building up of my body was paying off with interest—my faith in myself had been justified—all my wonderful dreams were at last coming true.

A few days later, Mama, Papa and Victor saw me off at Penn Station. There were the usual tears, the backslaps and the goodbye kisses. Papa gave me two bank-rolls of quarters.

"So long as you're going to be an actor, Joey, you got to learn how to tip. And don't be cheap about it . . . never less than a quarter." As the train pulled out I was walking on air. Not yet twenty-one and armed with a Universal contract and a ticket to Hollywood, I was on my way to fame and fortune in the Land of Make Believe. God was good—the World was good—Life was good! I felt I must surely burst with happiness.

My first day in Hollywood!

I awakened at four in the morning and rushed to my hotel room window, to peer out at the Palm trees—the Yucca trees—the Orange and the Lemon trees. I didn't **see** any . . . the sun wasn't up yet . . . ah but I knew they were there! Southern California—the West Coast—Movie Land—as someone once said, "The home of the Holly-

Fred Datig, Universal's head casting director.

From fake steamships to real palm trees—Universal's land of movie make believe.

In front of the studio's very own post office—and this was not a film set.

wood cocktail—a swimming pool with an actor in it!" And at last I was destined to be a part of this wondrous melange—to be a soupcon of the frosting on the Hollywood cake! The Kid from Coney Island had ARRIVED!

By five, I was showered, shaved and dressed, and impatiently pacing the floor. What was it going to be like out here? How long before I'd be a star and should I sign autographs Joe, Joey or Joseph Bonomo? Or maybe I should CHANGE my name to Vincent, or Noel, or Wallace or something. Finally I could stand it no longer. I went for a long walk, had breakfast, then grabbed a cab for Universal City. They probably didn't start work 'til ten but I could hang around and soak up the atmosphere.

When the cab pulled up at the studio entrance, you can picture my amazement at seeing thousands—actually THOUSANDS of people milling about.

I went through the big arch to the front door of the Executive Building. As I started up the steps I was intercepted by a big Irishman in uniform—a studio cop.

"It's okay," I told him, "I'm Joe Bonomo."

"I don't care if you're Joe Eskimo," he retorted. "Wait over there with the rest of the mob."

"Mind telling me who they are? . . . I'm new here."

"You MUST be," he said, sizing me up. "They're extras. They'll be workin' in THE HUCHBACK OF NOTRE DAME—the new Lon Chaney picture."

"I'll probably be playing in that," I said, "I'm a personal friend of Lon Chaney's," and I started up the steps again. But he suddenly had me by the coat-sleeve and jerked me down.

"It won't work, kid. If you're after a job, get in that mob with the rest of 'em. Now start movin'."

"Oh, I've got a job," I said. "In fact, I've got a seven year contract."

"I'll BET you have." He was propelling me down the steps. "What are you—some kind of Nut or somethin'?"

"And here's my letter of introduction to Irving Thalberg," I said, showing it to him. He stared at the letter, bug-eyed.

"Pardon ME, Mister Bonomo. Right in there." He waved me back up the steps to the main door. I went through it feeling nine feet tall. I was ushered right into Mr. Thalberg's office.

Irving Thalberg, top producer for the studio, was a small man with sharp but sensitive eyes. He shook my hand warmly and welcomed me to Universal City.

"Is everything I've heard about you true, Joe?" he asked.

"Well, I don't know, Mr. Thalberg," I laughed, "What did you hear?"

"Some fabulous things about your stunt work with Pathe. And I saw a film you made for Nathan Hirsh."

"Heck, Mr. Thalberg, I was only an amateur, then. You should see me **now**!"

He smiled. "Just don't try to do it all at once, Joe. We'd like to keep you around for a while."

Then he pushed a button for an assistant-assistant, and instructed him to show me around. I was introduced to a lot of big people, shown the dressing rooms, the special costume department, the make-up department and some of the studios. I noticed the stars all had their names on their dressing room doors. I wondered again if I shouldn't change my name to Vincent.

At the end of the tour I had a warm feeling of being "in". Then I was introduced to Fred Datig, the head casting director. He had adding machine eyes that were totaling me up as he shook my hand.

Lon Chaney—The Man of a Thousand Faces.

"As long as you're HERE, Mr. Bonomo . . ."

"Just call me Joe," I said.

"Well, as long as you're here, Joe, you may as well go to work."

"The sooner the better," I said . . . and I meant it.

He called another assistant-assistant. "Fit Mr. Bonomo to a Lon Chaney costume. He may be doubling in the 'Hunchback.' Then take him out to the Cathedral. So long and good luck, Joe."

What a thrill! My first day in Hollywood and I was doubling the title role in "THE HUNCHBACK OF NOTRE DAME." It wasn't quite like playing the lead . . . but Rome wasn't built in a day and neither is a Hollywood star.

Properly costumed, I was taken to the back lot where a replica of Notre Dame Cathedral had been erected. Lon Chaney spotted me immediately and seemed overly pleased to see me.

"Hey, Wally," he called to Wallace Worsley, the director, "our troubles are over. Here's that Bonomo guy I've been telling you about."

You will recall Lon had been one of the stars of "A LIGHT IN THE DARK" that I worked on with Hope Hampton.

Worsley seemed delighted. "Boy, are we glad to see **you**!"

I found out why as soon as he told me what my first assignment was to be. Whoever doubled for Chaney, as the Hunchback, had to slide down a rope, from the Cathedral tower to the ground —a good hundred and fifty feet. The slide had to be done fast, and they weren't sure it could be done successfully. At least, no one was willing to try it. A long, fast slide down a rope may look easy, but actually it is one of the most difficult of stunts, and all stuntmen know it.

"But Joe'll do it," Chaney said, recalling my

On the set of THE HUNCHBACK OF NOTRE DAME.

recklessness back East.

"Not so fast," I hedged, "let me see the equipment."

One of the other stuntmen eagerly handed me the heavy leather gloves that were to be used. I looked at them, then looked up at that hundred and fifty feet of rope, dangling from the tower window.

."And you want this done fast?" I asked.

"Gotta be one continuous fast slide," said Worsley.

"Not in these gloves," I said, "it would be suicide."

Worsley was nettled.

"You've changed since New York," said Chaney. "Losing your nerve?"

"No," I said cheerfully, "I've just gotten a little smarter. I'll need a couple of hours to get some special gloves made."

At this Worsley exploded. I might have been fired on the spot had not another stuntman, (Harry, I heard someone call him,) stepped in.

"Let **me** have the gloves," he said, "I'll do it."

I suppose he figured this was his chance to gain a reputation, even though he must have known how dangerous the stunt was. He evidently was willing to gamble.

He got into the costume, went up in the tower, the cameras started turning and he started down. (Those of you who saw the picture will remember that slide.) I knew he was going too fast. About two-thirds of the way down he let out a tortured groan, let go of the rope, and fell. When we reached him he had a broken leg, to say nothing of serious hand and leg burns. The gloves were still smoking—they had burned right through.

A consultation followed and Worsley asked me how long it would take to make the special gloves. I said about two hours; so while I hustled off to the costume department they switched to another sequence.

I made the gloves myself. I got the heaviest leather ones I could find and lined them with special thick sheets of tin foil . . . the same stuff used on gum wrappers . . . to insulate against the heat. I also had long strips of foil sewed on the inside of my tights, from crotch to ankle. With this equipment the stunt was easy. We got perfect footage on the first attempt. The slide was sensational.

It never occurred to anyone that the already scorched rope might have broken while I was coming down—but it didn't—which goes to prove that stunting is more dangerous than putting your head in an alligator's mouth. Incidentally, a bit later on in this story I do that, too—again proving that if you insist on using your brain, you don't belong in this business.

Well, that was my first day in Hollywood. I had appeared in THE HUNCHBACK OF NOTRE DAME. Though audiences would never know it was Bonomo, I was there just the same. And I had gained a reputation as an efficient and safe stuntman.

A classic scene from a classic film—Lon Chaney and Patsy Ruth Miller in the original HUNCHBACK OF NOTRE DAME.

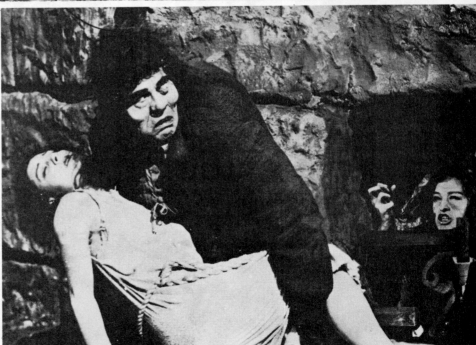

Universal's lavish production of THE HUNCHBACK OF NOTRE DAME was a spectacular introduction to Hollywood for me.

Chapter #10

The Cowboy FROM Coney Island

AFTER THAT FIRST DAY I was a top stunt-man. But that was only part of it. My contract also called for me to be a "stock actor," and any time a "bit" part went begging, they handed it to ME. I played pirates, Gypsies, adagio dancers, doormen, policemen, sailors, cowboys, . . . you name it . . . I played it. One week I'd be playing a Chinese Mandarin . . . the next week an African gorilla.

I was willing to do **anything**, and believe me, I did **everything**.

Then I was cast in the Pete Morrison series of two-reel Westerns. The real cow-punchers who were working in the series, resented the intrusion of a Coney Island Cowboy, and the tricks they played on this tenderfoot, were the next thing to mayhem.

The first day they gave me a horse and told me to ride it. I didn't even know how to get up into the saddle. But I remembered seeing a saddle-jump done in some movies, so I took a run, leap-frogged over the horse's rear and made a perfect three point landing with my feet in the stirrups.

It was the worst thing I could have done, for where they previously had only resented me, those old time cow-pokes now put me down as a smart kid and really decided to get me.

The next horse I got started bucking immediately and off I went . . . but I just grabbed the saddle horn and vaulted back into the saddle. A moment later I was down in the dust again.

Back up I went and back down I bounced.

"You ain't got the idea, Bonomo," a lanky Oklahoman drawled. "You're supposed to stay **ON** the critter."

I didn't say anyting—just jumped onto the horse again, only to be bucked off again and this time to land flat on my back. The laugh that went up could have been heard at the bunkhouse.

Then one old timer took pity on me. "Your trouble, son," he said, "is you don't know enough about horses."

Then he removed a three-inch stick from between my horse's rear and the base of his tail. Someone had placed it there so he couldn't get his tail down. All his bucking had been to try and shake the stick loose.

But that was only the first trick, of many. Someone would casually loosen my cinch-strap, and the next time we'd start up, off I'd go again. Once I was playing an Indian, wearing only a loin cloth, a feather and a pair of moccasins. While one cowboy held my attention, another sneaked over and put itching powder on my horse's back. I innocently mounted and started off. It wasn't long before I was out-bucking the horse. I even itch now when I think of it. These tricks they played on me and a hundred more, but I just laughed them off and bided my time. I got even when we started "bulldogging."

Bulldogging is when a man leaps from a horse to a steer, and twisting the animal's head, bears

I won my spurs in Westerns as I learned from the experts. This two reeler starring Pete Morrison (center), provided one of my first introductions to the wide open spaces.

him to the ground. To bulldog a man, you leap from a tree or a high rock, hitting a horseman across the shoulders, with both men falling to the ground. You've seen that many times in the movies.

Well, because of my tumbling training, I could always manage to land on top when we hit the ground, whether I was the jumper or the man jumped . . . and when my one hundred and ninety pounds landed on a man, it hurt. And when we'd bulldog into a stream, I'd suddenly get clumsy, and before I could get off the man he'd be almost drowned. And in the fight scenes, because of my strength and wrestling ability, I used to toss them around like rag dolls. It wasn't long before they asked for a truce. I was happy to call off the war, for I really liked and admired them a lot. Of all the men I've ever

worked with those cowboy stuntmen were the most courageous. They took chances every day that most men would back away from and they accepted injury or sudden death as all part of the game. Never sell a cowboy short.

Among those I worked with in those days were Floyd Criswell and Jackie and Bert Goodrich. These men and men like them were the REAL stars of the Westerns, doubling for the gun toting, spur jangling, swashbuckling Western star whenever a scene was shot where life and limb were at stake . . . and yet their names seldom, if ever, appeared on the screen. Whenever the audience acclaimed their favorite cowboy hero as he thrilled them with death defying stunts, it was really his "double" they were cheering. Not that the stars were incapable of doing the stunts themselves—many of them were crack riders possessed of great personal courage and daring—but an injury to a "name star" could wreck a whole production and cost the studio many thousands of dollars. Name stars were not expendable.

I recall when one of the cowboy "heroes" asked to see a script of the scene he was about to do. Floyd Criswell drawled "You don't need no script. You jes' ride into the town, sit like a chicken in the saddle, roll a cigaroot and kiss the gal. **We'll** make the picture!" And that's just about the way those pictures were made. We stuntmen were the ones who got the broken bones, who went over the cliffs and rode the rapids. We were the hombres who made those thrilling pictures thrilling.

Where did those cowboy stars come from? Usually right up from the ranks . . . and if there was such a thing as a producer's nightmare it was having star material in his hands and letting it slip through his fingers, only to see the actors and actresses he could have put under contract and made millions with, making the millions for some other producer.

A good example is the case of a cowboy named George Belden who used to work with the famous Buck Jones at the Fox Studio. What little they gave George to do he did well, but being overshadowed by the great Buck he never got a chance to distinguish himself or gain any real notice.

Came the day when Buck had a disagreement with the studio and left in a huff and they had

The great Buck Jones—a screen legend.

to find a quick replacement. Several of us suggested George Belden but Sol Wurtzel, head of the studio, had his eye on a young fellow who worked on the chuck-wagon as a waiter. He called himself Rex King, had a nice smile, wore Western clothes as though he'd been born in them and had a line of talk that would have charmed the devil out of his pitchfork.

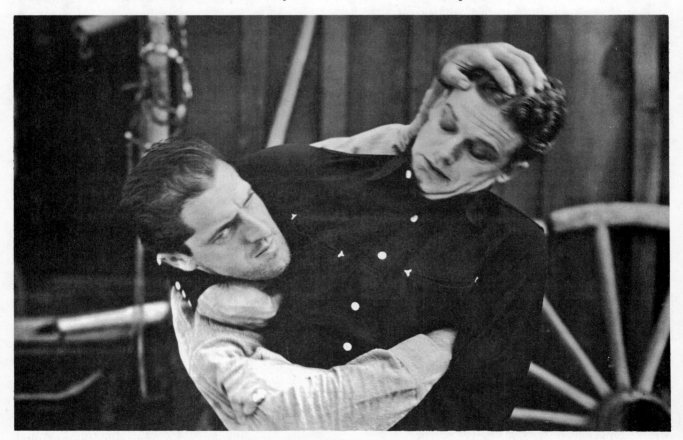

Rex Bell (right) dished out his share of movie thrills before becoming Nevada's Lieutenant Governor.

So against everyone's advice Wurtzel signed him to replace Buck Jones, without even giving George Belden a tryout or a second thought. He turned out to be impossible as an actor and after a disastrous couple of weeks Lefty Huff, the director, sent him back to the chuck-wagon. They then looked around for Belden but he was gone. Another studio signed him and not long after, he blossomed forth as a Western star in his own right as the great Rex Bell. He married the beautiful Clara Bow and came into political prominence as the Lieutenant Governor of Nevada, a position which he held until his untimely death in 1962.

I have often wondered how many potential stars just missed having a career by the mere turn of a card, one bad audition or the faulty judgment of some producer. A case in point was that of a personable young man named Leonard Slye. Paul Malvern, my good friend and fellow stuntman, had turned producer and was doing a series of pictures for Trem Carr at Universal.

Monogram Pictures had merged with Republic Studios and top man Herbert Yates had just brought out an unknown guitar player named Gene Autry who had made a big hit in a picture called TUMBLING TUMBLEWEEDS. Autry took the public fancy and almost overnight guitar playing cowboys became the rage, so Paul and Trem started auditioning every cowboy they could dig up who could twang a guitar and sing a little.

Among those auditioned was this Leonard Sly who seemed to meet every requirement . . . he was a good looking cowboy type, he had a good

Bronco Bonomo, ready to meet the West's roughest heavies.

singing voice and the guitar seemed to be his specialty. Why he was rejected no one seems to remember, but he was told he wouldn't do.

And so this young man went sadly on his way, not being heard from again until he turned up as Roy Rogers—and made a few million dollars.

A somewhat parallel case is that of John Wayne, whom Paul had in Republic's WESTWARD HO, a vigilante story which was distinguished, not alone for the presence of Wayne in the lead, but because it had 50 white horses pitted against 50 black horses. Shortly after this, Hollywood executives made a slight mistake . . . they said as a Western star John was washed up—finished —through. Not long after this momentous decision he was picked up for STAGECOACH and the rest is history.

Perhaps the most famous among our cowboy stunt group was Yakima Canutt. Yakima was a renowned rodeo star who, in competition with the best of them, had won the title of "World's Champion Cowboy." He could outride, outrope and outshoot any man he ever met. He originated almost all the really spectacular cowboy stunts in film history. He was largely responsible for the rapid rise of Westerns in popularity. He was the master . . . and his stunts were talked about half way around the world.

For instance, there was the stunt where the horseman overtakes the runaway stagecoach, leaps aboard from his galloping horse, works his way forward on the wagon tongue and reins the horses to a stop. This took a tremendous amount of athletic skill, horsemanship and nerves of steel. Another variation of this same stunt, that left

Gene Autry started the "singing cowboy" craze.

John Wayne and Yakima Canutt (right), the master western stuntman, who became the leading director of spectacular action for Hollywood.

movie audiences gasping, is where the man on the wagon tongue loses his balance, falls through to the roadway and is supposedly trampled by the horses and run over by the coach. (Remember that one?) Well, this stunt Yakima did by digging up a long section of earth between the wagon tracks, softening it up and smoothing it over. At the crucial moment he'd let himself fall from the wagon-tongue, in a sort of baseball slide, making a cloud of dust as the wagon passed over him. The danger was that one of the racing horses might stumble and fall as he hit the soft ground. This never happened, but the mental picture of the horrible tangle of horses, man and coach, used to keep us holding our breath every time Yakima did it.

Yakima was the only man who was ever able to transfer from a horse to a racing, covered wagon. He was the only man ever able to get a horse close enough. Perhaps it was the flapping

Before: Leonard Slye

After: Roy Rogers

canvas that caused the horse to shy away, I don't know, but no one else ever did it. No one, that is, but—Bonomo.

One day I bribed the prop men to rig a short pole on the wagon, on the side away from the cameras. This done, I bet Yakima twenty bucks I could duplicate the stunt. He went for it, hook, line and sinker. I was a fairly good horseman by now, and I could get my horse just close enought to the wagon so I could grab the pole. As I was on the other side of the wagon from where Yakima and the camera crew were, all they saw was my body swing forward and plump into the wagon as it sped away. I quickly untied the pole and Yakima was none the wiser. None of the prop men ever told him, and to this day I'm sure he wonders how that pseudo cowboy with the Brooklyn accent, ever did it.

Shortly after that stunt my friend Bert Goodrich almost lost his life. He was doubling a big Western hero, chasing some bad men down a road that curved around a giant tree. Bert was to cut off the road, cut across the curve, and intercept the villains. Well, down the road came the bad guys, galloping their horses at top speed —and not far behind came Bert, galloping his horse a little faster. The villains veered right, following the curve in the road and Bert started to pass to the left of the tree to cut them off. But Bert's horse had other ideas . . . he wanted to follow the pack. Frantically Bert tried to rein him to the left but, just as they reached the huge tree the horse cut sharply to the right and crashed into it, head on.

We could hear the sickening crunch a quarter of a mile away. When we got there both Bert and the horse lay in a doubled up heap. The horse had just been knocked unconscious but Bert had a broken neck. He was also totally blind for several days but with good medical care he made a complete recovery. And guess what? He went right back to stunting again.

I hope I'm not giving the impression that a stuntman's life was just a continuous succession of mayhem, broken bones and hospitalizations. True, we had our share but we had a lot of fun, too. In those days meeting schedules and deadlines wasn't as important as it is today and we had more time for clowning. Many of the tricks we played on each other were harmless enough . . . some were a bit rough . . . but there was one that wasn't to be recommended for anyone with a weak heart.

I first saw it when we were doing a series of two reel Westerns on location. The director had gotten his training under the famous William Wyler and like Wyler, he was a perfectionist. He knew what he wanted and in order to get it he often used to ride "rough herd" over the cowboy actors.

One day he became especially dissatisfied with the work of two of the stuntmen and, in no minced words, gave them a dressing down before the entire company. They were fairly thick skinned and I don't think they minded it much, but to keep from losing face with the rest of

Astride the mighty Silver King, Fred Thomson's famous screen mount.

the company they decided to retaliate. If the gag had ever been pulled before, none of us had ever seen it, and I'm sure the director hadn't.

They waited until the following day and deliberately bungled a scene. The director stopped the cameras and started bawling them out. They took it without a word until he had finished, then one we called Slim suddenly drew his six-shooter and moved in on the surprised man. As he thus engaged his attention, his partner slipped around in back of the director until he was standing directly behind him.

"Mister," drawled Slim, "I've had about as much as a man can take. There's only blanks in this here gun, but that shirt you're wearin' is mighty thin and I calculate the wad from one of these blanks will go about half way through ya at close range." Saying which he jammed the muzzle of his gun against the startled director's stomach . . . and at precisely the same moment his partner fired a shot directly behind him. I've had it pulled on me since and the effect is startling. The explosion of the gun behind you and the pressure of the gun shoved into your stomach synchronize so perfectly you can only conclude you've been shot.

The director's knees buckled, he clutched his stomach and looked for the blood before he realized he'd been taken. Then he joined in the general laughter and said he knew all the time it was just a gag . . . but it was a good ten minutes before his hands stopped shaking enough so he could light a cigarette. From then on we stuntmen did just about as we pleased.

When a large percentage of the shooting had to be done away from Hollywood on location, we had many free evenings when time hung heavy on our hands. When we tired of playing cards, checkers and chess, one of our chief diversions was practical jokes. They had to be new and cleverly devised as we had all been victimized at various times and were constantly on guard. On this occasion it took an old stuntman named Billy Jones to catch us with our

A formidable fivesome of silent era Western Stars—Yakima Canutt, Jack Dougherty, Leo Maloney, Bill Fairbanks and Jack Perrin.

guard down.

I recall we had just moved into a good hotel and had rooms on the seventh floor and on this particular night we had played cards until after midnight and were sitting around talking about things in general. Finally the subject of foot-racing came up. I have mentioned earlier that I did the hundred yards in slightly over 10 seconds, but if any of those present believed me, because of my size and weight they certainly didn't believe I could duplicate it, while I was just as sure I **could**.

Harvey Parry, my good friend and fellow stunt-man, who was also working in this picture, was a top athlete, thirty pounds lighter than I. He was sure he could beat me in a hundred yard dash and didn't hesitate to say so. The argument was waxing pretty hot when Billy Jones spoke up.

"Look boys . . . I've got an idea that will decide this once and for all. While you two strip down to your underwear, I'll pace off a hundred yards in the hotel corridor outside and you can settle it out there. Not only that, but I'll give twenty bucks to the winner. It'll be worth that to put an end to all this talk."

So while we stripped down to our shorts he went out in the hall and paced off a hundred yards—the other stuntmen checking it to make sure it was accurate . . . marking the starting and finish lines with a piece of chalk. As we were running on carpet we came out barefoot wearing **just** our shorts. All the boys gathered 'round, Jonesy hollered "On your mark . . . get set . . . go!" and off we went down the hall at full tilt.

Neither of us were used to running on carpet and I found it especially difficult. Harvey, being much the lighter of the two didn't find it such a handicap and beat me by about a foot. But when he turned to collect his twenty dollars there wasn't a soul in sight. While we were racing, Billy Jones and the others had hustled back into the room and closed and locked the door.

First we called but got no answer, then we started pounding on the door-panels. Several other doors started opening down the hall, from which annoyed sleepy faces peered out at us in amazement. Then the elevator door opened and the hotel detective stepped out and grabbed us. Billy had phoned the desk that a couple of characters were running around the hall, prac-tically naked, knocking on people's doors. We explained what we were doing and said if he could get Billy to open the door he'd verify our story. At the house detective's first knock, Billy opened the door and stepped out, followed by the others, all looking surprised and puzzled.

"Something wrong, officer?" said Billy. "I see you caught them all right."

"Yeh—but these looneys say they're friends of yours. Can you vouch for 'em?"

Billy turned to the other stuntmen.

"Do they look familiar to you boys?"

They all shook their heads in unison. Then Billy gave us a sad look.

"I'd sure like to help you birds out, but I can't lie about it. I never saw you before in my life."

Although a buckaroo from Brooklyn, I was ac-cepted into the ranks of the studio's real westerners.

And he closed the door.

It took us a half hour and the price of a box of cigars to talk our way out and if old Billy Jones is still alive I'll bet he's still chuckling. He never paid off that twenty dollars either . . . said he was phoning the house detective and missed the finish of the race.

Practical joking was not confined entirely to stuntmen. I think one of the funniest jokes was perpetrated by the inimitable Harold Lloyd, him-self. If my memory is accurate it happened during the first of the pictures he produced, directed and starred in.

As he had a genius for devising wild and dangerous situations, there was plenty of work for us stuntmen and a nice bonus upon completion of the picture. Lloyd was, and still is, a grand fellow and we all liked him and always gave him our best efforts, so we were quite surprised when Harvey Parry, who was doubling some of Lloyd's stunts, bungled a couple of easy ones. Lloyd gave him a puzzled look, but all he said was, "Try it again, Harvey."

As the morning wore on Harvey seemed to be getting more nervous and absent minded by the minute and kept looking at his watch. Just before noon he went to Lloyd and said, "Can I get off early today?" Lloyd said, "Get off early? Why?"

"Well," said Harvey, coloring up, "I'm getting married at four o'clock and I've got things to do."

"Great," said Harold, "I'll let you off right

Taking a break by the camera, while working on THE EAGLE'S TALONS, on location at Laguna Beach. Director Duke Worne is seated in the chair and Fred Thomson is at the extreme right.

after you double for me in this next scene.''

The scene took place down in a pitch-dark, musty, cob-webbed cellar into which Lloyd had fallen and he's trying to find his way out with the aid of just one lighted candle. In trying to locate a means of egress, he mistakes a tall step-ladder for a flight of steps, climbs to the top and steps off into thin air.

Harvey, doubling Lloyd, stepped off the top of the ladder, let out a yell and started to fall . . . but as he passed out of camera range, unseen by the audience, he was dangling on a piano wire, sixteen feet above the cellar floor.

"Are you okay, Harvey?" Lloyd called to him.

"Okay," said Harvey as he dangled in the air.

"Good," said Lloyd . . . and at a signal from him the background orchestra broke into the wedding march, everybody shouted "Happy marriage!" and walked out and left him dangling.

It took the poor guy three hours of twisting and turning before he could kink and snap that piano wire, after which he fell the full sixteen feet to the floor. He limped into the church five hours late for his wedding.

Oh, yes . . . the girl married him just the same. When you say "yes" to a Hollywood stuntman you've got to expect almost anything.

When Hollywood was growing up, practical jokes really had their place in the scheme of things, for in those days life had not taken on the sombre aspect it seems to have today. It was a happier, more carefree world where people took time out for pure, unadulterated fun, with practical jokes the order of the day. One such cause of hilarity to the perpetrator, I shall never forget.

One of my best friends on the West coast was Fred Thomson. Fred was one of the country's greatest athletes, who was married to Frances Marion, the well known screen writer. They had a beautiful ranch home in the hill section, with complete stables for their thoroughbred horses and a special stable for a fighting bull that Fred had imported from Spain, as sort of a live toy to play with. He housed the bull in a Mexican style stable with a low roof which, as you will soon see, becomes important to this story.

I first met Fred Thomson, who was also an excellent actor, when he was set for the lead in THE EAGLE'S TALONS, a serial out at Universal. I was chosen to play the heavy as the script called for a particularly athletic type of villain. It was the first time I had worked with him and he was constantly surprised by my strength and especially my tumbling ability, considering my size. He reached deeply into his bag of athletic tricks, but everything he did I duplicated with ease.

Besting me got to be almost a fetish with him and I smelled a mouse when one day he invited me out to his home to see the prize bull he had been telling me about. However, whatever the gag was to be I decided to go along with it.

The bull was a beautiful creature named Muro . . . young, strong and filled with fire. You can imagine his size when I tell you he had a 96 inch neck. He had arrived several weeks earlier and Fred immediately had rubber plugs put on his needle-pointed horns and been working out with him daily, wrestling with him and learning all about him. When I arrived and found Fred had also invited quite an audience of friends, I was sure something was up.

We all had lunch and then Fred suggested we go out to the corral and meet Muro. When everyone was at a safe distance, Fred let him out and put on an exhibition with him that would have done credit to most matadors. Using a cape he would approach the bull, say "NOW Muro!" and Muro would paw up the dirt, lower his head and suddenly charge like an express train. Although the plugs were on his horns, had Fred not leaped nimbly aside at the psychological moment, he could have suffered severe injury from being tossed by that powerful beast.

After several charges of this type, Fred dropped the cape, literally took the bull by the horns and wrestled him to the ground from a standing position, a feat that took great strength and knowhow. Then looping a rope about the bull's middle, with just a loop on top, he rode him about the corral like a bucking broncho. He brought the snorting, quivering animal to a stop just in front of me and said with a grin, "All right, Joe . . . now it's YOUR turn."

Although my knowledge of Spanish fighting bulls had been limited to a few film shots I had seen of them, I decided I couldn't let Fred get away with this without at least giving it a try, so I replied, in a matter of fact tone of assurance, "Okay, pal, let's have a go at it." And then the fun began. Muro took one look at me, his eyes started to turn red and he emitted an angry snort. For some reason he disliked me on sight. As I advanced toward him he pawed the ground for a moment, then lowered his head and charged full speed.

I had no cape to divert him but, as startled as I was at the moment, I didn't need one. I took a leap to one side that would have done credit to a bounding Basque. By the time he circled around and came at me again I had my coat off and, using it for a cape, I made like a real Toreador. On his third charge I went with it and got a grip on his horns.

I figured if Fred could throw him I certainly

Fred Thomson (center) backs away as I (right) prepare for a bit of villainy.

could, but what I didn't know was that Fred, being left-handed, had always thrown him from the left side . . . and I had him on the RIGHT side. Fred had thrown him so many times that the bull had gotten into the habit of going into a fall when he felt that left-handed neck twist, having learned from experience it was useless to fight it. But when I started twisting his neck to the right, he just couldn't understand it. He held his powerful neck as rigid as a bar of iron, except when he was trying to shake me off. We went round and round and I finally got him down, but I still don't know how unless he finally got tired of it all and decided to take the easy way out.

By this time my audience was hysterical and Fred offered to let me off the hook, but I had gone through too much to quit a loser. I said, "Put the surcingle on him and I'll ride him like a horse on a Merry-go-round." So we got it around the unhappy Muro's middle and I hopped on his back. But if I hadn't had enough, Muro had. He took off like a shot and headed straight for his stable . . . the one with the low roof. After miraculously ducking beam after beam I finally wound up in his stall, still perched on his back, where I intended to remain, for Muro was good and mad and had I gotten off in that little stall, he'd have stomped me to death or crushed me against the walls.

Then, in trying to keep him from turning his head and biting my legs, I wrenched at his horns so desperatley that the rubber knobs came off the ends and I suddenly found myself with two needle-pointed "daggers" to deal with . . . with Muro trying his best to shake, bounce or brush me off, so he could use those horns to do a little fancy "needle-point embroidery" on my anatomy.

When Fred and the others came running in, I was clinging to that bull's back like a jellyfish to a rock, the perspiration rolling off me in rivulets. Luckily no one had a camera or I'd have never lived it down.

As it was, Fred gleefully spread the story around and I never denied it . . . that is . . . I never ACTUALLY denied it. But whenever some kidder would say, "Hey, Joe, what's this Fred Thomson was telling me about Muro?" I'd say, "Muro? Oh, that's just a lot of bull." And believe me, he WAS.

Fred Thomson and his pet bull Muro.

A day at Universal was always interesting, and I enjoyed it all—from playing a cop in a comedy to horsing around with Fred Thomson and Silver King behind the sets on the lot.

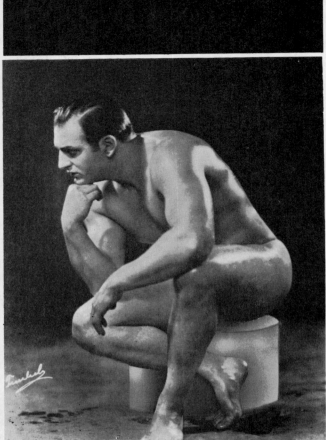

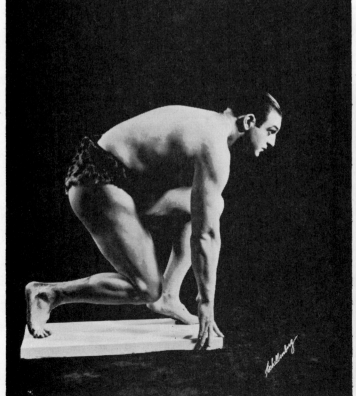

When the studio decided on a photo session they usually came up with interesting poses. Here are two of my favorites—"The Discus Thrower" and "The Thinker".

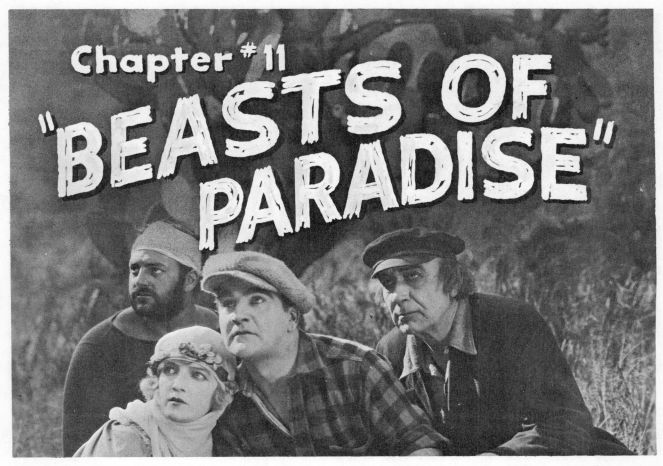

Chapter #11
"BEASTS OF PARADISE"

I REMEMBER I hadn't been with Universal more than a few months before I saw a stuntman lose his life. We were working on a stunt where a man was to fall off a cliff and be swept away in the rapids below. This fellow did the fall all right, but missed the "brake ropes" and was swept over a steep waterfall to his death.

I knew this man and I knew he was a secret drinker. The alcohol in his system had slowed his muscular coordination and threw his timing off just enough to make him miss. If I had ever been tempted to play around with intoxicants, I certainly had the notion wiped out of my mind when we fished this fellow's broken body out of the water below the falls.

In those days, I was then twenty one, I used to be up every morning at six, do some road work and calisthenics, shower, eat a good nourishing breakfast, (that's important) and be at the lot, ready for work, at eight. The picture business was a rugged grind and a demanding taskmaster. But I enjoyed it and never asked more of God or the Industry than that I be kept lucky by the first and busy by the second. I had a good car and good clothes, ate the best food, and was always good for a touch. For recreation I drove, read, and went dancing or to the movies in the evenings. I went out with girls, but I was always back to my room and asleep by eleven o'clock. The girls shook their heads despairingly but they couldn't shake my resolve. My first love was my career and no girl was going to come between us.

We made a lot of pictures in those days. The stories would change, the settings would change, the costumes would change, and the stuntmen would change. Some were killed and others permanently injured and forced out of the profession. Many others just walked away. I think they had premonitions of disaster.

I couldn't possibly remember **all** the pictures I made. There were hundreds of films with thousands of stunt sequences—serials, two-reelers and features. I played in settings and costumes that must have represented every nook and cranny of the world. The exhibitors gobbled up the pictures and yelled for more, and we kept grinding them out.

Quite often we'd spend weeks on location . . . making pictures away from Hollywood. Then— the singing around the campfires, the dances we'd put on, the parodies we'd do on the stars, and the stories we'd tell. Those were wonderful days and nights.

Oh—and I almost forgot—the crap games. I don't recommend gambling, but I was young, and when it rained there wasn't much else to do. One night I got lucky and wound up with more than half of Palm Springs in my pocket! No fooling, I had it, deeds and all! If I had hung on to it, I'd be a multi-millionaire today. But at that time Palm Springs was little more than a water-hole in the desert, so I sold it back to the fellow I won it from—for four hundred dollars! He promptly lost it back in another game. Then it passed through several periods of ownership—one character had it three times. I never knew what finally happened to it, but I often think how little the people in Palm Springs today, realize how many crap games their home sites passed through . . . and how many of them are there only because, many years ago, someone threw a seven when he was trying for a six—the hard way.

I had just finished my chores in the Jack Hoxie and the Hoot Gibson Westerns, when I was called in to do the fight sequences with Reginald Denny in THE LEATHER PUSHERS. I was winding that one up when Jack Dempsey arrived in Hollywood to make his FIGHT AND WIN series of two-reelers—and I was assigned to work with him in the fight scenes.

On the first day of rehearsal I'll never forget Dempsey's surprised look when I climbed through the ropes.

"Pretty Boy!" he shouted. "What are you doing here?"

"You told me to go to Hollywood, Champ," I grinned. "I took your advice."

Among other things, Jack and I did the exciting and dangerous, though comic, "Slavat" fight. In this, while Dempsey fought in the orthodox manner, I employed the Slavat system, boxing with my feet instead of my hands, delivering kicks in place of punches—high kicks, low kicks, side kicks and mule kicks. It made a great sequence, but I had to be careful not to injure

Hoot Gibson was always fun to work with.

the Champ. For one thing, he was too valuable —and for another, if he'd gotten mad he'd have probably annihilated me.

In a previous picture Jack had made, he'd been in the ring with a well known heavyweight, who shall be nameless. This misguided pug conceived the idea of knocking Dempsey out with an unscheduled "sucker punch." With the cam-

Reginald Denny (right), known in later years as a light comedian, was an able screen fighter. This scene is from the famous LEATHER PUSHERS.

70

eras going and the film to witness it, he figured it might get him a regular bout for the title. Of course, it was unethical, but he wasn't very bright to begin with.

As the cameras started rolling, he suddenly caught Jack with this unrehearsed haymaker, putting everything he had behind it. Dempsey shook his head, but he didn't go down. Instead, he landed some unrehearsed punches of his own —just four fast murderous blows that sent the unethical aspirant to the hospital with a broken jaw, a concussion and three broken ribs. When the guy was able to sit up, Jack gently admonished him with, "You really shouldn't have done what you did." Then he apologized and paid all the hospital bills. That was Jack Dempsey!

When we did the "in-fighting" scenes I always cautioned him. The man had such power in his punches that just a quick jab, using only the snap of his wrist muscles, would almost paralyze a man. A mere flick of those powerful wrists and I'd have another big red splotch on my ribs.

"Take it easy, Champ," I'd say in the clinches, "if I want to get killed by you, I'll do it for the championship and make some dough out of it."

A few years later I was to challenge Dempsey to a knock-down, drag-out brawl—"everything goes and the winner takes all " Of course, it was just a publicity stunt as I knew he wouldn't accept, for Jack was smart and no smart boxer will take on a strongman, a wrestler or a tumbler in a free-for-all. There are too many tricks in the wrestling, judo and Slavat repertoire. However, of all the men in ring history, I think Dempsey would have stood the best chance in such a combat. He was a rough and ready fighter, with the courage of a lion and tremendous power in every part of his body. And those murderous fists! I often wonder how I'd have come out if he HAD accepted the challenge.

Several years later I staged the fight sequences for Gene Tunney's serial THE FIGHTING MARINE, which added to my reputation as one of the top "fight scene" stagers in the industry . . . for when it came to fights I had about all the "natural equipment" you could look for. Remember, I was a wrestler, tumbler, acrobat, strongman, boxer and judo expert—I had super-quick reflexes and a seemingly special talent for working out spectacular falls and chair-throws —as many as six in advance. Add to this my hand-picked crew of trained acrobats and fighters and how could I miss! The fight scenes we put on were almost beyond belief. If I wore a hat I'd certainly doff it to that crew of mine. After I had been with Universal for about a year, I got the studio to build me a gymnasium on the lot. And, knowing a captain is no better than his team—and a team no better than its poorest member, I hand-picked my team with utmost care. Then I trained them so fight scenes could be staged with a minimum of danger and a maximum of excitement.

For many hundreds of hours, evenings, Saturdays and Sundays—whenever we could get time off—we worked. It finally got so that one of us could make an improvised or unrehearsed move and the others would react automatically. And violence was our specialty. Directors were amazed when I'd pick up a man and throw him across a room, into three of four others, as merely a prelude to a fight in which we would smash tables and chairs over each other's heads and hurl one another through doors and windows. It looked as though no one could live though the apparent punishment we were taking, but when the scene was over, we'd come up smiling. We'd be bruised and sprained, with perhaps an occasional broken bone, but no **serious** injuries.

After a while the directors got smart and shot all the scenes that were in a set, before turning "Bonomo and his trained lunatics" loose. For let us stage just one good fight scene and for all the good the set was after that, you could take it out and burn it! Boy, could we demolish scenery!

Danger and inconvenience were just everyday situations in the life of a movie stuntman back in the 1920's. In Universal's BEASTS OF PARADISE, I not only played the important part of

In character for BEASTS OF PARADISE.

"Big Jack", but also doubled for the hero, Bill Desmond. Paul Malvern was also working on this serial and he doubled for heroine Eileen Sedgwick. There was a scene in which Bill and Eileen were cornered on a passenger steamer named the Yale, that plied between Los Angeles and San Diego. As a gang of murderous seamen closed in on them they were to leap over the rail and swim for their lives. The stunt had one rather dangerous angle in that, after a 75 foot leap from the top deck to the water below, we had to do a quick water sprint to avoid being cut to ribbons by the vessels twin-screw propellers. That meant we had to land in the water without being knocked unconscious and, despite the clothing that would hamper us, we had to clear the stern of the moving vessel by a good safe margin. After that it was a full mile and a half to shore, through a rough breakwater, but we were told not to worry about that as we would be picked up by a rescue boat.

We donned our costumes, which duplicated those of Bill and the girl ... the time arrived and over the rail we went. We struck out at a fast clip and cleared the propellers okay, then started to look around for the rescue boat ...

but no boat was in sight. However, we were both strong swimmers and, struggling out of our costumes down to the swim trunks we were wearing underneath, we finally made it to shore through that breakwater ... but it was close. We came out on a rocky beach somewhere in the neighborhood of Wilmington. After limping a painful mile in our bare feet, over sharp rocks, we reached a road and luckily an empty taxi came along and picked us up. We taxied back to the studio, a matter of a good 25 miles. You can imagine what was on the meter by the time we made it back.

The studio was delighted to see us safe and sound. We said "Where was the rescue boat that was supposed to pick us up?" They said that at the last moment they discovered they had gone overboard on expenditures so they cancelled the boat. They knew we both could swim so they weren't worried. Then they congratulated us on the stunt, which was a photographic success, but regretted there was no provision in the budget for paying our taxi fare. After all, taking that taxi wasn't in the script ...that was OUR idea.

The crew revolts in this big clash with Bill Desmond.

Above: I am a man of great mystery in this secretive scene with heroine Eileen "Babe" Sedgwick.
Below: A perilous encounter, the conclusion of which was "continued next week".

Making a serial like BEASTS OF PARADISE involved a great deal more shooting than a feature picture and these films were actually the forerunners of today's TV series shows.

Entering the lair of evil.

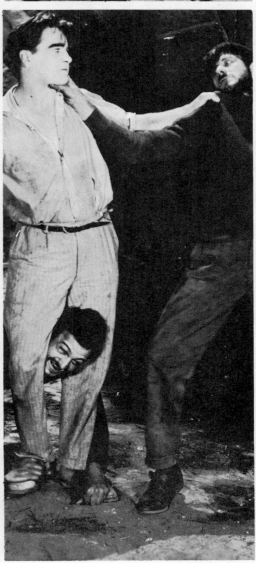

When Universal turned the cameras somebody's life was always in peril.

The making of motion pictures today is a carefully supervised business, operated for a profit to the stockholders. The expenditure of every dollar must be accounted for to financial experts who supervise and check the budget. In consequence, everything must be done as economically as is consistent with good picture making and the wasting of those precious budget dollars is not to be tolerated. This does not mean that many thousands of dollars are not expended for scenes and effects that wind up on the cutting-room floor, but at least the effort behind them seemed intelligent and justified at the time of shooting.

Such was seldom the case in the early days. Many directors worked on "a percentage of the ultimate cost" basis. That meant that the higher they could run the cost of the picture the more money they received for their directing stint. I won't say that many directors took advantage of this deliberately, but it obviously offered a great temptation to push the cost up to the "high water mark." At best it did not encourage economy. The pelican hunt is a good example of some of the things that happened under this system.

It occurred while we were making a comedy in which Clyde Cook was featured. . . .
There was a scene in which Clyde, in attempting a spectacular escape from a prison camp, dashes across an air-field where a plane is just taking off. As it rises into the air he manages to grasp a rear strut and is borne aloft by the plane . . . much to the delight of his fans and to the bafflement of his pursuers. It was a fairly dangerous stunt and I was doubling for Cook.

So far so good, but as I hung onto the rear of the speeding plane, my body streaming out behind like the tail on a kite, it occurs to the director that it might be a big laugh if a passing pelican swooped down and nipped me in the rear end. Unfortunately for the stockholders this suggestion drew a loud laugh from the cast and crew, which determined the director to achieve this effect at all cost . . . and all shooting would be held up until it could be accomplished.

But first . . . where to find a pelican. Someone recalled seeing some of the birds hovering about Buena Vista Lake, which lies about 60 miles beyond Bakersfield. I was put in charge and supplied with a closed truck, a driver, a cowboy, who was an expert with the lariat and Paul Malvern. The orders were to bring back at least a half-dozen full grown pelicans and bring 'em back alive. The cowboy was to sneak up on them and lasso them if possible—if not, Paul, who was an expert shot, was instructed to take a rifle along and wing the huge birds in flight, just sufficiently to cause them to fall to the ground where we could retrieve them. They were not to be killed or badly injured, which called for some really fancy shooting. When we brought them back, the most likely and ferocious looking of the lot was to be selected for the stunt and

Pelicans on Buena Vista Lake—the objects of an extremely unusual hunt.

the rest returned to the lake after any casualties, if there were any, had been patched up and nursed back to health. Remember, all this was for one 15 second laugh—IF it came off.

Also, as the pelican would have to be suspended on a piano wire so he could be guided to his target, the prop department was put to work devising and constructing an elaborate feather covered harness for him, which would be invisible to the audience.

So the cowboy arrived with his assorted ropes, Paul got a couple of rifles and a supply of ammunition from the gun department and we all climbed into a truck and started off on our weird safari.

When we arrived at Buena Vista Lake, after a hot, dusty and bumpy ride, we felt that luck was with us, for we saw before us a whole colony of the great birds. They were even larger than I had pictured them, being from 4 to 6 feet in length with a wing spread of from 6 to 8 feet. Their massive curved beaks were from 14 to 18 inches long. I took one look and decided to put a little extra padding on my rear end.

We crept as close as we could without disturbing them; then our cowboy unleashed his

first lariat and sent it spinning through the air. Before it reached its mark the intended victim was thirty feet up in the air and soaring skyward. After about twenty more unsuccessful attempts, those wily birds had him talking to himself, and he gave up in disgust. So Paul went to work with his rifle. He finally winged six of them, all of which fell into the lake which meant we had to swim out and get them. That was a project in itself, for they were strong and full of fight and those powerful beaks and beating wings were something to contend with. But we finally got them ashore and into the truck with only a few bad nips and bruises to show for it.

The long ride back to Hollywood was the worst part, crowded in that hot, stuffy, covered truck with those six oversized indignant birds, flapping their wings and snapping at us in an effort to escape. I regret to report that by the time we reached the studio only one was still alive, the others having died of heat and exhaustion, and **that** one lived only a few hours. So a taxidermist was called in and the largest of the pelicans was stuffed and fitted with a mechanical beak that had a clock mechanism in it that kept opening and snapping it shut for the "bite"

After another 24 hours of work and preparation they got me on a piano wire—the pelican on a piano wire—and everything synchronized for the great moment. The cameras turned, the plane came into view with me streaming out behind . . . but just as the pelican swooped down my wire kinked and snapped. Luckily my grip held and I didn't fall . . . but with its target gone the stuffed pelican hit the rear strut of the plane so hard it practically exploded in a shower of clock springs and feathers.

There was some talk about getting some more pelicans and trying it again, but it had already cost thousands of dollars in lost time and money, and the producer was starting to ask questions, so that bit was thrown out. The fact that the director wasn't fired is evidence that in those days of prodigal spending, such costly mistakes were not unusual or even severely frowned upon. The surprising angle is that despite such loose practices pictures made money. It may have been because whereas at times they would lean over in one direction, at other times they would lean just as far over in the other.

I doubt many ever realized the risks that were taken during the earlier days of picture making, to bring that magic element called realism to the screen—and I'm sure few realize the number of valiant men who sacrificed their lives to provide the thrills that held audiences breathless and brought them clamoring back for more. The writers were searching the history books for hazardous episodes to put into their scripts and, regardless of the dangers involved, there were always men like myself who were willing to take the big gamble.

One picture that meant a prodigal expenditure of both money and lives was —The TRAIL OF '98, the story of the gold rush to the Klondike. Today, with Hollywood's amazing ability to produce "special effects," such a picture would probably have been turned out right in the studios, with a maximum of safety. But those were the days of realism, so the entire company and working staff were transported to Alaska, poorly equipped to face the many unforseen perils of the far north.

To bring out my point let me describe just one day's shooting. In an attempt to make the crossing from Cordova to Sitka the story called for us to navigate the Copper River, which was fed by the Miles Glacier and was practically a series of treacherous rapids.

We had been warned that only one man, a fellow named Abercrombie, had ever shot those rapids and lived to tell about it, but it was in the script and the director figured if Abercrombie could do it, we could. However, he rounded up the stuntmen and said, "This may be a bit dangerous, boys, and I'm not demanding it of of you. If any of you want to back out, just say so." Of course that was a challenge no self respecting stuntman could ignore and there was not a dissenting voice. How little we realized what stark tragedy lay ahead.

To shoot the rapids they decided to use halibut dories; flat bottomed boats with flaring sides. Paul, Harvey and I were in the first boat, with Red Thompson, Gordon Carveth and several others. In case the boat capsized in the rapids

On location in Alaska for a spectacle of the Klondike's gold rush days.

Note the authentic backgrounds.

we all wore air-suits, which were considered to be an ample safety device to keep us afloat until a man in a Bosun's Chair, which had been rigged up to cover our route, could fish us out of the water. Everything seemed quite secure as we pushed off.

All went well until we struck the boiling waters of the rapids when, without warning, our 16 foot oak oars were snapped off like so many match-sticks, leaving us at the mercy of the wild, swirling cross currents.

Now the boat started spinning like a top and, as we were clinging desperately to its flaring sides, a wave came rushing down the river and tossed the boat into the air, spilling us all out into the rapids.

The air suits proved to be of no value whatever and eight men, including Red Thompson, either drowned or were suffocated in the foam. By some miracle the great wave picked up Gordon Carveth and tossed him ashore. Paul, Harvey and I were fished out by the man in the Bosun's Chair, who then lost HIS life trying to rescue another of the group. Altogether it cost the studio $270,000 and the lives of eight men, to get exactly 70 feet of film.

If you're interested in ironical touches, I later saw the picture at the Chinese Theatre. At the close of the scene I have just described, I heard a lady sitting behind me say to her escort, "Isn't it marvelous how they can fake things these days? You'd think all that actually happened." And he said, "You sure would, but of course we know it DIDN'T."

A long roof jump, which I performed without any special stuntman's assisting devices.

Did you ever wish you could see a great magician expose his tricks? Well, in all the world there's no greater magician than the Movie Camera. With its lens a hundred fold quicker than the eye, it tricks you into thinking you are seeing a thousand things that you're really not seeing at all.

Let me play the villain for a moment and sneak open that closely guarded Hollywood door, behind which are the secrets to the well meant and innocuous frauds that have, for years, been perpetrated against you.

Take the case of Harold Tumbleweed, the famous singing cowboy. He's so non athletic he's stoop-shouldered from that guitar slung around his neck—and he's been in pictures so many years you wonder if he creaks when he walks. Yet you see this character, who has never jumped onto anything higher than a bar stool, approach his horse from the rear—and·a tall horse at that —take a couple of steps, and suddenly, while

strumming his theme song, vault through the air into his saddle—while the kid in the seat in front of you screeches, "Look Ma—no hands!"

Or you see your favorite Private Eye, Mike Mallet, pursued across a roof-top by a couple of murderous thugs. His only salvation is to leap to the roof of the building across the street . . . a good thirty feet away. You recall that Jesse Owens' Olympic record for the running broad-jump, 26 feet 8¼ inches, wasn't bettered in twenty-five years, but the dauntless Mike Mallet doesn't know that, so without the slightest effort, he jumps a full thirty feet through the air and lands safe, sound and smiling, on the roof across the street.

Or you see Super Bird-Man, who through the power of his mind has "mastered the force of gravity," leap to the window-ledge as his enemies are breaking through the door. And there he goes—out through the window, over the house tops and soaring off into the sunset!

Astounding? Breath taking? It is until, traitor

that I am, I give you the three magic words—spring boards, trampolines and piano wires.

I employed the spring board in some of my "amazing" jumps in THE CHINATOWN MYSTERY and have used all the above, at various times, to mystify you.

Ever see a man jump from a fire-escape to a horizontal flag-pole and hang on? Sure you have—and yet—it can't be done, and never has been. I was working on one picture where a chase sequence called for a man to jump from a fire-escape to such a flag-pole about twelve feet away, and slightly lower down. You wouldn't believe that, for a well conditioned athlete, there would be any danger in this. All he had to do was jump, catch the flag-pole, swing himself up and go in the window. Child's play!

I was somewhere down below, shooting the breeze, and the director was up on the fire-escape with Johnny Connell, a young fellow who was working with me. They were about to start when, by some lucky chance, I glanced up.

"Hey, Johnny!" I shouted, "Get down from there before you break your neck!"

"Quit your kidding," he called back, "I'm just jumpin' out to the flag-pole."

"Oh, no you're not," I yelled, "not without a safety net under you."

"Why not?" the director yelled back impatiently.

"After you've rigged the net I'll let him jump and you'll **see** why not!" I called back.

The director argued, but I was adamant and in charge of all stunts and the net was finally in place. Johnny jumped and caught the flag-pole, but was immediately, snapped off and landed in the net four stories below, lucky to be alive.

What neither Johnny nor the director knew was that a horizontal flag-pole, firmly anchored, springs at the farther end. It has a whip-like rebound that makes it impossible to hang onto. As Johnny jumped and caught it, his weight swung him, pendulum like, under the pole, which bent with him. But just as he reached the end of his swing, the pole snapped back the other way, tearing itself out of his hands.

Making a successful flagpole jump proved to be no easy task. This is the actual photo of my doing the stunt that almost never wound up on film.

The deceptive part of the stunt was that it looked easy . . . so easy in fact, that several of the other men in the crew bet me they could make it—each figuring some way to hang on. I won every bet and made two hundred dollars extra that day. And that was one bet the men didn't mind losing. They had learned a valuable lesson at a bargain price.

When the master shots were made I did the jump, myself. I fell, too, but we faked the film so you never knew it. I jumped, caught the flag-pole and was snapped off out of camera range. Then shooting stopped while I walked up the stairs to the window from which the pole extended. I climbed out on it, hand over hand, and started to swing back and forth. Then the cameras started again and showed me swinging back into view, just as though I'd never been snapped off. And the public never knew they'd been fooled.

Perhaps the most spectacular "deceit" of my career was a "free jump" I made from a ninety foot tower to the ground. The usual procedure was to rig double safety nets below you. In case you broke through the first, the second would hold you. The trouble with this was that the public never saw you land. They just had to assume you made it.

Jay Marchant was directing this picture and he wasn't satisfied with this.

"Joe," he said, "I'm going to mount the cameras above you, on the tower, and we'll get the shot from **overhead** as you fall to the ground."

"Swell," I said, "but how will the audience see me through the parachute?"

"What parachute?" he said.

I started to walk away.

"If you think I'm going to make a jump, ninety feet to the ground, with no safety nets there, either you're crazy or you think **I** am. And if we **use** nets they'll **show**."

He confessed he hadn't thought of that—and then I got an idea. We got a crew of workmen to dig a huge pit in the ground, below the tower window from which I was to jump. The pit was about fifteen feet deep, and halfway down in it we strung a safety net. Then, at the surface of the ground, a "give-away" canvas was stretched and covered with dirt, concealing the pit completely.

Before making the leap I strapped myself up, tightly binding my elbows, wrists, knees, ankles and most of my body. I also donned a crash helmet under my costume hat. Even with all that I had misgivings. Of course, if the give-away canvas didn't hold me I still had the safety net under it, but from ninety feet up I'd be coming down with terrific force, and you never can tell! However, I went up to the tower and signalled the director I was ready. I looked down at that little splotch of ground for a long moment, then I took a deep breath and stepped off, arms outstretched. Down I plunged, keeping straight up, but watching that spot. I'd better not miss it and the ground was coming up awfully fast! I bent my legs, leaned back slightly, and hit the dirt

Being in top condition has always been a necessity for all stuntmen.

A dangerous explosion sequence that was filmed at Santa Cruze Island. The chances for stuntmen to survive the fall into shallow water, just as the tower was being destroyed, were so slim that dummies were used instead.

I refused to do this tower jump because it would have meant certain death.

in a more or less sitting position. Into the canvas I plopped, and a moment later, in an agony of anxiety, I felt myself sag to a stop. The canvas had held . . . the safety net wasn't even needed.

The boys ran over with shovels and dug me out. Though unhurt, I was temporarily blinded from the dirt explosion as I had hit. But the shot was sensational and the public could never figure out how I did it without being killed. After all, they saw me fall ninety feet and hit the ground—or they **thought** they did! Barnum said, "You can fool all of the people some of the time, and some of the people all of the time," but we fooled all of the people MOST of the time!

I have had many questions regarding the state of a person's mind during long falls and if one loses consciousness. Many believe that suicides, who jump from high places, are dead or unconscious when they hit the ground. This, I can testify, is not true. The mind is quite acute during the entire course of a fall. In repeating this same tower jump, on a later occasion, I challenged a friend of mine to write some words on a slip of paper, and hand it to me just as I jumped. I read it on the way down and threw it away before I reached the ground. I later repeated the message to my doubting buddy—"If you miss that spot your goose is cooked." Parachutists

often drop thousands of feet before opening their chute and, unless they faint, are fully conscious and alert during the entire time.

The trampoline is probably the most extensively used of all stunt apparatus. It covers a multitude of frauds. A small one, just big enough for one foot, for example, is often planted in the ground, with the top just level with the surface, then camouflaged with dirt. That was what our movie hero used to jump-bounce onto his horse. For fights and acrobatic work, trampolines of all sizes are planted in table tops, chairs, sofas, stair-landings,—in any spot where a stuntman needs an extra bounce. I recall one picture where I jumped from the roof of a building, four floors high, in making a getaway. This four-story jump was done with no safety net. How then? By employing special trampoline awnings on the building I was in, and on the building across the narrow street. I jumped from the roof of the first building, down onto the fourth floor awning below me. Then twisting, I bounced to the third floor awning across the street—then to the second floor awning on the original building—then to the first floor awning across the street—and finally down to the ground. This was a stunt that was spectacular and humorous, but it was terribly dangerous. One wrong twist—one miscalculation —and I'd have bounced right into eternity. I never tried it again.

While I'm on the subject I must caution my readers, especially the younger ones, against the use of trampolines, so popular today, without constant and adequate supervision. The trampoline is a dangerous plaything. I know you've seen acrobats bouncing around on a trampoline with great ease and assurance, and it seemed like a lot of fun—and it **is**, IF you know how to control it. But in my opinion it is more dangerous than the high-wire or the trapeze. The muscular control required can not be overestimated. The slightest wrong bounce and you're apt to go flying almost anywhere, crashing into poles—landing on your head—breaking your bones. Children have been killed by trampolines and many badly injured, some crippled for life. So unless you're an expert, or have an expert supervising you every minute you're on one, better leave them to the professionals.

I never went into trampoline jumps without previous preparation. In addition to body padding I wore special shoes with thick sponge-rubber soles. Yet even with these precautions I broke no less than eleven bones.

There were times when fooling you with our Hollywood cameras exacted a high price. Take the case of my friend Mack, from Brooklyn. He was the second of the Black Cats to feel the cold, damp kiss.

Mack and I had worked together on stunts, back in New York, and one day he wrote me his mother had died and he wanted to come West and could I do anything for him? I could—and I did—and out he came to work with me in Hollywood.

We went through many stunts together and Mack became known for his recklessness. He'd tackle any assignment and the more dangerous the better he seemed to like it.

One day we were having lunch together when he suddenly said, "Joe, if anything should happen to me this afternoon, see that I get buried alongside my mother, back in Brooklyn."

I stared at him incredulously.

"What's the matter, Mack? Don't you feel well?"

"Oh, I feel okay," he said, "I've just got sort of a crazy premonition."

I knew about premonitions and I had a lot of faith in them . . . and I knew he was scheduled for a tricky fire-escape stunt.

"If you feel that way take the afternoon off. I've got plenty of stuntmen around. I'll get one of them to take your place."

"Thanks, Joe" he said, "but I'm not turning yellow . . . and maybe I'm wrong about this. But just in case, see that I'm buried beside my mother."

I went back to where I was working in a jungle scene and Mack went to another part of the lot. That was the last time I saw him alive. The scene he was in involved a fight on a high fire-escape and one of the men, (Mack, in this case) was to be knocked against a break-away side of it, which would give way, and he would fall out of camera range and presumably to his death. This sounds dangerous, but if the proper precautions were taken, it was more or less a routine stunt. The hinged side of the break-away fire-escape could be easily caught and although the fight would take place four stories above the street, with a safety belt on, Mack would be in little danger.

As they started the sequence there was no net below—for what reason I can't recall. Then someone noticed that Mack was not wearing a safety belt. When his attention was called to it, instead of taking the time to get one, he carelessly tied a length of sashline around his waist and fastened it to the break-away side of the fire-escape saying that would suffice if anything went wrong. Had I been there I'd have insisted on his using a regulation safety belt . . . but I wasn't there and my friend was killed that afternoon.

With the cameras going and the fight in progress, the side of the fire-escape broke away as planned, but for some reason Mack missed his grab at it and fell. He had fallen only a few feet when the sashcord "safety-line" was used up. It snapped taut and broke like a piece of string and Mack plunged the four stories to the asphalt pavement below.

Because of his statement during lunch and his failure to wear a safety belt, which came out in the inquest that followed, the insurance company refused to pay off, claiming it was deliberate suicide. The only settlement was the usual $5,000 state workman's compensation paid to a sister back East.

I didn't agree with the insurance company, but who knows what's in the other fellow's mind. I saw to it that he got his last wish . . . he was buried beside his mother.

As the tower explosion turned out, nobody could have lived through its furious destruction.

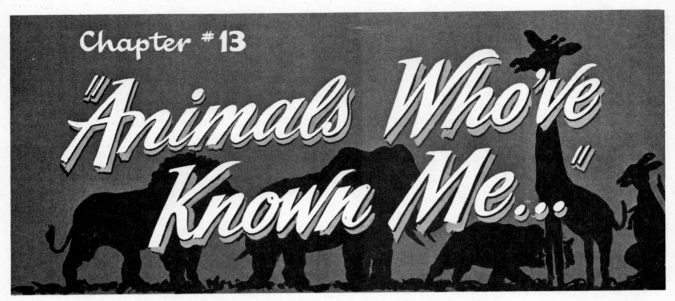

Chapter 13

"Animals Who've Known Me..."

THIS CHAPTER I AM DEDICATING to animal lovers the world over—and include me in. To paraphrase the late Will Rogers, "I never met an animal I didn't like." And most of them have liked ME. Those that didn't undoubtedly had valid reasons for disliking mankind in general. Take the big cats as an example. A little brutal treatment from their first keeper or handler could impress upon them that the strange two legged animal known as man was not to be loved or trusted. And even with what we term the best of treatment, we must realize they have been torn from their natural habitat and way of life and relegated to a life-term of servitude within the confines of a cage, with scarcely room enough to pace, much less jump and run as their creator intended.

Their only respite is when they are driven, at the end of a sharp pointed stick, into a larger cage, where a man with a chair, a whip and a revolver, puts them through torturous and frightening hours of learning to do a lot of, what to them, are meaningless things that they were never meant to do. And no matter how hard they may try to please, their only reward is to be prodded back into that hateful little cage again, to be brought out the next day to do the same silly things all over again. It is small wonder they rebel.

I believe that certain animals, such as seals, some horses and certain breeds of dogs, perform for the love of it and for the tasty reward that follows each successfully done trick. Chimps and monkeys are natural "hams" and I've even seen performing bears who seemed to definitely enjoy their work. But the big cats must be taught and controlled largely through fear, which hardly establishes a good relationship. We can scarcely like them less because they fight to retain their natural birthright of dignity and freedom.

As I've said many times, I never enjoyed working with the big cats because of the constant risk involved, but I have always admired and respected them.

Of course, there's an element of uncertainty working with any creature. I once attended a performance of the Flea Circus on 42nd Street in New York, when a member of the "cast" got loose and hopped up the "professor's" pants leg, inflicting several healthy bites before it was finally retrieved. I've never assayed training a flea, but I've been involved in some things almost as weird. For instance—how would you like to break an ostrich to the saddle? Sounds easy? Try it sometime.

In the first place, there is nothing docile about an ostrich and he has no intention of ever letting anyone strap a saddle on him and climb aboard —and he has a couple of very definite ways of expressing his displeasure.

To begin with, he stands from seven to eight feet high and weighs in the neighborhood of 300 pounds. He has a huge, flat beak that can inflict a nasty bite that will leave a scar you will carry for years, and if that isn't sufficient to discourage you, let me tell you about his feet. He has only two toes, the third and fourth. The third is much the bigger and bears a short, hoof-like nail. Using this as a weapon he can kick either directly forward or sideways with either foot and with such force that men and even horses have been killed by the first blow. You will realize from this that an ostrich is nothing to fool with . . . especially an angry one. But as I have said before, a good stuntman will try anything.

The whole thing came about when the studio decided to make a picture that called for a thrilling race between a thoroughbred horse and a famous racing ostrich that had supposedly been brought to this country from Africa, to spring a surprise on the American racing fraternity. This was not as fantastic as it might sound as the Bedouins, on their fleet Arabian steeds, can seldom keep pace with one of the big birds. An ostrich in full flight can cover as much as 25 feet in a single stride.

There was no difficulty in getting an ostrich. A fine specimen was selected from among 1500 to be found on the California Experimental

Ostrich Farm . . . but there wasn't an ostrich jockey in the country . . . or anyone who knew how to train one for the race. None of the cowboys would tackle the job; I think mainly for fear they'd be laughed at, so it was put in the stunt category and again the questionable honor fell to me. I didn't know the first thing about how or where to begin, but I figured I could learn.

The ostrich was brought from the farm to the studio in a large horse-van and we turned him loose in the middle of one of the corrals that had a high wire fence around it. Then they gave me a small English racing saddle and their best wishes and left me to figure it out for myself. Luckily for me, Pete Graham, one of our regular animal trainers, stayed behind to "watch the fun."

Remembering that a bird in the hand is worth two in the bush, I decided the first thing I had to do was catch him. I advanced toward him

beat a hasty retreat I decided discretion was the better part of valor and I'd better try a long distance operation. I figured if you could rope a wild stallion you ought to be able to rope an ostrich, so I came back with a couple of lariats. As they were something new to him I had no trouble dropping the first noose over his head, which he didn't seem to mind. But in order to rope him about those dangerous legs I'd have to drop a noose over his body . . . and no matter how large I made it I couldn't get it past his wings and tail-feathers . . . and with those legs still free I didn't want any part of him. I'd probably still be working on it if Pete hadn't finally come up with a suggestion.

"I never seen it done, Joe . . . fact is, I never even seen a ostrich before, but I've heard tell

with my best smile, making friendly little clucking noises, as he eyed me with evident distrust . . . and for each step I took forward, he took two steps back. A few minutes of this and I was getting no place but winded, although Pete, who had perched himself at a safe height, on the corral fence, seemed to be enjoying it thoroughly.

"Hey, Pete," I called to him, "know anything about birds?"

"Nuthin' bigger than turkeys."

"Well how am I going to catch this thing? Don't you have any suggestions?"

Pete chuckled.

"Try puttin' a little salt on his tail."

Your first thought might be that a big, overgrown bird would be easy to outsmart and outmaneuver . . . but not an ostrich. He's wary, alert and full of fight when he's cornerd. I decided to wait until he got used to me and then try a sneak attack. After a bit, he stopped watching me and started pecking away at some alfalfa, I think it was. His tail was now toward me so I started cautiously moving in. He apparently didn't see me until I was almost within grasping distance of him, then he suddenly wheeled and let go with a vicious kick that just missed me by inches as I jumped back. As I

that if'n you can git a black bag over their heads, so they cain't see nuthin', they's gentle as a lamb."

Anything was worth trying so I put a double hitch around one of the fence posts and pulled Mr. Ostrich over by the noose around his neck, until he was flush against it, and had Pete hold the rope taut while I hustled over the the prop department where they dug me up a black cloth bag.

By the time I got back Pete was having his troubles with that 300 pounds of angry, squawking ostrich who by now was heartily resenting the situation and, at the risk of hanging himself, was trying desperately to get within kicking distance of Pete.

I joined Pete on top of the fence and, after a couple of tries, managed to drop the black bag over the struggling creature's head . . . at which, an amazing thing happened. He suddenly relaxed, ceased his struggles and became completely docile, offering no resistance as I strapped the saddle on him, slipped the bit into his mouth and mounted to his back.

I sat there for a while, expecting that at any moment he would make a flying leap into the air, but nothing happened. Gaining courage from this I gently removed the black bag. He blinked a couple of times to get accustomed to the light again and then, with a whoosh, he took off.

I have ridden bucking bronchos, wild steers, Brahma bulls and even camels, but I never had a ride like that. He just spread those great legs and we must have gone a dozen times around the corral, at jet propelled speed, before he even slackened his pace. I didn't attempt to steer him . . . I was too busy hanging on, with my face full of ostrich feathers and my mind full of the things I was going to call Pete, who kept emitting Indian war whoops and yelling and waving his hat every time we went by, scaring the poor bird even more. I could have done a rolling fall off his back, but I had a feeling he wasn't too kindly disposed toward me and would probably double back and kick me into Kingdom Come before I could ever reach the safety of the fence.

Then my wits suddenly returned and I thought of the black bag that all this time I had been clutching in my hand. By inching up on his neck I finally managed to once more get it over his head and—he came to an immediate stop. As I slid off his back, over his tail, to avoid a possible side kick in case he was just playing possum, Pete came running over.

"Greatest exhibition of ostrichmanship I ever seen," he chuckled. "And what a stepper. Who says fine feathers don't make fine birds!"

And as it turned out he WAS a fine bird. I discovered his weakness was chopped beets, green alfalfa and oranges and that the way to his heart was definitely through his tummy. We got to be great friends and it wasn't long before I could ride him at will and he seemed to enjoy it as much as I did.

But something went wrong—the picture was called off and I never got the chance to race him. I hated to see him go back to the ostrich farm but you can hardly keep an eight foot 300 pound bird for a pet. Even Hollywood stuntmen aren't permitted to be THAT crazy. But I still think that bird could have given Citation and Swaps a hundred yard start and beaten them to a fare-thee-well. Too bad he never had a chance to prove it.

Now let's go to Queenie. Queenie was a member of the Universal Zoo family and an accomplished actress who worked with me in THE GREAT

CIRCUS MYSTERY. Queenie was a leopard, a beautiful animal almost four feet in length from the tip of her nose to the root of her tail. She was yellowish fawn in color, with black spots. Beautiful as she was, when I met her she was regarded with a healthy fear by the zoo keepers.

The reason big-game hunters will say "Never underestimate a leopard" is that, because of its smaller size and inferior weight and power, it is not generally regarded as being as formidable and dangerous as the tiger, whereas the truth is that because of its superior quickness, agility and quick-wittedness, it is the tiger's peer.

With Queenie on the set.

Queenie had definite likes and dislikes which seemed to be governed largely by her sense of smell—and to her, most human beings did not measure up to her olfactory standards. They apparently smelled unfriendly and dangerous for, after her first sniff of the average stranger she would arch her back, snarl and strike out with her scimitar sharp claws extended. I must have used the right soap for she took to me from the first moment and with me she was as playful and gentle as a kitten. When we were on the set I would release her from her cage and she would follow me around like a faithful dog . . .

and although I kept her on a leash as a precaution, I'm sure she would never have attacked anyone while I was present, for she seemed to have eyes for no one else and would obey my slightest command.

I could handle her physically and, no matter how roughly I treated her, she never resented it. I could even pull her four foot tail and never a claw came out.

I did many stunts with her for pictures. On command she would leap into my arms from the branch of a tree . . . she would ride with me on the wing of a flying plane . . . we would stage fake fights together, wrestling about for minutes at a time and on no occasion was I bitten or even scratched.

You cat lovers know how keenly you can miss just an ordinary house cat when you have to go away and leave them. Well, when I finally moved on and had to say goodbye to Queenie I actually choked up. They say you can never

shoes and could dress and undress herself and although "a perfect lady" in most respects she had one really unladylike habit. If she didn't like the food served to her she would promptly throw it back at the person who served it and her aim was as accurate as a baseball player's. She also like to smoke and enjoyed a cigarette, a cigar or a pipe with equal relish, puffing away like a veteran. At such times it was not advisable to stand too close, for she had seen some smokers expectorate and would proceed to do so with great abandon and no regard for bystanders.

Chimps have always amused and interested me and I used to spend most of my studio spare time watching Josie and her antics . . . and as I was regularly receiving cases of candy from Papa's candy factory in Coney Island, I never failed to bring some along for Josie, together with a banana, a carrot or whatever I thought might appeal to her. It wasn't long before, whenever she saw me coming, she would jump up

Queenie was a fine animal actress and worked well with us during a film's actual shooting.

learn to love a wild animal so I guess it wasn't love, but I've never stopped missing her and even to this day I never see a cat without thinking of her.

Another Hollywood actress who seemed to capitulate to my questionable charm—one who really had a violent "case" on me—was Josie. If you think this will be an expose of "monkey business," with a Hollywood setting, you're quite right, for Josie was a chimpanzee, better known as a "chimp"—an anthropoid ape, smaller and less ferocious than the gorilla and, with the possible exception of the whale, ranking second to man in intelligence. The cat, the dog and pig also rank high on the intelligence scale but are far outstripped by the chimpanzee—and Josie was one of the best.

She could do innumerable difficult tricks after only a lesson or two . . . she could imitate other animals and many of the picture stars who had outstanding characteristics . . . she chewed gum without swallowing it . . . she wore clothes and

and down, rattling the bars of her cage trying to get out to me, the while emitting little squeals of delight.

It never occurred to me that Josie misunderstood my attentions, but as I previously stated, Chimps are not far removed from humans and Josie ranked higher than most . . . but whether she thought I was another Chimp or that perhaps she was a human being, in her own strange way poor Josie had fallen in love.

I suddenly realized it one day when I brought along one of our stock actresses when I paid my regular call on Josie. This time there was no jumping up and down or rattling of the cage bars in delight at seeing me. Ignoring the fruit and candy I passed in to her, she grasped the bars of her cage, bared her teeth in an ominous growl and suddenly lunged out with a long, hairy arm, at the little stock actress who barely ducked away in time, while Josie glared at her with eyes filled with jealousy and hate. And now realizing she could not reach her "hated

Josie was a temperamental chimp with an "emotional problem."

rival," she snatched up the candy and fruit I had brought her and started pelting the frightened girl with it.

That ended my visits to Josie, although as long as I was on the lot, whenever I received another shipment of candy from Papa, I sent a couple of boxes to her by way of her keeper.

At Universal we also had a powerful chimp named Joe Martin, who was just naturally mean. When a visitor came by he had a habit of thrusting his hand through the bars of his cage, apparently for a handshake, but woe to the unwary one who fell for that little trick . . . for when the unsuspecting visitor took his hand to shake it, Joe would pull the man's arm though the bars and almost break it off.

One day I chanced to see this happen and offered to break Joe of the habit. I knew how strong he was but I figured I was just a bit stronger . . . so the next day I stood in front of Joe's cage and offered him my hand. He took it, ready to pull my arm through the bars, but I pulled first. With a mighty jerk I yanked him against the front of his cage and held him there while he screamed bloody murder. And I kept

him there a full two minutes, letting him ease back a little and then bumping him again and again against those steel bars. It was the surprise of his Simian life and he never tried that trick again.

Contrary to what you may have heard there is not a wild animal in existence that cannot be trained and tamed if the right trainer gets him. But also, there is no wild animal that can be entirely trusted, regardless of my experience with Queenie. They tell me I was just lucky, for no matter how thoroughly trained or tamed, the average wild animal will kill you if it gets the chance.

A common question is "What is the toughest animal to train?" To my mind it is the zebra. In their natural habitat, zebras are considered virtually defenseless animals. In captivity they are among the meanest. They will trample you on the slightest provocation or with no provocation at all. Of all the animals used in my pictures, and that included elephants, chimps, tigers, crocodiles, hyenas, giraffes and a two-toed sloth, the zebras gave us the most trouble.

W.S. Van Dyke, who had spent much time in the African jungles, told me it would be impossible to train a rhinoceros . . . and I was quite ready to believe him as these strange beasts are looked upon as the most ferocious of jungle animals. Yet to everyone's surprise, including my own, I eventually accomplished it. I worked with a rhino for just two months, feeding him and caring for him until the beast believed I was his friend . . . and at the end of those eight weeks he would roll over and play dead on command and eventually became so tame that Johnny Weismuller, in a Tarzan picture, rode him like a jockey.

One of the most difficult tasks was when a tiger had to be trained to ride on the back of an elephant . . . the two being natural enemies. This was accomplished by training the animals separately. First a platform saddle was built to fit a horse, covering him so he would be fully protected. Then the tiger was taught to mount the platform and, after several weeks, he got used to staying up there while the horse was in motion.

At the same time a large dog was put on the elephant until he became accustomed to having an animal on his back. When the time came to shoot the scene the tiger was merely substituted for the dog and both animals got along fine. Audiences who were amazed to see a tiger riding an elephant, as though they had been friends all their lives, did not realize that this on little episode had taken many weeks of patient training.

What a wild animal doesn't understand he fears. That even goes for strange smells . . . as in the case of Queenie. A trainer who gets into an animal cage with liquor on his breath is taking his life in his hands. There are several recorded instances of trainers having met their death because of this.

In subsequent chapters I shall tell of my experience with lions, elephants, pythons and such but for a slightly more humorous note . . . I'd like to tell you the story of the boxing kangaroo.

One was called for in a comedy scene in a picture I was working on and it seemed the only boxing kangaroos in this country were already booked in vaudeville and circus acts. Our only alternative was to get one and teach him to box. As I was also operating the gym on the lot and supposed to be an expert on things pugilistic, I was stuck with the job. I rather looked forward to it—it sounded like an interesting and easy assignment but then, I had never met a kangaroo face to face.

The studio rounded up a big fellow, who had recently been shipped over from Australia, and had him delivered to the gym. He had evidently been confined in his crate for some time for, when I opened the lid, he bounded out like an animated rubber ball and started bounding around the gym in huge delighted leaps that sent everyone, including me, ducking for cover. All I could do was let him bounce himself out, which he eventually did, settling down finally on a wrestling mat. I might add that by this time he and I were the only two left in the gym, the others having made a hasty exit as he came bouncing in their direction.

I first closed all the doors and windows then, spying some vegetables that had come in the crate with him, I got a handfull and approached him cautiously. He eyed me with the same suspicion the ostrich had, but to my surprise and relief, when I got close enough to timidly extend a carrot, he took it daintily in his short front paws and started nibbling on it, peacefully as you please.

I followed through with one vegetable after another until I felt I had firmly established myself as a friend, then I spoke a few soothing words to him and, moving a bit closer, I reached out to give him a friendly pat. In the twinkling of an eye he rocked back on his big tail and brought up his right hind foot in a vicious kick that, had it connected, would have ripped me open from stomach to chin. As I leaped backward he just gave me a mild stare and went back to peacefully eating his vegetables. It was then I decided I needed a little help.

I phoned for a couple of animal men who arrived with a large net. Even between the three of us it took some doing, but we finally got the net over our Australian friend so he couldn't use those powerful hind legs. We then got him back into the crate, after which, it took several days of personal feeding and gentle treatment to make him realize I was **really** his friend. Once that was established I named him Oscar, put a collar and chain on him and he used to hop around after me like a tame rabbit.

There is no animal as ungainly as the kangaroo, often called Nature's Mistake or Nature's Practical Joke . . . and yet, to me, Oscar in repose had

a certain dignity and charm. He had a fawn like head with beautiful, large, expressive eyes . . . and once he felt you could be trusted he was really a gentle soul. But the studio didn't want a gentle soul with large expressive eyes, they wanted a boxing kangaroo, so Oscar's training had to begin.

I had some special boxing gloves made for him that would fit tightly over his small front paws. I had them made especially long so he could slap with them. I knew I had nothing to fear from that angle as a kangaroo has comparatively little strength in his forepaws. It was those lethal hind legs that worried me.

While teaching him to box I also had to teach him not to kick, which was his first impulse if he though he was being attacked. To accomplish this I tried several methods. First I fastened heavy iron dumbbells to his hind feet, but I underestimated the strength in those hind legs. He started flailing around with those dumbbells as though they were cork and smashed up several valuable pieces of apparatus before I could quiet him down and get them off him. Next I stretched a steel wire between us so whenever he kicked, the wire caught the force of the blow, and hurt him enough to discourage another kick. That worked the first couple of times, then he just hopped over the wire and again I had to beat a hasty retreat. I had punched him around a little while boxing and he had decided I wasn't his friend after all. The next day, after he'd simmered down, I attached his hind feet to the floor with short chains and floor rings so each

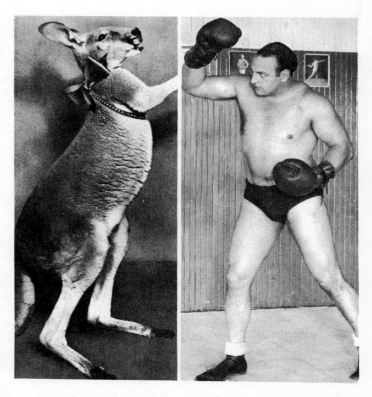

My new sparring partner — Oscar the kangaroo!

time he tried to kick he would practically upset himself. This worked and broke him completely of the habit of kicking while boxing.

The final result was that he became a safe opponent who relied entirely on his front paws for offense and defense. Just between you and me, Oscar was never much of a boxer, but he never knew it and, if ignorance is bliss, he must have been very happy and proud. We used him in several pictures and as naturally, the audience was always pulling for the kangaroo, we invariably let him win by a knockout. Yes, Oscar must have thought he was quite a fellow.

As I check back over the many animals I have tangled with, there is one that still sends a shudder along my spine—and it wasn't a lion, or a tiger, or a gorilla—it was a wild boar who fought me to the death on Catalina Island.

Catalina is now a rather famous resort and tourist attraction but at that time, before the concessionaires moved in, it was fairly wild and primitive, being overgrown with trees and heavy shrubbery. And how they got there is a matter of conjecture, but it numbered among its animal population a goodly sprinkling of wild boar. (I understand Howard Hill, the famous archer, still hunts them there with bow and arrow.)

For those of you who have never met a wild boar face to face—and let's hope you never will —I'll describe one. I had always thought of them, when I thought of them at ALL, as a sort of oversized pig—and in this respect I was right— only I was missing a few important details.

Although the wild boar is the general ancestor of our present day domesticated swine there are radical differences. The average pig is a fairly docile and tractable animal, but the wild boar is a ferocious, cunning and swift footed "bundle of dynamite." Because of its extreme courage, coupled with its superior strength and toughness, it is a dangerous and most formidable adversary. It is much larger than the domesticated swine and is covered with short, grayish-black, wooly hair, thickly interspersed with stiff bristles that assume the form of a crest along its spine. A young boar has great sharp tusks protruding from its lower jaw which eventually curve up over its snout and are then replaced, as weapons, by the teeth of the lower jaw which protrude and curve outward. With either the tusks or teeth it can quickly slash its victim to death.

Have you ever noticed that sometimes the worst things happen to you when you're trying to do somebody a favor? Well, we were doing another "Western" and the director had asked me if I'd look around for a different type of locale in which to stage an Indian sneak attack on a wagon train that was trying to push its way through a patch of wild and uninhabited country. That seemed to sound like Catalina so, having a Sunday free, I decided to look the island over for some possible good location spots. Luckily I asked Steve Barry—I think that was his name—to accompany me. Steve had been a trick bow and arrow shot with Ringling Brothers Circus and we were using him for some spec-

tacular bow and arrow work in the Indian sequences. Happily, as it turned out, he decided to bring along his bow and a quiver of arrows in the hope he might bag some small game with which he had heard the island abounded.

We rented a small boat with an outboard motor and put-putted across the San Pedro Channel to Santa Catalina as it's properly called. We started wandering around and found it ideal for our sequences, it being heavily wooded with many hills and deep gorges . . . perfect for Indian surprise attacks.

We were about to turn back when we saw a sudden movement in some dense shrubbery to our right and caught a glimpse of a pair of beady eyes staring at us. Without questioning what it was Steve whipped an arrow into his bow and let fly. There was an immediate hoarse squeal of rage and, bursting through the shrubbery, on the attack, came a huge, infuriated young boar. Steve's arrow had just grazed his side, but sufficiently to draw blood and make him realize we were enemies. As he came at us, with those short legs pounding, I was reminded of nothing so much as the charge of a mad rhinoceros. For some reason he had selected me as his target and was coming straight at me, at a furious pace, his great tusks at the ready.

While working on a Western I made the mistake of going on some location scouting.

A wild boar is best left alone!

I had no weapon, not even a stick with which to fend him off. Had it not been for my training as a tumbler and acrobat he'd have had me down and been slashing at me with that first rush, but I leaped high into the air and to one side as he went under and past me. However, before I could quite recover my balance he had made a lightning fast turn and was headed for me again. I started to do a porpoise dive over him but I wasn't quite fast enough. I was barely a foot off the ground when I felt the violent impact of the massive head. He had missed with his tusks but I was tossed in the air and landed on my back with most of the wind knocked out of me. As he came at me again, intent on the kill, I struggled to my knees and, going backward with the impact of this attack I was able to grasp one of his tusks and a fore-leg.

At times I used to think most of my great strength was going to waste, but at that moment, I thanked the good Lord for my muscles and my wrestling skill. But, strong as I was, I thought for a moment I had met my match, for the power in his neck and body as he tried to shake me off was unbelievable. Then, for just a split second he relaxed to alter his mode of attack—and that split second was all I needed. With those razor sharp tusks practically at my throat I gave a terrific heave that threw him over on his back with his three free legs kicking in the air, but the next instant he was rolling over with me

trying to shake me off and I could feel my grip on that tusk already weakening from the strain.

During this struggle, which takes so long to describe but was so lightning fast that it actually consumed but a few seconds, from the corner of my eye I had seen Steve trying to line up a safe shot with one of his steel tipped arrows. One arrow missed, on the boar's second rush and then we were so closely embroiled he was afraid he'd get **me** instead of that snorting animal—and there was a good chance he **would.**

As we stopped rolling that great pig must have thought he had me for he was now on top of me and, with a violent wrench he shook his tusk free and reared back to make a slashing lunge for my throat, but he was a second too late. As he reared, to drive that tusk home, Steve's bow twanged and an arrow went directly through his heart. With a gasping grunt he rolled off me and was dead.

As, a bit shaken, I was dusting myself off, Steve said, ''Let's stick around a while . . . maybe they hunt in pairs and I can get his partner.'' But even as he spoke I had started for our boat. I had had my fill of wild boars—enough to last me for the rest of my life.

I reported to the studio that I didn't think Catalina would be suitable and, on my recommendation, we shot our Indian sequences on Gopher Flats. Gophers I can handle.

CHAPTER 14

THE WILDERNESS TRAIL

My next assignment was in WOLVES OF THE NORTH, in which I portrayed the nastiest looking French Canadian heavy you'd hope not to meet on a dark night. My name was Pierre and Mama and Papa would never recognize me in this one, either.

WOLVES OF THE NORTH was all about fur piracy in the Hudson Bay region, so, with Hollywood "realism," we filmed it at McCall, a summer resort on the Salmon River in Idaho. But we shot it in mid-winter and I guess they figured that after all, snow is snow, and you can't argue with **that**.

The cast included William Duncan, Edith Johnson, Esther Ralston, Melvina Polo (Eddie's daughter), three repulsive looking characters— Frank Rice, Harry Woods and Joe Bonomo,— and a couple of German-Shepherd police dogs to be camouflaged as "wolves." We also brought along Scotty Allen, who had set an overland dog-sled record from Nome, Alaska, to some

I was a tough character to tangle with.

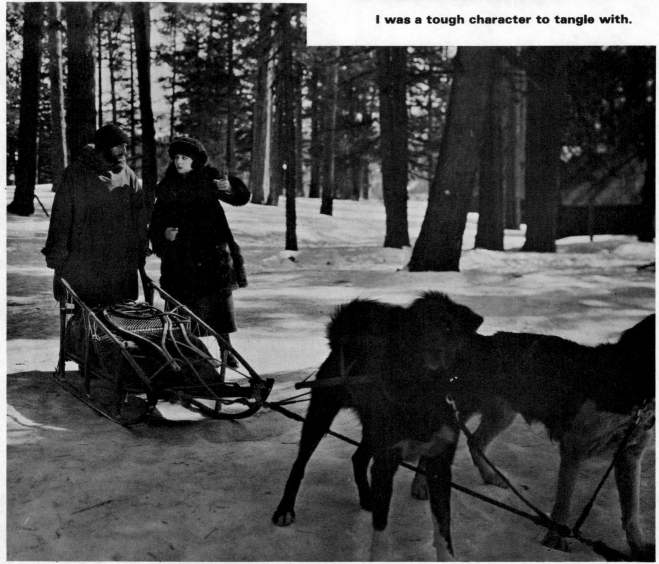

Edith Johnson points out the rugged trail ahead.

place or other. Scotty really knew his business. It was a good thing somebody did!

Honestly, from all the furs, dogsleds, and junk we took along you'd have thought we were headed for the North Pole. For the "mush" sequences, Scotty brought along two dog teams, real huskies, who bit almost everyone including each other. He also brought along some Eskimos. They didn't bite but they looked at us as though they'd like to. As they couldn't speak English and we couldn't speak Eskimo, I never found out why.

It took us three days just to learn how to "mush." The "Hee!" (go left) and the "Haw!" (go right) that we shouted at the huskies came easy enough, but try to run a few feet on crusted snow, behind a speeding dog-team sometime. This was my regular routine—I'd step off the sled runners, take a few steps, break through the snow and go flat on my face, while the huskies went yapping away . . . with their yapping sounding suspiciously like a "horse laugh." Of course, each time I took a dive, the snow would be all mussed up, and the whole company would have to move on to another location. It cost the studio thousands of dollars for Bonomo to learn how to mush, and frankly, I don't think it was worth it.

And those snow-shoe chases were a panic. (Those are treacherous things, too.) Frank, Harry and I would steal an armful of furs and race off across the hills on snow-shoes, pursued by a couple of actors dressed in Canadian mounted police uniforms. That is, we'd race for about ten yards when one of us would go down. Another sequence ruined and another location used up. We used to bet ten bucks apiece on who would be the first to fall, and the cast was making bets on who would be the first to be fired! At the speed we traveled on those snow-shoes, the **real** mounted police would have arrested us for **loitering**!

Even the horses had to wear snow-shoes. Ever see a horse on snow-shoes? We strapped webbed discs, about the size of frying pans, to their hooves. They had their troubles, too, but after they got used to them they wouldn't budge out in the snow without them.

There was one particular sequence that was

Harry Woods, Frank Rice and I close in on Esther Ralston and Bill Duncan.

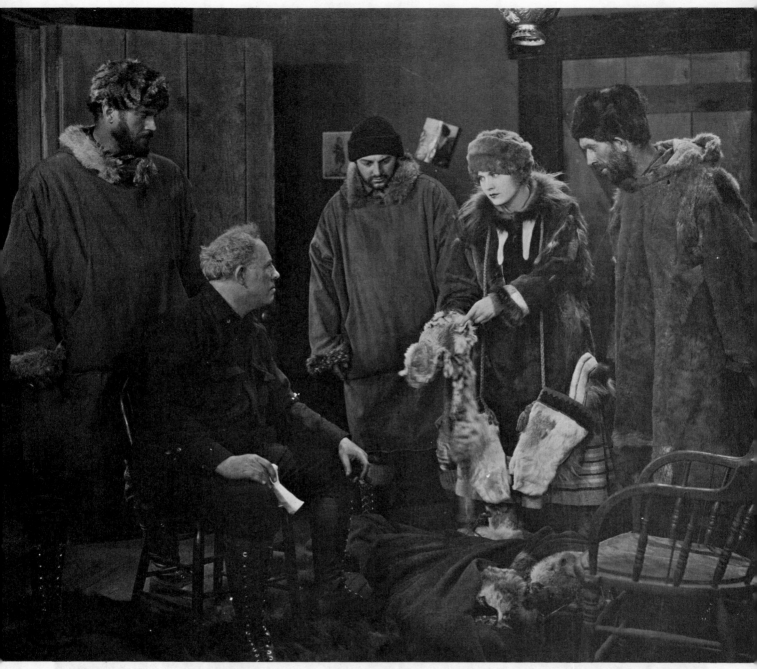

Esther Ralston shows the stolen furs to Harry Woods, Robert Homans, Frank Rice and myself.

a chiller-diller—mostly a chiller. Harry, Frank and I were to fight in a canoe, upset it in the river and be swept over the rapids.

We protested that to be dunked in that icy water didn't sound exactly like fun, but the director barked that we weren't up there for fun and he wasn't going to say it twice! So out to the river we went. It was below zero and the summer hotel where we were billeted wasn't equipped for winter living, but we figured if we got bundled up in a flock of blankets, dumped onto sleds and hustled back indoors before we got a chill, we'd be able to survive it. The hotel was heated by about forty of those little, round oil stoves we had brought with us. It also boasted

a big open fireplace which was dandy for toasting marshmallows, but sent half its heat up the chimney.

Most of the river was frozen solid but we found a center lane of running water, got the canoe into it and staged the fight. As a climax we tipped the canoe over and into the icy water and down through the rapids we went. We managed to swim to the snow-covered ice on the edge of the river, where we were hauled out and helped through the waist-deep snow to the solid bank, where the men with the blankets were waiting. Shivering and shaking we were wrapped up like bundles of wet-wash laundry, (our clothes were still soaking wet) and the

Preparing to meet the raging rapids.

Bill Duncan (center) starts a free for all and we heavies ready ourselves for the fight.

whole party headed back to the hotel. Picture our consternation when, as we approached it, we saw smoke pouring from the windows. But the hotel wasn't on fire . . . it only looked that way. Some well meaning idiot had turned the forty oil stoves way up so there'd be plenty of heat for us. Every stove was belching smoke and all the windows had to be opened to clear it away.

When we finally got in, the place was freezing cold from the opened windows, so they thawed us out before the fireplace, where they kept turning us like pigs on a spit. By the time we got dry we were almost crisp. I knew how an Idaho baked potato must feel. Why we three pirates didn't get pneumonia I'll never know but we didn't even catch cold.

Some days we had blizzards that made shooting impossible. Then the card games would start. We were there a little better than seven weeks and "Mighty Joe" returned to Hollywood with nothing more than his life and his memories. I had had my first experience with card sharks who hire out as bit players, extras, crew men or anything they can get . . . just to go along on location . . . and the experience had been a costly one. And I wouldn't have believed it, but the slickest card sharks of them all were those Eskimos!

Despite the difficulties, "Wolves" was another serial hit and suddenly I was put in for the starring role in a projected series of two reel action films. I was known as Gregg, the "College Cowboy," and while the series didn't last beyond the initial production, this film did serve to introduce me to the public as an action "star."

In action in my first starring film — THE COLLEGE COWBOY.

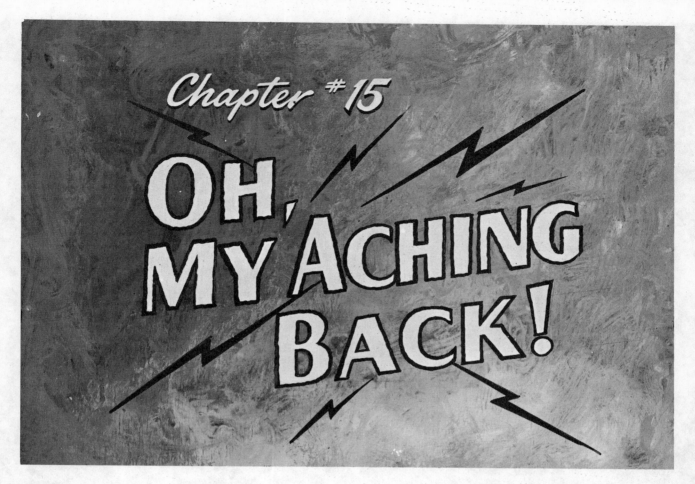

Chapter #15

OH, MY ACHING BACK!

WHILE MAKING THE COLLEGE COWBOY, in which I played a sort of a "handsome Harry" hero type of leading man, sometimes I'd put my makeup on at home and drive to the studio all ready to go to work. On one of those occasions I was driving along, wearing full greasepaint makeup, when I was blocked by a repair truck which had stopped to make some road repairs and had not pulled far enough to the side of the road. I tooted my horn and a couple of big rough looking guys came strolling over. When they saw the makeup, with the accentuated eyebrows and the lipstick, they evidently got the wrong impression. One of them said, "Well, well—get the **pretty** boy!"—and the other put a hand on his hip and said, "Lah--dee-DAH!"

Now "pretty boy" I could have overlooked but that "Lah--dee-DAH" got me. I climbed out of my car and walking up to the larger of the two, a strapping six footer, I said, "I'm afraid I'll have to teach you a lesson." He said, "What d'ya teach—ballet dancing!" with which he took a healthy swing at me and in a moment we were engaged in a rough and tumble free-for-all. He was well muscled and he knew how to fight but he was no match for my superior strength. I was afraid to hit him as hard as I could for fear I'd break his neck so, after a bit of sparring around, I closed in with a couple of wrestling holds and it was amusing to see the surprised look on his face when he felt the power in my

arms. I held him helpless for a moment or two and then, with a "La-dee-dah to you!", I picked him up like a sack of laundry and tossed him four feet through the air into the arms of his astonished partner.

By that time the rest of the repair gang had run over and a couple of them recognized me. When they told my chagrined opponent who I was we had a good laugh and a handshake all around. It turned out that he was the champion heavyweight of their local boxing club and they voted me in as a member of the club on the spot.

When they asked me, at the studio, how my make-up got so smeared I told them about everything EXCEPT "La-dee-dah." A thing like that could get AROUND and I didn't want to have to fight half the guys in the picture business.

Papa used to say the Turkish people were the luckiest people in the world . . . because they were all born Turks. Due to the fact that I am only part Turkish, although my luck has been pretty good, I am not a hundred percent immune from misfortune. I had this proven to me in THE COLLEGE COWBOY.

As you now know, I usually had my own crew of "fight men." These were either regulation stuntmen or well trained and athletic stock actors. Actually, we had hundreds of such men to draw from for riot scenes, gang fights, battle scenes, etc.

In THE COLLEGE COWBOY the studio had gone out of its way to show off acrobatic skill

Veteran screen villain Harry Woods was an impressive adversary in THE COLLEGE COWBOY.

which they seemed to think was rather exceptional to find in a strongman. In making various films I had done every stunt the writers could dream up, so to give this picture a slightly different slant and some added color, they made the background a Mexican village.

The script called for some Mexican brigands to harass me, so the casting director put out a call for Mexican stuntmen and came up with some good ones. I worked out with them for three or four days, staging some realistic fight scenes filled with good fast action and a lot of film viciousness. We then came to the big scene, where my Turkish luck ran out.

This scene was built around an adobe house, two stories high. A sort of Mexican fiesta was going on inside and, as the scene opened, I was doing a whirlwind dance with Melvina Polo. (As I promised nothing but the truth in this book I must tell you that, when the picture was shown, the New York critics said. ''The dance was terrific, but why did Joe Bonomo have to wear such

tight pants?'') Well anyway, just as the dance was concluded the Mexican bandits swarmed in and we all went into a battle royal. Badly outnumbered, I fought them off as long as I could, then I vaulted over a piano, picked it up and tossed it on top of them and leaped through a window, glass and all.

The next sequence called for me to be cornered on the roof by the bandits. As they advanced on me, one with a lariat was to attempt to lasso me. I was to grab the lariat from him, twirl it over my head and lasso a flag-pole on a building across the street. Then, throwing the first bandit into the others I was to do a dangerous ''pendulum swing'' from the roof, land in the saddle of my horse, waiting in the street below, and gallop off to safety. It was a risky stunt, but I had done similar ones before and I figured this should come off all right.

Luckily I decided to rehearse the swing before they started shooting. It's a good thing I did. They had forgotten to blindfold the horse and

As the hero, I defended the heroine's honor and upheld right.

when he saw me come swinging down at him he let out a frightened whinney and took to his heels. Then they blindfolded him . . . after I had picked myself up out of the dirt.

This should have been a warning to me, but I've always been an optimist, and I figured bad luck wouldn't hit twice in the same scene.

However, on this ill-fated day, unknown to me, Louis, one of my best Mexican stuntmen had to go to a wedding . . . so he got his cousin Pedro to take his place. I don't know what Louis told Pedro—evidently not much—for Pedro, who had never worked in a picture before, didn't have the slightest conception of what was going on.

I was busy getting my rope set and my horse in position and neither I nor the director noticed the substitution. When you get a half-dozen Mexicans in makeup and costume, who the heck is going to know the difference, anyway? If the other stuntmen did they didn't say anything about it.

As the scene opened I, closely pursued by the murderous bandits, climbed hand over hand up a drain pipe to the roof while they dashed up the stairs to intercept me up there. I had successfully swung the lasso across the street, snagging the flag-pole, when they converged on me. We knocked each other about for a while, then I made for this Pedro, thinking, of course, it was Louis, who was the one I was going to pick up and throw into the others. I must have had a ferocious look in my eye—or put too much realism in it—for poor Pedro, who apparently didn't realize it was all make-beleive, started backing away and backed right off the roof.

I ran to the edge and looked down, just in time to see him bounce off an awning and land in a crumpled heap on the sidewalk. I rushed down to see what could be done for him. I found his right leg had been broken and he was in considerable pain. Ignoring the director who was yelling for me to come back and finish the scene, I rushed him over to the Universal hospital to see that he received proper medical care as well as the compensation to which he was entitled. As I walked out the hospital door I little suspected that in less than an hour I'd be in the bed next to him.

Back on the set we performed the fight scene again. The lassoing footage was all right, so we didn't have to do that over . . . just went right into the fight. But while I was at the hospital, some nit-wit, who had no business to touch my rope, must have figured I was going to travel hand-over-hand along it to the flag-pole across the street, so he had helpfully tied the long loose end to a pipe on the roof. As we were behind schedule by now I didn't think to check it.

The fight scene over I straddled the rope, grabbed it and jumped. I hadn't gone ten feet when it snapped taut between my legs with such violence that it whipped me off, slamming me so hard into the side of the building that I was knocked unconscious and, with my back to the wall, slid down to a crash-landing in the street below. It was the only time in my life I've been unconscious, but it proved to be a life saver for me. Being unconscious I wasn't resisting, so although I was badly bruised I had no broken bones.

When I came to, you can imagine my surprise to find myself in the hospital, just one bed removed from poor Pedro. As bad as I felt I

A romantic interlude.

More dashing than Zorro and the Cisco Kid, I dazzled Melvina Polo in my Mexican disguise.

The roof fight and lasso episode that ended in a near disaster for me.

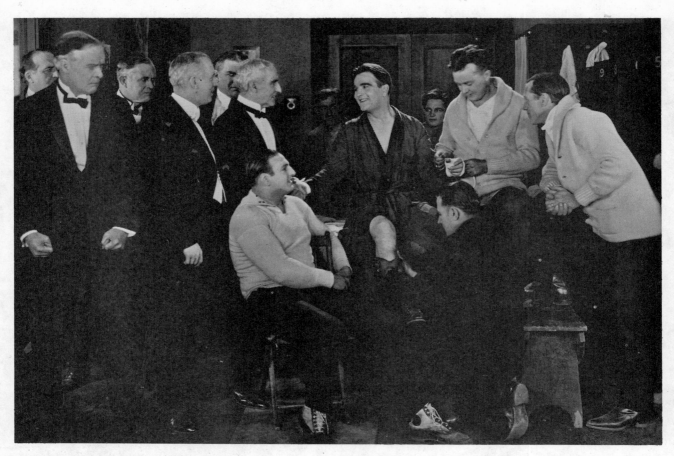

During my term as a Universal stock player, I never knew what the day would bring when I arrived at the studio in the morning. Here I am with William Desmond in THE PHANTOM FORTUNE.

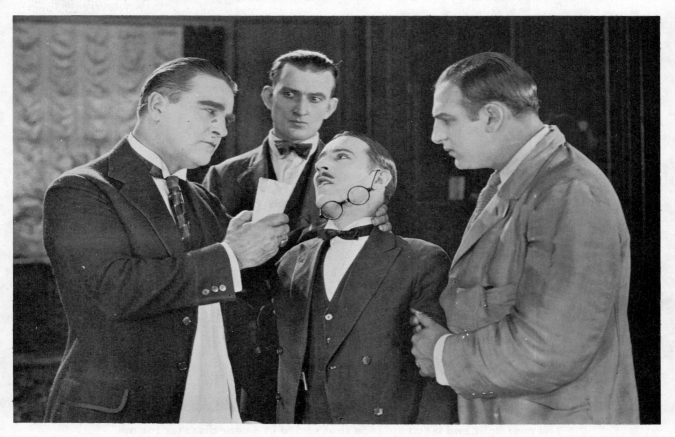

As a man of many disguises I romanced, menaced and fought for Laura LaPlante in THE THRILL GIRL.

couldn't help grinning.

"I sure scared you, didn't I, Pedro?"

"Si, señor," he replied, wincing from his hurts, "you scare me pretty good." Then he eyed my bandages and tape.

"Señor—"

"Yes?"

"Who scared YOU?"

Even though it almost killed me, I laughed for a full minute. Pedro must have thought, "Strange people, these gringos."

I was back on the set in the morning. It had just been another day in the life of a Hollywood stuntman.

Universal tore up my contract and gave me a new one, with a nice big bonus to boot! Once THE COLLEGE COWBOY was finally edited and assembled I guess the studio executives felt they had a potentially popular action star on their hands. ACTION was King at Universal and their now legendary serials, or "cliffhangers" as they were called, constantly needed new faces in the hero role. In my case I could perform the dangerous action sequences **myself** that other stars were doubled in. I was now set to walk the road of Hollywood stardom, or rather to **run** it, while being pursued by wild animals, vicious cutthroats and everything else the studio could possibly send my way. Stardom, back in the 1920's, did not mean that an action performer like myself was to be relieved of his stunting chores. On the contrary, the jobs got tougher and tougher. But, I loved my work, and risking my neck daily was the most exciting part of it!

A daring pickup by plane. The type of stunt which many times has gone wrong, with deadly results.

Chapter #16

The BLACK CATS

IS THERE A SPIRITUALIST in the house? Anyone who has taken "that step beyond?" Or perhaps someone who was tottering on "the brink" when some mysterious force suddenly snatched him away from the icy hand of Death? Good—then I'll tell you about "The Black Cats." You practical folk who pooh-pooh all forms of psychic-phenomena, Guardian Angels, and "warnings from beyond the grave", may skip this chapter and receive a five percent rebate upon request. It came about like this:—

One day, not too long after I'd started stunting, a Hollywood publicity man drank a "double-coke" at his favorite "soda-fountain," and had a brain storm. He wrote an article entitled "The Black Cat Club." It was strictly a figment of his imagination, but it made exciting reading. It depicted thirteen of us Hollywood stuntmen, who he stated had formed this club where we laughed at Death and toasted the Devil. The name came from the fact that we were sure-footed as cats and apparently had nine lives. He then painted us as thirteen hare-brained and happy-go-lucky daredevils, who gloried in doing death-defying stunts and regretted we had but nine lives to give to the Movies. He said we limited our membership to thirteen—and called ourselves Black Cats—to show how recklessly we flaunted superstition—despite the fact we were living doomed lives that could end only in sudden death. Yes, it made great reading.

But when the article came out we didn't like

what it started us thinking about. A fellow who is risking his life every day mustn't do much thinking, anyway. While no one likes to consider himself superstitious, in this age of scientific enlightenment, men working in dangerous jobs can't help having a shadow of superstition creep into their lives. You try to laugh it off, but one of the men is killed the day after a picture suddenly fell off the wall in his living room. Then you think of that day a bird flew in your window. Your air-hose broke in that diving scene and they just got you up in time.

Your mind begins to work. You're sure you had a funny feeling, a premonition of danger, just before the stunt was attempted. Maybe you didn't, but you begin to think you did. Then someone points out that the last three men killed were all wearing green shirts, or something just as silly. But it may not be as silly as it sounds and it starts to interfere with your work.

I make no claims to being psychic, but on quite a few occasions I have had a queer feeling of impending danger before doing a stunt, and each time, something went wrong. I would be doubly careful, but someone else, that other element over which I had no control, would miss up on timing or judgment—or just goof —and I'd get hurt.

You may call these premonitions, a sixth sense, or just plain hunches . . . but whatever you call them, I eventually began to respect them. And whenever I got that queer feeling,

A typical end of serial chapter situation — a potential disaster for any stuntman.

regardless of what others thought of me, I would refuse to do the stunt . . . and more than once I saved my life by heeding the warning of this "inner voice."

Perhaps, because we were all in the same profession, we had the same premonitions and fears, and we didn't like this publicity guy unceremoniously dumping us into this "Black Cat Club" of his—"the club of the doomed!" It sounded too much like the "kiss of death". And as things turned out it wasn't far from it. Within nine years there were only three of us still alive. The nine lives of the other "Black Cats" had run out. The sole survivors of the original group were Paul Malvern, Harvey Parry and myself.

It was only a few months after the Black Cat article appeared that the first of us did his last stunt. This tragedy showed us only too clearly how this kiss of death and our own premonitions were to work hand in hand through the years.

In one picture there was a sequence in which a stuntman was to double for the hero when he changed from an airplane to a speeding freight train. Now, I had already done so much of that kind of work that the director naturally chose me for the job. It didn't sound especially difficult when we talked about it, and I agreed to do it. Just another stunt, I thought.

However, the next morning, when we were all on location, that warning voice inside me told me not to go up. I didn't like the flyer who was to pilot the plane. Somehow, I didn't have confidence in him. The regular pilots that we usually worked with were nowhere around, and believe me, the life of a stuntman depends so much on the skill of his pilot in this sort of stunt. So I told the director I wouldn't do the stunt unless Al Wilson—another of the Black Cats—piloted the plane. Al was the pilot I usually worked with, and I was sure he knew his job. Al, incidentally, was the last of the Cats to go —killed in 1933 stunting at an air carnival. But he was a heck of a good man and we were close friends. On this particular day, Al was working another job. I was sorry, I said, but I just didn't like the looks of the guy who was to pilot for this stunt.

The director became angry, and refused to change pilots, muttering something about "temperamental stuntmen with no guts." He insisted that this pilot was thoroughly competent.

"What's the matter with you, Bonomo," he said. "Running out of gas?" (This was a common movie expression for losing your nerve.)

"I'm sorry," I said. "But maybe that's it. You do the stunt if you want to, and I'll direct the cameras."

There were a few more nasty remarks passed, and finally the director, losing his patience, sent for a friend of mine to do the job.

This other stuntman (I'll just call him "Lefty" here) was a close friend of mine. We had worked together, on and off, for several years. He was a specialist in this kind of stunt, too. When it came to coolness under fire, and courage at all times, well, Lefty had no master. A great guy.

After about an hour, Lefty arrived, and the director told him what had happened. I was standing some distance away, and I couldn't hear what they were saying, but the director occasionally glanced at me with scorn. Pretty soon Lefty nodded his head and grinned, and I knew he had agreed to do the stunt. The director went back to his camera crew, and I approached Lefty. He was getting into his belts and other straps, the natural protection all stuntmen wear.

"You going up, huh?" I said.

"Sure, Joe. Why not?"

What could I tell him? I had no logical reason why not. Just a feeling. "I've just got a bum hunch about this pilot," I said.

"What's he got to do? Just fly the plane, that's all," he replied.

"Lefty;" I said, "Don't go up."

I'll never forget that look in his eyes. It seemed to tell me that he knew I was right. It's a funny thing, but he understood the way I felt. Since the fight with the director I had been left alone

The great stunt pilot Al Wilson.

Helping a fellow stunter out of a tight situation. One slip and he'd fall to his death!

on the lot like I had leprosy. But here was a guy who understood. He seemed to hesitate a moment, but then he broke out in his usual grin, tightening his protective chest belt.

"What the hell, it's a job," he laughed. "I'll see ya later." He jabbed me playfully in the gut and walked off to talk to the pilot.

They took off a few minutes later and the train was started way down to the left, coming up toward us. The thing was to be timed so that the transfer to the train happened just in front of us. The plane circled as the train picked

rungs on the swaying, free-hanging ladder, but it was not enough. The plane, doing probably seventy miles an hour, slapped him up against the side of the moving freight train, dragged and bounced him over the top, and he was lost to view on the other side.

When the train had passed, we could see the plane rise a little, with Lefty still hanging on to the ladder. We were all screaming our lungs out, trying to wave the pilot off, but he misunderstood the signal, I guess, and thought the director wanted another try.

A tricky rope ladder transfer to a plane.

up speed. Instead of overtaking and settling down on the train from the rear, can you imagine our horror on the ground when this pilot who was supposed to be so competent, approached the train from the **side**! There was no radio in the plane; our only communication with the plane was by hand signals. And the dummy in the cockpit probably had all he could do to fly the plane, probably didn't even look down.

There was nothing we could do but wave at him, and that having no effect, stand by and watch the tragedy. Lefty was down at the end of the rope ladder. The plane was coming in too low, and at right angles to the train. At the last minute, we saw Lefty try to climb back up the ladder. He managed to get back up a few

By this time the train was some distance down the track, and we saw the approach from sort of behind. The plane approached again, and again too low. Lefty, battered and probably broken in a dozen places, couldn't climb up and he couldn't let go to fall to the ground. It was probably only on sheer guts that he hung on at all. We all stood looking with a helpless sick feeling, as into the side of the train he was swung again, bounced and dragged over the top again. He hung on for maybe fifty yards on the other side, then slipped off the ladder and fell to the ground. He hit and bounced almost as high as the low-flying plane, then hit again, rolled a few more yards, and lay there.

When we reached him, Lefty was still conscious.

In this type of transfer stunt balance is very important—you must let the plane lift *you* up. Pulling down on the rope ladder can actually throw the plane off and cause it to crash.

Instead of blaming the stupidity of the pilot, he apologized to the director for ruining the picture.

"I'm sorry I missed, Bill," were the last words he said. He became unconscious, and about a minute later he died, almost every bone in his body sticking out through his flesh in jagged splinters. The first of the Black Cats had been kissed.

The pilot responsible for this boy's death didn't do any more work in films, you can bet on that. The plane had circled the scene of the accident a couple of times, and the pilot must have looked down and seen what had happened. He wasn't too bright, but I'm sure he must have known whose fault it was, because the plane just flew away. The guy never even showed up to collect his pay.

You'd wonder why a tragedy such as this didn't send us all packing—scurrying around for nice safe jobs where the money was just as good and you didn't have to risk your life for it— but stuntmen don't seem to be happy unless they ARE risking their lives. And they certainly don't do it for the money there is in it. In a sense they're playing a game, with Death as their opponent, and there's no game on earth quite as thrilling. Remember the Crystal Pier in Santa Monica? Well, if you used to see a bunch of muscular young fellows, risking their fool necks, doing water dives from the roof of a two story building, into soft sand in place of water—even including double back flips—you saw the Black Cats. You'd think we'd have had enough stunting all week at the studios, but Sunday afternoons would find us at Santa Monica, risking a trip to the hospital, just for kicks. A poor jump could mean a broken bone or two —and sometimes did—but with us, bones were expendable. After all, didn't we have two hundred and six to play around with? You see, we **did** think things **out**!

Stunting is like a recurrent fever. Even after a stuntman moves up to a directorship or a producer's status, the old urge is liable to break out at any moment. Whenever Paul Malvern was producing a picture and a stunt would go wrong, he'd either show the stuntman how, or

An actual movie car crash—one where the stuntman didn't make it.

One of my specialties—a high dive off the mast.

An interesting biplane stunt, where I climb up the craft's landing gear.

do it himself.

On one occasion, they were out on a schooner, filming a sea picture. The hero and the heavy were to stage a fight in the rigging. It wasn't going too well so Paul went up to the top of a tall mast to show the stuntman how it should be done. He was supposed to be hit, just as the ship rolled, and fall into the ocean. Well, this day the ocean was rough. The fight started, Paul himself playing the heavy; but just as the hero hit him, the ship took a sudden lurch, Paul lost his footing and fell the **other** way, down to the deck, fifty feet below. Fortunately he was able to twist in the air and grab a guy rope, breaking his fall a bit. But he burned the skin off his hands and hit the deck on his back.

When they brought him to he was spitting blood from internal injuries and was partially paralyzed. It sure looked as though Fate had claimed another one of the Cats . . . but Paul was a pretty tough hombre and eventually recovered. However, a new contract was drawn up, forbidding him to even so much as show a stuntman what he wanted.

From then on Paul went along steering clear of all stunting, living up to this contract . . . until . . . one day they started ribbing him on the golf course. "Poor old Paul, he's sure not the man he used to be." So without a word, Paul went into his specialty, which was a round-off flip-flop. He'd show them!

In this acrobatic stunt a man flips, going forward, with only his hands and feet alternately touching the ground. It is something like a cartwheel, only directly forward, like the front flip from a high diving board. After doing several flips forward the round-off comes. The man flips high in the air without touching his hands

to the ground, but twists his body so he lands in a standing position, facing in the direction from which he started.

Well . . . Paul went into it, but the grass was damp that day and a bit slippery. At the end he came down in such a way that he tore loose the main ligaments in both legs and practically severed his Achilles tendons. Into the hospital he went for many days while all the ligaments and tendons were painfully wired back into place.

After that he concentrated on producing, turning out such pictures as HOUSE OF DRACULA, ALI BABA AND THE FORTY THIEVES, and many others.

When he heard I was going to do this book he said, "Never mind warning them against **stunting**, Joe—warn them against **golf**. Look what it did to ME!"

So the only member of the ill-fated club still stunting is Harvey Parry . . . still one of the top men in the profession. In the old days Harvey was a lot of laughs. He had two front pivot teeth that were continually getting knocked out, and it seemed he spent half his time running to the dentist to have them replaced. It wasn't so funny to Harvey, but **we** enjoyed it, and I'm sure the dentist did. I liked Harvey a lot—and I have never killed a man in my life—but I almost made Harvey the exception.

We were doing a picture up at Feather River, and he and I had to stage a fight on the edge of a sixty-foot cliff, with both of us going over into the rapids below. Four brake ropes were stretched across the river, with strips of white muslin draped over them, so we would be sure to see them. When the rushing water is hustling you downstream, bouncing you off the rocks, a brake rope is easy to miss. That's why we always used four, just in case you missed one, or two, or possibly three.

We have already seen how a man could be killed by being swept over the falls below that last rope. In fact, several top Hollywood stuntmen met their deaths at this very spot. To be crashed on the rocks below, and survive, was considered impossible—'til that day when Harvey did it.

We were finally ready, the cameras started, and Harvey and I began our fight. In the struggle, as we went over the cliff, my knee accidentally struck him in the mouth—but we were on our way down and I didn't think any more about it.

We hit the water, were immediately picked up by the current, and away we went! I caught the first brake rope, but Harvey missed. He'll get the next one, I thought, as I watched him tumbling downstream. But he missed again. And he missed again. And he missed a fourth time! Then I saw him go over the falls.

I pulled myself to shore as fast as I could, but by the time I got there, others had reached him and had him on the bank. He was sitting up, alive, but coughing like mad. Finally he was able to tell us what happened.

Just as we went off the cliff my knee had knocked out those two front teeth. They had lodged in his throat and almost strangled him as he went into the rapids. Struggling for breath and on the verge of choking to death, he had

missed the ropes. When he hit the bottom of the falls the jolt dislodged the teeth and he swallowed them. Why he wasn't killed, no one will ever know.

"Now, Joe," Harvey concluded, grinning through the empty space in his mouth, "since it was your knee that knocked out those lousy choppers, how about paying for the **new** ones?"

I was so happy to see the guy alive I'd have gladly bought him a full set of both uppers and lowers . . . and let him BITE me with 'em.

While I'm still on the subject of Harvey I must tell you about another experience that brings out a long forgotten phase of picture making. Before the inception of the Guilds, to monitor and patrol the industry and protect the interests of those employed in it, underpayment was the rule rather than the exception. A few of the stars made big money, but the rank and file grubbed along on barely a living wage and in some instances didn't even collect THAT. Studios with impressive sounding names would spring up overnight, make a picture and, once the film was in the can would fold their tents like the Arab and silently steal away, leaving the hard-working performers and crew to whistle for their money.

One such outfit was—let's call them The Giles Studios. They opened with a big fanfare, signed up a lot of people, including Harvey and Paul,

There was always a chance for injury on a jump from a speeding train.

and went right into production. The heads of the outfit were two brothers named Bronsky . . . a couple of prosperous looking, smooth talking lawyers from the east, who painted rosy pictures of the future and were long on promises although, as it turned out later, a little short on cash.

The picture was to be one of those "death before dishonor" yarns with the locale centered about a place called Serpentine Point, on the Feather River, in Alaska. The story was a contrived affair about love and passion amid the arctic snows and consisted mainly of the trials and tribulations of the beautiful and virtuous heroine trying to escape from the clutches of a handsome but wicked rascal who was pursuing her, intent upon bending her to his evil will. In those days the plot wasn't too important as long as there was plenty of action.

There was apparently enough money to get the company up to Alaska and the shooting commenced. There was one exciting chase sequence where the girl tries to escape by paddling down the river in an Eskimo kayak with the villain pursuing in a canoe. (As this entire sequence presented some dangerous aspects, Harvey, in a blonde wig and feminine attire is doubling the girl and Paul is doubling the heavy.) In a burst of furious paddling the girl reaches the shore just a few yards in the lead, leaps out of the kayak and runs into the woods, her long blond tresses streaming in the wind, with the thwarted heavy in close pursuit.

We next see them racing along the edge of a cliff, a hundred feet above the river. Now, poised on the cliff's edge, with the villain closing in behind her and the swirling waters a hundred feet below, she must make her choice between dishonor and almost inescapable death. With a whispered prayer on her lips she leaps to the angry waters below, pulling him with her as he reaches out to stop her.

Now this may not sound like much of a feat for two experienced stuntmen, but the Feather River was something to contend with. The current was rushing by at from 35 to 40 miles an hour and, at the jump point, there was a bend where the water kept piling up in miniature rapids. The morning of the shooting, they had gone to the top of the cliff and dropped big boulders down to test the current. What they learned wasn't too comforting. The water was going by so fast the boulders didn't even sink but went right on down the river with the current.

It is doubtful they would have gone through with the stunt except for one thing. They had bought some liquor, made by an old moonshiner up there, that was concocted from fermented reindeer milk, bay leaves and pine needles, to name just a few of the ingredients. Whatever was in it, it had what they needed, and after two or three good belts of it, over the cliff they went. They were buffeted about, cut by jagged rocks, somersaulted through the rapids and finally pulled out more dead than alive. It's a miracle they both weren't drowned.

After a few more days of shooting and several more tough stunts the picture was finished and they all packed back to Hollywood. An hour after Hap Depew, the head cameraman delivered the negative to the lab, the news came out that the studio had folded, gone into bankruptcy, and

A difficult pendulum swing from a great height.

120

Making a high dive escape into the studio pool.

no one would be paid.

When these sad tidings reached Paul and Harvey, who had $350. coming, they resolved not to take it lying down, so they called on me for help. The brothers Bronsky had gone into hiding, but we finally located one of them in a room on the 9th floor of the Christie Hotel on Hollywood Boulevard. He was a small man who was apparently trying to drink his weight in a wine elixir, a prohibition ''tonic'', of which he had a whole case.

When Harvey and Paul asked for their money he just waved them grandly away. They tried to explain the hazardous job they had done for him . . . they jumped on and off the bed to illustrate the cliff bit and then swam around the floor, using the carpet as a simulation of the swirling Feather River. Mr. Bronsky enjoyed their performance as he polished off another bottle of tonic, but he was adamant. The studio had folded . . . he'd like to pay 'em . . . nice boys . . . but no money.

Just then Harvey conveniently discovered he was out of cigarettes. He hustled down to the lobby and called Hap Depew to get the negative back from the lab and dash over to the hotel with it. As he left the room I passed a whispered word to Paul and, without further ado, we seized Mr. Bronsky, lifted him into the air and carrying the startled man to the open window, held him out nine stories above the street . . . head down . . . each of us grasping a leg.

Suddenly sober the frightened man tried to scream but the voice froze in his throat.

I said, ''All we have to do is let go, Mr. Bronsky. Right, Paul?''

''It'll be a pleasure,'' grinned Paul, bouncing Mr. Bronsky up and down a little. ''We'll just tell everybody he jumped.''

The panic stricken Mr. Bronsky suddenly found his voice.

''No, no,'' he screamed, ''don't drop me. I'll pay . . . I'll pay.''

''Fair enough,'' said Paul . . . and we hauled him back in through the window.

Without another word, Bronsky rushed to the telephone and called his brother who arrived with the money just as Harvey and Hap Depew got there with the film. Without even stopping to explain, the thoroughly shaken Bronsky counted out $350 with trembling fingers.

''Wait a minute,'' said Paul, ''you're not through yet. Now pay off Depew.''

Bronsky was in no mood to argue.

''Okay,'' he said to Hap, ''here's your money.''

''Thanks,'' said Hap, ''here's your film,'' and handed the astonished man the negative he had retrieved from the lab, which the Bronskys would have never gotten if they hadn't paid off. Best of all, they were so frightened that the following day they paid off the rest of the company, too . . . proving that some situations call for heroic measures. I doubt that anyone would have dared try THAT one but a couple of Hollywood stuntmen. It sounds risky but we used to take bigger chances than that almost every day of our lives.

My stuntman's sneakers betray my true assignment in this epic of the desert.

CHAPTER 17

CHARLIE AND THE CIRCUS

ALL STUNTING WAS DANGEROUS, but everything was worked out to the most minute detail. Then, if things went according to plan, it wasn't any more dangerous than your first shave with a straight-edge razor!

But now and then the ball took a bad bounce, as they say at the ball park, and sometimes that meant the ballgame. But after all, that was the stunt business. You were taking risks daily, but you always knew about what to expect and could take precautions against it.

Working with animals was a different story. An animal was a living thing, less predictable than the law of cause and effect and less dependable than a human being. But it was my job to do anything I was called upon to do, and unless it was "illegal, immoral or fattening," I did it.

In consequence, in addition to fighting humans, I have tangled with virtually every animal from free-swinging gorillas to boxing kangaroos. I have wrestled lions, pythons, alligators, bears—I have even fought sharks, underwater.

Have you ever thought of engaging a man-eating shark in a battle to the death? If you have, you'd better hurry to a head-shrinker. But I'm sure you've seen it done in the movies and I'm one of the guys who did it. And there's really nothing to it, that is, the way we do it in Hollywood.

It was in BEASTS OF PARADISE that I fought my first shark. How was it done? Well, first of all, we had to **get** the shark, so the studio sent out a call to fishermen along the California coast . . . a hundred dollars to the man who could bring in, alive, the largest man-eater. In a few days there were so many we could afford to be choosey, and we picked the biggest, ugliest baby in the lot.

After they got some underwater swimming shots of **me**, they put the shark in a large glass tank and got some shots of him, both underwater and with his fin zipping along the surface. All these shots could later be spliced in. Then out we went to the clear waters off Catalina.

On the way out the prop men went to work on the shark. They wired his nasty mouth shut and put a harness on him, on either side of which was a small loop or "handle." During the fight I was to hold these handles and literally "ride" him until he was played out. But I'd have to hang onto him—and he was a monster and full of fight—and I knew if he ever shook me off, that one blow from his slashing tail could break my neck.

But when they arrived with him, he was so quiet I thought they'd doped him on the way. I soon had that impression corrected.

A man in a camera bell was lowered for the underwater shots, with another camera to cover the surface shots and I climbed on that man-eater's back and got a firm grip on the handles. Then this seemingly torpid shark and I were lowered beneath the surface. I'd heard sharks

A shark in his natural environment is even more dangerous than he looks.

were smart, but I never knew they could "play possum," but when we hit the water I felt I'd suddenly been transferred to a roller-coaster. That fish came to life so fast I almost fell off him through sheer astonishment. Then around and around, up and down, in and out of the water he twisted. I was never so busy in my life! It seemed like hours before he was played out enough for me to relax a little . . . satisfied that the camera-men had gotten all the film they needed. But then he suddenly came to life again with a sort of "second wind"—and no bucking broncho ever fought harder or gave its rider a rougher deal. But that was his final effort. As he gave up, exhausted, I swung under him, drew my belt knife, and dispatched him. The grisly job done, I swam back to the boat.

I never knew I could feel sorry for a man-eating shark, but after the fight that one put up, I've always felt he was, at least, entitled to a **draw**.

Sometime later, in another picture, I was called on to kill another man-eating shark. The film was to be done the same way, but when we were lowered into the water, can you imagine the scare I got when I saw five other sharks in the water with us? And no harness or wired jaws on any but the one I was hanging onto!

Without even taking a second look I let go of my shark and struck out. Now I was a fairly fast swimmer, having set a few meet records at different times, but never, before or since, have I swum that fast. Every moment I expected to feel a leg torn off—or worse. I fairly flung myself into the boat, with a groan of relief.

"What happened, Joe?" Francis Ford, the startled director, asked.

"Sharks!" I gasped. "A whole school of 'em!"

"Oh, those?" He laughed. "They're leopard sharks—perfectly harmless. I should have told you."

"Yeah, " I snapped, "it **would** have been nice!"

I was pretty angry and everybody was laughing. Everybody that is, but Francis Ford—for it had suddenly occurred to him that far out into the blue stretches of the Pacific—wired jaw, harness and all, had fled our man-eater, never to be seen again.

Even such a serious and hazardous job as tangling with man-eating sharks can have its humorous side. One of the funniest true stories that ever came out of Hollywood centered about what started to be a rather gruesome affair— a fight to the death between a killer shark and a pearl diver. In the course of the fight the man was to outmaneuver the shark, plunge his knife into the creature's soft belly and kill it.

The fight was to take place in a glass tank, simulated to look like a section of the ocean and I was elected to double the pearl diver, a big name star who was playing the part but couldn't swim for sour apples. However, even with an expert swimmer, in the fairly small tank provided, the odds would have been greatly in favor of the shark, had it not been for one thing. Before dropping this eight foot marauder into the tank they had sewn his vicious mouth shut with invisible cat-gut thread, leaving enough opening in the center for him to partially open his jaws, but not to open them wide enough to inflict the terrible bite he was normally capable of. In consequence, I anticipated little or no trouble as I climbed down the ladder into the water, my knife between my teeth. I figured I

Mixing character parts with stunts.

With a shark in a tense situation.

could avoid the slashing tail and with that ugly mouth sewn shut I had only to put on a good show until the moment came for the kill.

What everyone failed to take into consideration was the effect on the shark of not being able to open his mouth. He couldn't understand what was wrong and it drove him into a frenzy of blind rage which he proceeded to vent on ME. I had to resort to every trick in the book to avoid the savage rushes of this powerful, maddened creature who was trying to smash me against the glass sides of the tank.

After about three wild minutes of this, while the delighted director had the cameras catching it from all angles, you can imagine my relief when the signal came that it was time to move in. My knife was long and razor sharp and I had no doubt I would be able to end this one-sided contest with a single stroke. But I had again figured without the shark. As, with my knife poised, I swam to meet the lunging monster —my eye on the very spot where I would sink the blade—the big fish suddenly turned and dove directly AT me.

Panicked by this sudden surprise attack I slashed out wildly with my knife. It wouldn't

have happened once in a thousand years, but this time it DID. The razor sharp blade swept just close enough to sever the cat-gut stitches that were holding the shark's jaw closed—and his mouth suddenly snapped open exposing a frightening array of equally razor-sharp teeth.

I took one horrified look, then broke all my previous records getting back to the side of the tank where I scrambled up the ladder just as the still angry shark made a final desperate effort to dismember me—only missing me by inches. I dreamed about that shark for weeks and as long as I worked as a stuntman they could never get me into a tank with another one. They said it couldn't happen again in a **million** years but somehow they could never convince me.

Some of the more enjoyable moments I spent working with animals were spent with Charlie, Universal's prize elephant. Charlie was just about the biggest thing alive. How many tons is the biggest full grown elephant in captivity today? Well, Charlie was bigger.

But for all his great tonnage, Charlie was by far the most gentle, most sensitive animal I have ever known . . . and he had an intelligence and understanding almost human. You could ride on his head or neck during a running chase and just whisper into one of those big ears for him to slow down, or go faster, or turn left, or right —and he'd never make a mistake.

Charlie Murphy, his trainer, used to boast that Charlie could master any trick, however intricate, in just one rehearsal. That might have been a slight exaggeration, but Charlie would come through if he could, which was pretty good for an elephant. At a word of command he'd pick me up in his great trunk, being careful not to squeeze me too tight and gently place me on his neck. Or I'd lie down with my head on a wooden block and he'd kneel over me and gently touch his cheek against mine—and all the weight of that massive head would be light as an angel's wing on my face—for Charlie liked me—and he knew I liked **him**.

Which leads me to something I've often wondered about. How far could animals go if it weren't for the limitations of their animal bodies . . . if they could learn to talk, for instance, or had other human attributes and advantages. Even with Charlie's unwieldly bulk he could walk a narrow plank—even balance himself on a rolling iron ball. Had he possessed an I.Q. of a hundred and sixty could he have done much more with those ponderous twelve-inches-across hooves of his? Even his sensitive trunk, with which he could pick up a pin, had its limitations. There was only one of it, unlike the two hands we possess that can work together in perfect co-ordination.

Yes, Charlie was handicapped and he knew it. In working closely with him I could sense that he was conscious of his limitations. He'd look at me as though to say, "You've got to help me with this one, Joe—after all, I'm only an elephant and I can turn only so fast and jump only so high." And when, for the first time, he'd try a new trick I was teaching him, his funny little eyes would actually study my face, to read in it approval or disapproval. Yes, Charlie was smarter than any horse, dog or chimp I've ever known.

Carl Laemmle brought Luciano Albertini, a famous Italian stunt and aerialist star, to this country—and I was assigned the top "heavy" role in his serial vehicle, THE IRON MAN. That meant I was playing the villain again, but it was a great part and by the time the serial had played the theatres, I was as well known as any of the leading men. So, I was given top billing as "Landow the Strongman" in a great new

Up to no good in THE IRON MAN.

Routining an exciting fight with Albertini in THE IRON MAN.

I was out to get Albertini in THE IRON MAN, and have a good time while doing it.

Somehow directors always got me onto high places as a means of adding some jumping stunts, which meant action!

When it came to the perennial "dirty work afoot", I was always in the midst of it.

serial, THE GREAT CIRCUS MYSTERY. At long last, Joe Bonomo . . . Hercules of the Screen . . . had ARRIVED!

I was handed the shooting script to study, and as I read it, I got an idea . . . and had it not been for my youthful desire to bask in the glory of the bright lights, this idea would have made me a big Hollywood producer. I had suddenly realized the obvious—that we were wasting time and money by shooting serials, one two-reel episode after another. Why not plan the entire TEN episodes in a coordinate form and shoot them all at once? The complete script was there —all that was necessary was to figure out how many scenes were to be shot, how many costume changes were needed, and the relationship of the characters, in advance. Then, when all the sequences had been shot, they could be spliced together in the cutting room, and we'd have the whole ten two-reelers at one fell swoop.

I sat up most of that night drawing up schedule charts and took them direct to Mr. Laemmle the following morning.

"It's never been done that way, Joe," he hedged. "It sounds feasible, the way you explain it, but I'm afraid it would wind up in a mish-mash."

"Not if you follow these charts," I retorted.

"Shoot twenty full reels, each with hundreds of short sequences? They could never keep track of the film."

"They could if each piece of film was marked to correspond with the **figures** on these charts, Mr. Laemmle."

"Joe," he said, "we're budgeted at $200,000

Carl Laemmle, the man who founded the empire that was Universal.

Performing (in black outfit) a stunt fight on the wing of a plane actually in the air.

The complete company of THE GREAT CIRCUS MYSTERY. "Murph" Murphy, who ran the Universal zoo, and Eddie Polo's brother Sam (in turban) are on the ground with Queenie the leopard. Seated in front of me are Julius Bernheim, the studio manager, Carl Laemmle and producer Bennie Zeidman. Director Jay Marchant (in bow tie & white shirt) is standing in front of the camera on the right.

for THE GREAT CIRCUS MYSTERY. We're **sure** we'll make money the old way."

"Mr. Laemmle," I said desperately, "shoot the picture **my** way and you'll make twice as much."

"And if we should take a loss?"

"I'll personally make it up out of my salary," I said. He reflected a moment.

"What's your angle, Joe? What do you want out of it?"

"Just the satisfaction of being right!" I said dramatically. That clinched it.

"All right, we'll try it, Joe, but I'll hold you to your bargain."

As we shook hands on it I thought, "Bonomo, you'd **better** be right, or you'll be working for the rest of your life for **nothing!**"

THE GREAT CIRCUS MYSTERY was a real spectacular. The studio engaged top performers from Ringling Brothers, Barnum and Bailey, and other top circuses. All kinds of acts were brought in, to give the picture the thrills and excitement of a **genuine** circus. As the great Landow, I was called on to perform feats I had never before attempted. I could tumble, juggle, work with animals and amaze audiences with my feats of strength, but I was a little apprehensive when

THE GREAT CIR

featuring B

IS

The out to

Ballyhoo it to the skies! the greatest show on ea nomo, the world's stron a serial built for 10 big

A CYCLONE of THRILLS AMAZING ENTERTAINMENT

"The **GREAT** Circus Mystery

Featuring

BONOMO

THE WORLD'S STRONGEST MAN

with

LOUISE LORRAINE

UNIVERSAL ADVENTURE PICTURE

Crowd-attracting Advance One-Sheet
Plaster Your Town Like a Circus and Clean Up in Big Style

To the many lovers of the Big Top, this film's authentic circus atmosphere meant a great deal.

told I would also perform on the high trapezes with the famous Flying Cordovas—Frank, Al and Mary. Because of my weight I couldn't do the actual flying, but they wanted to use me as a "catcher." As I had done a lot of catching in ground tumbling acts, and was quick and powerful, I figured it wouldn't be too tough—so up into the "cradle", or catcher's trapeze, I went —and started catching.

There was a net underneath us, so nobody was concerned when I missed a few times— and after a while I began to catch rather well. I had been hanging upside down for perhaps a half-hour, when Frank Cordova said, "Okay, Joe, that's enough for the first day."

"I'm just getting the hang of it," I laughed, "this is fun."

"But not for your back," said Frank. "Give it a rest."

"My back can take it," I replied. "I'm always in top condition."

He warned me again, but I wouldn't listen— and as I was the "white haired boy" of the picture, we continued for another hour or two. However, unlike an experienced catcher who eases his arms down at the moment of the catch, I held my arms **out** and took the strain in my legs and back. What was the difference? I felt fine.

Finally the Cordovas insisted that was all they were going to do that day, so I **had** to stop. I jumped down to the net, flipped over the edge the way pros do, took one step—and fell flat on my face—with such a pain in my back I thought it was broken. Then it suddenly spread to my legs, and I lay there in agony, unable to move from the waist down. I was carried to my dressing room and laid out.

Jay Marchant, the director, was in mortal fear that the whole picture would have to be shelved, but the Cordovas assured him my condition was no more than they had expected and that I'd be okay in a few days.

Though it felt like I'd broken my spine, all I had done was pull the many small sacroiliac muscles around the spinal column. Joe Bonomo had been using muscles he didn't know he had! With heat therapy and gentle massage, although I was in the most agonizing pain of my life, in four days I had completely recovered.

Fortunately, the "schedule" had allowed Marchant to shoot around me, so no production time was lost. When I came back, the Cordovas advised me to catch some more, though they said the pain would come back, but less severely. They were right, and I spent another two days in bed. But finally, just as those great aerialists had predicted, my sacroiliac muscles were stretched and toughened to the point where I could catch for hours with no after effects.

But I got even with those muscles. I showed 'em. From then on I worked 'em to death!

Getting a good workout with "top mounter" Cecil Whitworth.

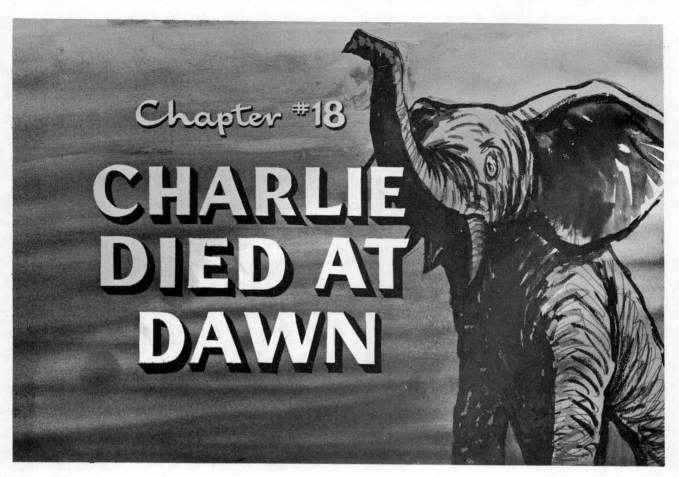

Chapter #18

CHARLIE DIED AT DAWN

FEW, IF ANY, can foretell the way they're going to leave this life—and Hank, another of the Black Cats, who had risked his life a thousand times, was about to get "the fatal kiss" in a manner, I'm sure, he would never have dreamed of.

We were shooting a circus panic scene in THE GREAT CIRCUS MYSTERY. Hank was to be performing on a high-wire when the big tent would suddenly start collapsing—an effect we had been working hard on. As the collapse came, the spectators would panic, the animals would stampede and Hank would apparently do "a death fall" from the high-wire to the sawdust, fifty feet below. Thus a wildly exciting scene would be achieved, crammed with Hollywood "realism." As it turned out it was **too** realistic—for both Hank and Charlie the elephant.

As I related earlier, Charlie seemed to have an almost human mind inside that massive head. We had worked together so much, I actually felt closer to him than to many of the actors. Once, Charlie had killed a man, but few blamed him for it. It had been one of the trainers at Universal—a nice enough guy I guess—but the wrong man for training animals. He lacked the inexhaustible patience that is the first requisite for animal trainers.

When handling an elephant, because his hide is so tough, an elephant-hook must be used. It has a sharp point on one end, with a short, curved hook branching off, just below the point.

This permits a double action. You can jab the elephant with the point—or catch and pull him with the hook. This is the only thing the huge beast can feel . . . and he responds accordingly. However, big as an elephant is—and Charlie was the biggest—he does have tender spots. But this impatient trainer would hook wherever he happened to hit, often catching Charlie around the eyes, or hooking him inside his sensitive mouth. This must have hurt like fury because one day, when he hooked Charlie in a sensitive spot, Charlie just casually wrapped his great trunk around him and crashed him against a wall, crushing his skull.

How much malice there was in the action is debatable. Knowing that elephant as I did, I think it was just his way of saying, "Take it a little easy, fella, that hurts!"—only Charlie didn't know his own strength. A sort of inquest followed, and on the testimony of several of the other trainers, Charlie was exonerated. He was not malicious—and he had a long record of intelligent and cooperative movie work behind him —so he was returned to his home in the Universal zoo, with a clean bill of health.

But now, several years later, disaster was about to strike. We had Charlie with us as we started to shoot the final sequence which included the faked collapse of the Big Tent, a faked fire breaking out, the ensuing panic among the spectators and finally the stampede of the animals. The stampede was to be faked in the cutting room,

Polishing off the heavies in THE GREAT CIRCUS MYSTERY.

With Charlie the Elephant, a super-intelligent animal.

for to actually panic animals could be disastrous.

Well, like the best laid plans, something miscarried. Through some miscalculation, helped along by a sudden storm that blew up, the Big Top really **did** start collapsing and a **real** panic started. To make matters worse, the smudge-pot man, thinking it was the fake collapse, began filling the tent with smoke to get the fire effect. Charlie, frightened, trumpeted and ran. We tried to stop him but it was no use—he had definitely panicked.

Now everybody was dashing about trying to get out, men were shouting orders, women were screaming—the smoke was getting thicker, visibility was practically zero.

This all frightened Charlie even more and he went charging blindly through the smoke-filled big-top. He knocked over some of the tent poles and more of the canvas came down. More screams and suddenly the **people** stampeded, knocking one another down and trampling each other in the wild rush to find the exits.

I was trying to fight my way through to where Hank was lying unconscious near the center ring. He had been knocked out by a glancing blow from one of the tent poles that came crashing down, knocking him off the high wire. I was within a dozen feet of him when the terrified Charlie came trumpeting out of the smoke. The unconscious Hank was directly in his path. Even in his panic I saw Charlie endeavor to avoid him. He broke his stride and tried to change his direction . . . but it was too late. His huge rear hoof dragged over Hank, breaking his neck. Hank never knew what hit him.

Charlie finally blundered into an exit, lumbered out and ran trumpeting down the street toward the zoo. "Get back home," his instinct was telling him, "get back home and everything will be all right again."

Mrs. Murphy, the wife of the head trainer, heard the screams and the trumpeting and ran out into the street in front of the frightened elephant. Fortunately, he recognized her . . . she was a friend . . . he slowed down. She spoke quickly and calmly to him and in a matter of moments, had him under control. He gladly followed her back to the zoo where she locked him up.

The following week Charlie was tried for murder. I know that sounds idiotic, but sometimes people **are** idiotic. He wasn't at the trial —and he couldn't defend himself. But there were lots of pleas in his behalf—mine as well as many others, for Charlie had a lot of friends. We said it was obvious this was purely an accident— Charlie had worked faithfully in more than a hundred pictures—he was a kind and sensitive animal—he had tried to avoid hurting Hank. All this and more.

But we were only wasting our breath. Charlie was a two-time loser and they couldn't risk a third killing. So poor Charlie the Elephant was condemned to death.

Now came the question, "How do you execute an elephant?" Shoot him? "But suppose the

From circus fires to deck fights **THE GREAT CIRCUS MYSTERY** boasted some of the most elaborate production value ever seen in a serial.

In the 1920's when a producer signed a performer to star in a serial, the first question asked was—"Can you defend yourself?"

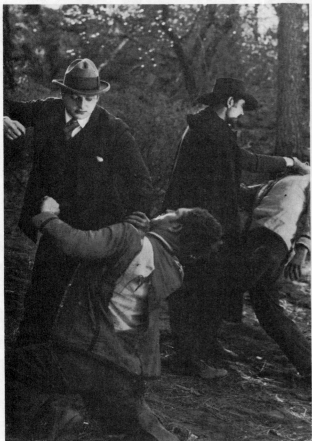

I trusted Charlie with my life many times, and he was no lightweight.

As Landow the Strongman, and the film's star, I had to support the rest of the cast.

shot doesn't kill him?'' said the man from the Humane Society. "The pain would madden him and who could guess what damage or additional killing he might do.'' Gas him to death? Where could you find a gas-chamber big enough for an elephant. Chloroform him? Electrocute him? It was finally decided that Charlie would be hanged . . . and as inhuman as this will sound, here is what actually happened.

Four big holes were dug, spaced the same distance apart as Charlie's ''feet''. Into these holes concrete was poured, with heavy steel rings about two-thirds submerged in it. When the concrete hardened, Charlie was brought in, heavy steel chains fastened about his legs and then run through the rings, so he was unable to move. Then, with Charlie securely shackled, two long heavy chains were passed around his neck, one leading off to the right, the other to the left. Now the end of each chain was secured to a five ton truck . . . the two trucks facing in opposite directions.

All work had been stopped for the execution, and all of Charlie's friends who could stand the pathetic sight, had turned out to witness the killing. We stood around, sick at heart, as the trucks were brought into position.

If you have ever had a ringside seat at a circus, you've noticed that when an elephant is under

a strain—when he is walking an elevated narrow plank, for example—his eyes water. He looks as though he's crying. I don't know whether this is an emotional or a purely physical reaction, but on this day it caused an emotional reaction within **me**. Charlie's eyes were more than watering—big tears were coursing down his cheeks . . . and Charlie's tears were not the only tears that were being shed. We knew what he must be thinking—"Why are they doing this to me? What did I **do**?'' It was the most pathetic sight I have ever witnessed.

The trucks were positioned now, and the chains all in place. Then the trucks started moving— very slowly—in their opposite directions . . . and dear old Charlie the Elephant was slowly, methodically, being strangled to death.

It was then that I turned and walked away— sick with pity. I couldn't stand any more. And most of the others left with me. We went back to the lot, where many of the boys broke out the bottles . . . and that was one of the few times in my life I was tempted. Had I been a drinking man I'm sure I'd have gotten roaring drunk.

Charlie's skeleton was sent to a museum and his brain to a medical school for study. Thus, even after death, Charlie The Elephant continued to serve mankind—even though mankind had betrayed him!

Getting to dry land was always a welcome relief!

147

The rest of THE GREAT CIRCUS MYSTERY was completed far ahead of schedule and then came the splicing, cutting and reassembling, based on the Bonomo Chart. It was a stupendous job but it went smoothly, as we had been meticulously accurate in the marking and classifying of practically every foot of film as it was shot.

The day following the preview, I was notified to report to Mr. Laemmle. My ego was more than a little inflated as I was shown into his office.

"Joe," Mr. Laemmle said, "have a seat."

I had one—and waited for him to continue. He puffed slowly on a big, expensive cigar, and gazed out the window for what seemed like an eternity. Finally he turned to me.

"Have you seen the production figures on the circus picture yet?"

"No, I haven't, Mr. Laemmle."

"Um-m-m," he said, and paused. He looked at me again. "I'm tearing up your contract, Joe."

You could have knocked me down with a puff from that cigar. I felt as though ice-water had been suddenly poured down my back. What could have gone wrong? Then he was talking again.

"Joe,—the budget on this picture, using your system, totaled one hundred twenty thousand. You saved us exactly eighty thousand dollars."

At last I could smile—and he smiled back.

"A slight token of the studio's appreciation," he said—and handed me a check that made my eyes dance. It was for five thousand dollars.

"But Mr. Laemmle," I stammered, in happy confusion.

"That's only the first installment," he said. "This idea of yours will save us millions in the future. Every serial is going to be shot this way from now on."

I just sat there—too happy to comment.

"But here's the **best** news, Joe—you're coming in with **me**. You're too valuable to get yourself killed as a stuntman . . . or to waste your genius being a movie star. You'll never be a **great actor**, Joe, but I think you **will** make a great producer."

He sat there, puffing on his cigar, beaming at me. He was dumping a golden opportunity in my lap, and he knew it . . . only I didn't want it.

"Mr. Laemmle," I faltered, trying to find the right words . . . after all, when a man hands you a check for a million dollars—even if you don't **want** to be a millionaire—you don't throw it back in his face. I tried again.

"Mr. Laemmle, . . . it's wonderful . . . except— I don't **want** to be a producer. Maybe in twenty years I might—but not now. You made a star out of me . . . and that's what I want. I don't want to be a producer."

I shall never forget the incredulous look on Carl Laemmle's face. Sort of like the way Papa looked, when I told him I didn't want to be in the candy business.

"Now I **will** tear up your contract," he said.

That's when I got mad.

"Mr. Laemmle," I retorted, "I've shed my blood

Is the mighty Landow finished? Come next week and see if he can escape from the "chains of death"!

THE GREAT CIRCUS MYSTERY meant action all the way—up in the air or on the ground. The bearded cyclist is the mysterious actor—stuntman Slim Cole.

Straying far from home base in **THE GREAT CIRCUS MYSTERY**, I help Slim Cole to the top of a freight car as stuntman Floyd Criswell sneaks up behind us (lower right).

and broken a lot of good bones for this studio —then I save you eighty thousand dollars—and now, because I won't let you kick me upstairs you want to kick me **out**! Well, go ahead. There are other studios—where I can make **more** money. And as for this check—you can light your next cigar with it!" And I tossed the check on his desk and started to walk out.

"Bonomo," he said sharply, "come back here and sit down."

It was like when Papa was mad—so I went back and sat down.

"Okay, Joe," he said, "you want to be just a movie hero? All right, we'll build you up. You're making a big mistake, but you'll have to find that out for yourself. Only don't get yourself killed doing it . . . we've got a lot of money tied up in you. We'll use you for public appearances, maybe even give you a vaudeville tour.

Universal will make another Eddie Polo out of you, if that's what you want. How does **that** sound?"

Well . . . I was grinning now.

"That's swell, Mr. Laemmle," I was saying, "you won't be sorry."

"I'm sorry already," he said, "I just hope **you** won't be." Then shaking my hand, "When you grow up a little and change your mind about producing, come and see me. And pick up that check—I forgot to tell you a nice boost in salary goes with it."

P.S. I picked up the check.

Change my mind about producing? Heck, I'm an actor, I thought, as I left the office, I know where I'm going. Laemmle's a nice guy, all right —he just doesn't know Joe Bonomo. Though I had no way of knowing it at the time, I had probably just made the blunder of my life!

Fights were my meat and the front office made sure we'd always have enough of them to please thrill-hungry matinee audiences.

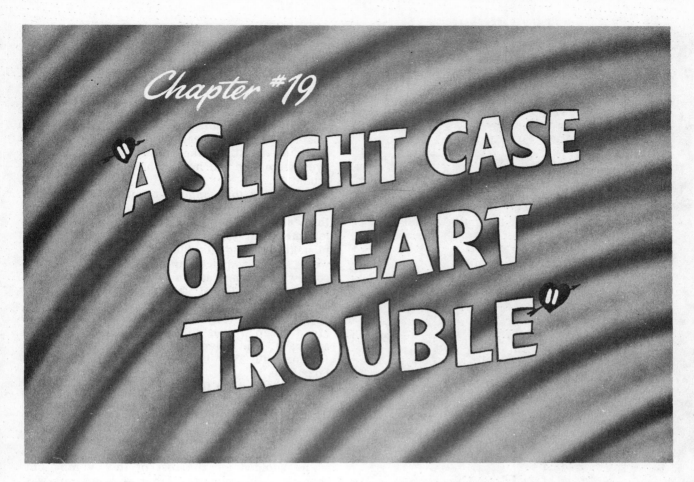

Chapter 19

"A Slight Case of Heart Trouble"

IT WOULD UNDOUBTEDLY STEP UP PUB-
LIC INTEREST in this book if I now included
a chapter called "The Secret Love-Life of Romeo
Bonomo, the Cagey Casanova," revealing my
torrid affaires d'amour with some of Hollywood's
most beautiful Pin Up Girls. And I **could** include
a chapter like that—and I could name names—
and I could be sued for libel—for if there is one
thing I **wasn't**, it was "a great lover."

Oh, I liked girls—but my life had been dedicated
to building up my body and turning my physical
prowess into a career—and girls weren't on my
daily training schedule. It is also possible I am
one of those enigmas known as a "one woman
man" . . . and I just hadn't met that one woman.
Had I known that someday I might need a spicy
chapter for this book, I might have done some
high, wide and fancy stepping out, and written
it all down in a diary.

Turning down Mr. Laemmle's offer of a pro-
ducership may have been a mistake, but almost
immediately, a lot of good things began happening
to me. And undoubtedly the **best** was an evening
I spent at the "Cinderella Roof" in Los Angeles.

The "Cinderella" was a famous ballroom where
many of the finest dance teams in the country
competed in weekly contests. I had kept up my
dancing, mainly because it helped keep me in
shape, but suddenly it looked as though it might
pay off. There was a leading role coming up,
in a feature production, and I stood a good
chance of getting it if I could find a talented

girl partner with whom I could work up some
good dance routines.

I had inquired around—several agents had held
auditions for me where I met some excellent
girl dancers, though none of them had exactly
what I wanted . . . but I didn't go to the Cinderella
Roof that night hoping to find my "dream girl"
there. I went to act as judge at a dance contest
they were holding. That's how innocently an
unsuspecting lamb can walk to the slaughter!

The contest had barely commenced when I
found my eyes constantly drawn to one particular
girl . . . a beautiful, statuesque blonde who seemed
to have everything. She moved with the effortless
grace of a panther, making the most difficult
dance steps look simple. She was more than a
pleasure to watch—she was exciting! You felt,
instinctively, that she had been born to dance.
I know she had a partner, but I doubt that many
noticed him, for she captivated all eyes as she
fairly floated across the dance floor, a blonde
vision of loveliness and grace, wholly unconscious
of the audience, lost in the rhythm of the dance.

I was fascinated—I never knew anyone could
dance like that—and it was with complete honesty
that I named her and her partner the winners.
I **think** it was with complete honesty. Frankly,
I hadn't even seen what the other contestants
were doing. Anyway, she and her partner got
the cup.

I immediately rushed over to Bill Lederer, who
ran the Rose Room there.

Laguna Beach is a far cry from Coney Island, but a beach is a beach and I loved the water, especially when Ethel was with me.

"Bill," I said breathlessly, "that blonde dancer —I've got to meet her."

As he led me over, at the very least I expected him to introduce her as Dianne Du Maurier, or something equally flowery—so I was a bit let down when he said "Meet Ethel Newman." But after all, I was Joe Bonomo, and there's nothing very flowery about that, either! However, she was all I had expected—and more. All I could think of, as she looked up at me, was that her eyes were like patches of blue sky over Coney Island.

We chatted for a minute or two about nothing in particular—she was even prettier close up than she had been on the dance floor, and it left me a bit tongue-tied. Then I made my big mistake. I suddenly blurted out, "If we could work out a few dance routines together, in private somewhere, I can get you in the movies."

The Coney Island sky in her eyes suddenly clouded over.

"You'll have to get in line, Mr. Bonomo. There are a dozen wolves ahead of you with the same approach. And when I want to get in the movies, I'm sure I'll find it safer to buy a ticket at the box office."

As I watched her float away I could have kicked myself clear to Pismo Beach . . . What a dope! The oldest line in the book, "I can get you in the Movies!" But as chagrined as I was it amused me to be mistaken for a Hollywood wolf. Me, of all people!

She avoided me the rest of the evening but that didn't dampen my ardor—I knew she was the girl I had been looking for. I got her phone number from Lederer and went home to plan my campaign.

For the next few days I phoned her repeatedly and I'd never been so "hung up on" in my life. I tried disguising my voice—speaking with an accent—talking through a handkerchief—but all I got, after the first few words, was "click!"

So I started writing her letters, sending telegrams and having flowers delivered to her daily . . . but she still hung up on me.

I finally decided on the direct approach. I drove around to her house and rang the front door-bell. She came to an upstair's window and I got my first real ray of hope. She said, very sweetly, "I'll be down shortly, if you don't mind waiting." I said, "I'll be **glad** to wait." But I didn't have to wait long. In a couple of minutes a police car pulled up and it took me ten minutes to talk my way out of it.

The next day I got a stroke of genius. I sent her a dozen of my "stills" from pictures I had made. I even included one in a gorilla suit, hoping I might look good to her by comparison. I later learned her mother salvaged them from the waste-basket and read the letter that had accompanied them.

"After all, Ethel," she said, "for all you know, Mr. Bonomo may be the most sincere man in the world."

"No, Mother," said Ethel, "he's just the most persistent."

But now that her mother had taken up the cudgel in my defense, she did a little checking ... and as blind luck would have it, Ed Stinson, a character actor, lived next door. He must have said the right things about me, for the next time I phoned, Ethel listened.

Well, to make a long story short, we worked out a few routines together, and then a few more. We entered many contests and won most of them, and we did some movie work together ... and before I realized it, I had fallen head-over-heels in love. Now I **was** in trouble. I knew Ethel liked me, but whenever I'd start to border on the romantic, she had a way of changing the subject. I didn't know **where** I stood—and I wasn't about to find out. As you might suspect there were several young men with good looks, money and social position, who were more than anxious to slip a wedding band on Ethel's fourth finger. They didn't have my muscles, but they also didn't have to say goodnight to a girl at ten thirty, so they could be in bed by eleven, which was a **must** with me. I was doing **a** lot of picture work involving many dangerous stunts and the slightest let down, resulting in poor coordination, could have snuffed me out ... and I wanted Ethel in **this** world—not the next! I didn't know **what** to do. I was starting to wonder how love got so popular—it sure wasn't making ME happy.

Ethel, when I first met her.

On the beach with a few of the dancing trophies we won together.

Then something happened that set my courtship back to virtually the minus column and through no fault of my own. I was winding up a picture—this was the final footage and we were working that night to get it completed on schedule. We decided that after the last scene was shot we'd hold a little celebration party at the studio where a reel or two of the picture would also be shown as a sort of sneak preview for the company. I had a great part in the picture and I thought if Ethel could see me in it, it might boost my stock with her considerably . . . so I invited her to drive out, watch the final shooting and stay for the party. I wasn't at all sure she'd come, but it must have sounded a bit glamorous to her, for she arrived on schedule, looking more beautiful than ever.

All went well, except the shooting took longer than we had figured on and consequently the party started so late it was almost three in the morning before it broke up. I wanted to drive Ethel home, but she knew I had to be up early the following morning for some retakes, and she wouldn't hear of it. She assured me she'd be quite all right so I reluctantly let her drive home alone.

Now Ethel's father had looked upon me with a jaundiced eye from the start; in his book any movie actor had two strikes against him as far as being a suitor for the hand of his darling daughter was concerned and with my history

as a strongman and stuntman he had me categorized as some sort of freak . . . definitely not to be trusted . . . or even tolerated.

All the way home Ethel was picturing the family explosion if he heard her drive in at three thirty in the morning but fortunately, he retired early and was a sound sleeper and she hoped to be able to sneak in without awakening him and, had all gone well, her plan would have been a good one.

At that time they were living in a four apartment frame house that had, in the rear, outside wooden stairways leading to sun porches, with individual garages just behind them. Ethel figured that if she shut off the lights and ignition and noiselessly coasted into their garage, her father would sleep on undisturbed and be none the wiser. But unfortunately a heavy fog had rolled in from the Pacific and, when she cut her lights, she couldn't see a foot ahead and, in rounding the building, she cut it too close and knocked the supporting beams from under the wooden stairways. The stairways promptly collapsed, bringing down the sun porches with them, with a deafening clatter and roar that brought everyone, including her father, leaping from their beds yelling "Earthquake!" Poor Ethel had wrecked her car, wrecked the rear of the building and almost wrecked our romance. Her dad blamed it all on me and forbade her to ever see me again —and I wouldn't have blamed her if she hadn't,

A publicity shot of some of Universal's finest, including (left to right) Margaret Quimby, myself, Laura LaPlante, Patsy Ruth Miller, Norman Kerry, Bill Desmond, Mary Philbin, Arthur Lake, Hoot Gibson, Jack Hoxie and Jean Hersholt.

Cecil Whitworth and myself making a personal appearance at a big first run house, which broke all matinee records with the opening of THE GREAT CIRCUS MYSTERY.

for he made her pay for the damages and repairs out of her savings.

Then, to make matters worse, "Circus Mystery" was released and the Exploitation Department sent me out on a public appearance tour, traveling up and down the West coast, appearing in a different theatre each week, heralded as "Bonomo —the World's Perfect Strongman—in daring feats of inhuman strength. He snaps railroad spikes with his fingers—bends iron bars and ties them

into knots.'' I could only hope that Ethel, between her dates with my rivals, was reading my billing and press notices.

Before gaping thousands I pulled two ton circus wagons, loaded with kids, through the streets —I broke iron chains with my chest and my "mighty biceps"—I tore telephone books—I bit the heads off railroad spikes—I pounded nails through thick planks with my bare hands and let men with sledge hammers smash huge rocks

Breaking into first runs!

Booked by the Victoria Theatre, Altoona, Pennsylvania, which has never run a serial before! A big first-run, weekly change house--1500 seats.

Produced and Distributed by
UNIVERSAL

Universal presents
BONOMO
the world's strongest human
in
THE GREAT CIRCUS MYSTERY

Directed by
Jay Marchant

An ADVENTURE PICTURE

People in the trade have told me that THE GREAT CIRCUS MYSTERY was Universal's top all-time serial attraction, as it opened new markets for their serials, being the first of its kind to play top First Run theatres.

An opening day promotional stunt, which featured my pulling a circus wagon loaded with local children to a theatre playing THE GREAT CIRCUS MYSTERY.

into powder, on my bared chest. "Mighty Joe Bonomo!" the crowds screamed, but not loud enough for the gorgeous Ethel to hear them, back in Hollywood. At least she didn't write. I was beginning to wonder if my dream girl wasn't merely a dream after all.

Now the publicity department arranged a vaudeville tour for me. Though they had to book me for less, the studio paid me my full salary, the salaries of my company and all our expenses, and the cost of publicizing me from coast to coast. They let me plan the act and engage my supporting cast. By offering Ethel the feminine lead in the act I saw a chance to kill two birds with one stone—the two "birds" from Beverly Hills who had been making a play for her during my absence. Her parents were a bit reluctant to let her go on the road with me—someone having told her father all Turks went in for harems—but I finally won him over after Ethel assured him she just looked upon me as a big brother—which I was beginning to suspect was true. Those sparkling blue eyes still turned to ice-cubes when I got **too** close.

Universal made up a three-minute trailer for me to use as an introduction to the act. This trailer realistically showed me diving off Suicide Cliff, in Herculean fights and doing death defying stunts, ending with "And now . . . in person . . . Joe Bonomo—World's Strongest Man—the Hercules of the Screen!"

The audience, all prepared to see a big gorilla in a leopard skin step out, were taken aback when "Hercules," in white tie and tails, entered with the dazzling Ethel and went into a fast dance number. The surprise never failed to get us off to a good start with our audiences. They loved Ethel on sight, which was okay with me.

I figured there was safety in numbers.

I then performed some feats of strength, twisting a six foot, two and a half inch iron bar into a veritable pretzel—snapped a steel chain tested for six hundred pounds resistance and lifted a bar-bell over my head with a whole cluster of stage hands hanging from it. Then Cecil Whitworth and I did a routine consisting of acrobatic stunts and hand balancing, and I finished with

Ready to take on all comers.

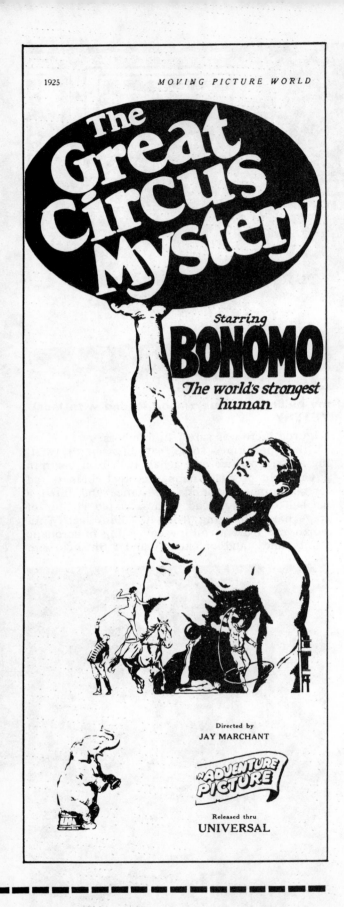

The Great Circus Mystery

Starring
BONOMO
The world's strongest human

Directed by
JAY MARCHANT

An ADVENTURE PICTURE

Released thru
UNIVERSAL

My serials were very popular in Europe. In Italy I was billed as the "American Maciste", an early equivalent of the popular "Hercules".

a fast dance routine with Ethel. As an encore Ethel and I danced a beautiful tango. The act was a tremendous hit wherever we played it.

It was during this period that a most unexpected incident occurred—an incident that was calculated to discomfit me but which boomeranged to my advantage, and which centered about another professional strongman, one Warren Lincoln Travis. To do him justice, you could not enumerate the five great strongmen of the world without including him. He stood about five feet ten and a half inches, had huge shoulders, a barrel chest and oversized hands so large he had special weights and contraptions built that no man, with normal size hands, could possibly handle. He appeared as the strongman with top circuses such as Barnum and Bailey, Ringling Brothers, etc.; and he was no fraud. He really performed many astounding feats of strength, such as having a big cannon suspended from his shoulders while someone fired it . . . and he did spectacular lifts of great iron balls that bordered on the impossible.

I first met him when I was just a boy in Coney Island and he was featured there. And I learned a lot from him, spending every spare moment watching him and pestering him with questions. Many years passed before I saw him again. I had grown up and gone to Hollywood, he was making a world tour, and I lost track of him completely.

It was while I was making this personal appearance tour, billed outside the theatres as "The World's Strongest Man," that he again came into my life. He passed a theatre where I was playing, saw the billing, and it was more than he could bear. He had always billed **himself** as the world's strongest man and here, this little kid from Coney Island, this little pipsqueak he had brushed off as a juvenile nuisance, had grown up and was stealing his thunder.

If he had come backstage I would have welcomed him with open arms, but he was too angry and indignant for that . . . he had his own scheme to avenge what he fancied was an insult to his reputation. So he rushed to the newspapers and took full page ads proclaiming himself as the world's strongest man and challenging me to a public performance where he defied me to match his feats of strength, offering to forfeit one thousand dollars if I could duplicate his act, using his weights, barbells and other apparatus.

Luckily I knew where the catch was . . . in the fact that everything he used was specially made to fit his oversized hands. The average hand could handle a one inch to one and a half inch barbell; he had his made two and one half to three inches. Anyone with normal hands would find it impossible to work with them. They could lift the same weight barbells, but not HIS . . . and the same thing applied with all his special apparatus. Had I not known this from my boyhood association with him I could have fallen into his trap and been badly beaten.

So I invited him to appear on stage in MY act and compete with me, using **my** barbells

THE GREAT CIRCUS MYSTERY boasted more of *everything* than most major features of its day.

Warren Lincoln Travis' big challenge—as he advertised it.

and apparatus, but all such offers were ignored. Instead, he spent the entire period of my engagement, pacing up and down in front of the theatre where I was playing, proclaiming himself to anyone who would listen, as the world's strongest man and waving aloft a one thousand dollar government bond which he said he was willing to wager that I could not match his feats of strength.

To his chagrin, rather than hurting me, this proved to be excellent publicity and sent many an extra dollar wending its way through the boxoffice. Literally hundreds of people who had no previous intention of attending my performance, did so just to see what all the hullabaloo was about.

Warren Lincoln Travis is now dead, leaving an unsolved mystery behind him. He had never married and was known to have accumulated a large personal fortune. However, like my uncle Yousiff, he distrusted banks and, as fast as he made his money he converted it into diamonds and other precious stones, which he concealed in some secret hiding place.

Did he stash them away in safe-deposit boxes under names other than his own, leaving no record of their location? It is said that Bernarr MacFadden buried much of his great wealth—in currency—in isolated spots on Long Island. His widow had patches of ground dug up where she had reason to believe some of his millions were buried . . . and several thousand dollars were found . . . some of the bills bearing his fingerprints.

Did Warren Lincoln Travis perhaps also follow this pattern? Nobody knows. He died, leaving no will and, although many searches have been made, the hiding place has never been discovered. The location of the Travis horde is still one of the unsolved mysteries of show business and of the world. Anyone for a Treasure Hunt?

By the end of the tour I was more in love than ever and thought I detected signs that Ethel was thawing a bit toward me, but I didn't try to press my luck. A couple of times before, what I thought was the lovelight shining in those azure eyes, turned out to be a stop light! And I couldn't have gotten a worse dressing down from a traffic cop. Her father should have done his worrying for ME!

Well, so much for my unrequited love . . . . again I had other fish to fry. The tour helped greatly in building me up to star stature and led not only to many personal appearances in theatres, but led me into still another field. I began to get requests to speak at Parent-Teacher meetings, to address Boys' Clubs, Rotary Clubs, high school assemblies and such. I must have lectured to hundreds of thousands of men, women and children over a period of time. I spoke on the benefits of clean living, proper eating, obedience to parents, and abstinence from tobacco and alcohol. And I still practice what I preached.

Years later, during a period when I was literally "hanging on the ropes" and could have used the money handily, I turned down a lucrative offer from an advertising firm, rather than pose with a cigarette in my hand, for their cigarette advertising. I just couldn't let the kids down. Stupid? Perhaps, but that's the kind of guy I am, and I guess there's nothing that can be done about **that**.

As a result of my health talks, fan mail started flooding in, from youngsters and their parents, from all over the country. Hundreds of letters a week and it kept growing . . . and every letter with questions to be answered. The studio assigned a couple of secretaries to help me keep up with the avalanche of mail, but it was simply too much. We kept falling farther and farther behind. There were now thousands of back letters piled up.

So when I was approached by a Mr. and Mrs. Charles Ludwig and asked if I'd be interested in putting my health rules and my knowledge of physical culture into organized courses for mail-order distribution, I felt they were Heaven sent. The Ludwigs were a charming, retired couple who had operated a most reputable mail-order business in Kansas City. I wrote up the courses,

At the height of my film career my mail order business started, and in a big way.

had an artist and a photographer illustrate them, and turned over the entire operation, fan mail and all, to the Ludwigs. In return I was to receive a percentage of the profits. The Ludwigs were back in the mail-order business and the Bonomo Physical Culture Institute had been born.

About this same time I was also approached by a Roger Barrows—a genial, smiling "promoter's promoter." He had conceived the idea of having me front for an adult health camp, up in the mountains. The camp was to be located on a beautiful lake—he had the location all picked out. He would take care of all details and run the whole operation. All I had to do was lend my name to the project, go up there on Sundays, give a health talk to the guests and put on a swimming and diving exhibition in the lake. In return for this I would receive a brand new Cadillac and a bungalow at the camp. This sounded all right to me . . . I liked this Barrows guy . . . and the thought also occurred to me, that if I had a "honeymoon cottage" all ready for occupancy, I might be able to persuade Ethel to marry me and move in. So I went along with the idea.

The camp was built, with about twenty cabins, in addition to the very nice Bonomo bungalow . . . and I got my Cadillac. I don't know where Roger Barrows raised the money for all this—there must have been a hundred thousand dollars invested—and he paid spot cash for everything.

At last the final nail was driven in—all was perfection and the camp was ready to open for business—then tragedy struck. Someone discovered that the beautiful lake the camp was located on, was not a lake at all but a **reservoir**! The camp was there . . . the cabins were there . . . and all the utilities—but you couldn't use the water for anything but the view!

I was afraid poor Barrows might drown himself, but I guess he found out you couldn't even use the water for **that**. He just quietly dropped out of sight.

I didn't tell Ethel about the Health Camp or the "honeymoon cottage." It's hard to propose to a girl when she's laughing at you.

My good friend wrestler Al "Andre Adoree" Baffert helps me answer some fan mail.

Chapter #20
SEE NEXT WEEK!
GARCIA

THE WEEKLY SERIAL has long since run its course—completed its cycle—and while there are few who will contend that the serials were great cinematic art, they did, nevertheless, have a place in the history of American entertainment that is unique. More American, probably, than the dime novel and the Horatio Alger books, there was nothing before the serials quite like them or anything since to take their place.

If you can remember those days long ago (so short in time actually; so long in recollection); if you belong to those generations which as kids, watched Eddie Polo, Elmo Lincoln, William Desmond, Charles Hutchison, Pearl White, Eileen Sedgwick, William Duncan and the others who followed, you will recall with some nostalgia the happy part that the weekly serial played in American culture.

The serial used to be the one big entertainment of the week. The features came and went, each was enjoyed, and remembered, and each would pass on with a "What a swell picture!" or "Was it lousy!" But the serial went on forever . . . it was the staple, the bread of the meal, more fascinating and longer remembered than most of the features.

All week long you had waited patiently through school and chores for Saturday to come. How was your hero going to get out of what was too hopeless a situation for mortal man to overcome? Of course, you knew he'd escape; he was bigger than mere mortality, and he had many tricks up his sleeve. You had talked about it during recess at school, trying to figure out the answer. And you already had too many reasons why whatever solution which might be presented to you was impossible.

But now, at last, it was next week. You joined your group of three or five or seven and walked the long way to your Rialto or Bijou or Crown. You spent whatever money you had above the price of admission, filling your pockets with candy, some of which you ate as you waited outside with the hundreds of other kids from strange neighborhoods and other schools. Remember the struggles for places in line, the arguments and fist fights that were common as you waited there? Remember the playful pushing, and the laughter, and the continued talk of the hero's perilous situation as you mimicked the scenes, played all the parts, from the "good guys" to the "bad guys"? As the moment approached when the doors would be opened, the excitement of anticipation mounted. And the noise mounted; everyone had to shout to be heard by his closest friend. The struggles for the places in line became more frantic. Little kids got stepped on, and looked up to the bigger kids' mere bigness. (It was an achievement in childhood just to get older). Finally the doors were opened, the tickets were being sold, dimes were pushed into the cashier's holes, tickets and little brothers were grabbed, and you scampered up to the balcony, your spot of happy isolation,

trying to be fast enough to get a seat where you could rest your chin and elbows on the brass rail that ran along the balcony edge. The excitement eased off for a while, then started to build again as others argued and fought for seats. Papers were thrown about the balcony and some over and down into the orchestra. The noise and the laughter and the talking mounted as the theatre filled. Whistles, and shouts, pierced the air as you all, in your different and mixed emotions, remained still individual, still isolated little islands of humanity. But then the house lights dimmed, and the noise hushed quickly, and you became a social group with a single thought, "Now, at last, the movies! What will we see today?"

The screen came to life, and you went through the preliminaries. There was the newsreel, and then a short comedy. Maybe two comedies, if you were lucky. In later days, there was the second feature first. But in those days, as **millions** watched each Saturday, on came the serial. Now the solution!

The week before, you had **seen** the heroine get pinned under the falling timber in the old abandoned gold mine, had **seen** the hero trying to pull her out, and **b-o-o-o-o-m**! The blast had blackened the screen and "See Next Week!" was the invitation. Now, Next Week having finally arrived, you see the hero pick the heroine up, carry her outside the mine, dodge to one side of the entrance, and **then** the explosion. You joined in the laughter and the hoots of derision at being cheated, directed at the innocent man in the projection booth. The smaller kids, who maybe couldn't remember last week so well, looked around and wondered what you were hollering about.

But no matter. The swift plot quickly swept up young and younger alike, and you all went speeding through the present sequence of fights, chases and other adventures, finally ending with the hero and the villain wrestling in the old sawmill. The villain hits the hero a sneaky blow and he sprawls unconscious in front of the whirling buzz-saw. As he is being slowly drawn toward it and as the smirking villain lays his lecherous hands on the saintly heroine . . . "See Next Week!"

And so it went. Hundreds of kids together in a theatre, millions throughout the country, all laughing, and thrilling, and shouting together. Then the long walk home after the picture, re-enacting the scenes, and trying to pre-resolve Next Week again. At this time, to bring back old memories, I'm including a few releases which were sent to exhibitors. They read like screen plays, and in many cases there was very little more than this used for a shooting script:

In the quiet days before our country grew up the Saturday Matinee was a spectacular event.

HERE'S HOW REAL SHOWMEN
PUT OVER THE GREAT
ADVENTURE SERIALS

This is the kind of matinee you can build up on
ADVENTURE SERIALS!

"I recommend Universal Serials to exhibitors as sound box office bets. They're made uniformly good from the first to the final episodes."

O. L. Meister, Mgr.
WHITE HOUSE Theatre,
Milwaukee, Wis.

As "The Swiss Family Robinson" we braved the hazards of a savage new world.

Title—**"Perils of the Wild"**, a Universal Picture.

Brand—Adventure picture.

Featuring—Joe Bonomo & Margaret Quimby.

Directed by—Francis Ford.

Story—Adapted from "The Swiss Family Robinson".

by Isadore Bernstein & William Lord Wright.

Footage—Ten two-reel episodes.

CAST

Captain William Robinson	**Alfred Allen**
Frau Mitilla Robinson	**Eva Gordon**
Frederick Robinson	**Joe Bonomo**
Jack Robinson	**Jack Murphy**
Ernest Robinson	**Howard Enstadt**
Francis Robinson	**Francis Irwin**
Emily Montrose	**Margaret Quimby**
Sir Charles Leicester	**Jack Mower**

No. 1. "The Hurricane"

Frederick, eldest son of the Swiss family Robinson, and mate of the ship Providence, of which his father is master, goes ashore to round up the crew, who refuse to sail with the dangerous cargo of powder and flintlocks. After a fist and sword fight with the insubordinate crew, in an ale house, in which Frederick subdues but fails to win them, Sir Charles Leicester, a gallant buccaneer, offers himself and his hard looking men to supplant the crew. With misgivings they are signed on, and the ship sails for Australia.

Nearing a tropic island, Sir Charles leads a mutiny and takes the ship for the pirates, together with the beautiful passenger, Emily Montrose, who was to join her father in Australia. But one of Sir Charles' men has dropped smouldering ashes on some dry hemp in the powder store. A great storm rises and the ship burns, with Frederick in the powder hold.

—See Next Week!—

No. 2. "The Lion's Fangs"

The Swiss Family Robinson, miraculously saved from the burning ship Providence by a great storm which extinguished the fire, make for the shore of a tropic island near which the ship has foundered, carrying with them stores and utensils from the wreck, and put up a tent which they call "tentholm".

It's a shame that serials like PERILS OF THE WILD can't be shown for young audiences today. Unfortunately, this old film, THE GREAT CIRCUS MYSTERY, and many of my others deteriorated with the passing years and all that remains is their memory and these photos from them. I'd certainly like to see them again myself.

Sir Charles Leicester, gallant captain of a gang of pirates who started the fire, has escaped with Emily Montrose, a beautiful passenger, to another part of the island where his friends await him.

Tonio, rough leader of the waiting party, accuses Sir Charles of softness, and has himself elected leader of the gang. They duel. One of them is sent tumbling over a precipice.

In the meantime, Francis, the youngest Robinson, has brought home a lion cub which he has hidden in a sea chest in the tent. During the night, a full-grown lion comes into the tent looking for the cub. Frederick springs from his cot and faces the brute with an axe.

—See Next Week!—

No. 3. "Flaming Jungle"

Sir Charles Leicester bests Tonio in a duel (it was Tonio, then, who went over the precipice) and re-establishes his leadership of the pirates.

Frederick, eldest son of the Swiss family Robinson, on another part of the island, beats off a ferocious lion that enters the tent at night to rescue a cub brought home by little Francis, who then takes the cub back to its home in the jungle.

Frederick sees pearl shells under water and sportively dives for them while his father and brothers are engaged in freeing the domestic animals from the wreck of the Providence. He is witnessed by Tonio, who chuckles with delight when Frederick is attacked by a shark.

The raft containing the other boys and the chickens and animals is being towed out to sea by a big turtle which they have lassoed.

On the other side of the island, Emily Montrose, menaced by the pirates, exhibits her "miraculous power" with a burning glass to intimidate the superstitious men, and sets fire to the jungle.

—See Next Week!—

No. 4. "The Treasure Cave"

Frederick Robinson frees himself from the shark, and Emily Montrose, on the other side of the island, runs from the burning jungle to a promontory, where Frederick gets a momentary glimpse of her as she is seized by the pirates and dragged back into their lair. One of the pirates steals a flintlock from the tent of the Robinsons and returns to the gang with the good news that there are more guns and powder to be had. They plot to raid the Robinson family. Frederick discovers footprints in the sand and, with his father, follows the tracks to the treasure cave of the pirates, where they find a wealth of precious stones and gold. An

The weird stone "Face on the Cliff" sets the mood for this scene.

The cover of one of Universal's famous weekly publications.

Protecting Margaret Quimby, whose appearance really fitted the role of a "maiden in distress".

alligator and a leopard attack them simultaneously. In an effort to escape, they fall from a great height into a pool of black water. As they struggle to escape from the pool, they are menaced by the alligator. Emily frees a carrier pigeon with a message of distress in the hope that it will bring a rescuer from somewhere.

—See Next Week!—

And so it goes, through ten thrilling episodes, concluding in this fashion:

No. 10. "The Rescue"

The pirates, trapped in the treasure cave by the falling earth, find a way of escape. While they are making their way through the jungle, the Swiss Family Robinson sights a ship just off shore. They try to signal with smoke and other means, but are unsuccessful. The ship, bearing Emily's father, passes on, and they turn back to camp dejectedly to be attacked by the pirates, who best them by superior

numbers and are about to massacre them when they are faced by the ship's crew, who have landed around the point.

As the party happily embarks for home, Captain Robinson presents the pirates, who have elected to remain on the island, with a Bible, and prays for their redemption. After reading the golden rule, they decide to quit piracy and lead upright and exemplary lives.

Sir Charles receives news from Prof. Montrose that his aged father has decided to forgive him, so he sets sail for home with a light heart that is untroubled when he sees Emily embrace Frederick, the man of her choice.

—The End—

Some "Perils" from

PERILS OF THE WILD

THE SERIAL VERSION OF
Swiss Family Robinson

Great care was paid to all detail to bring this classic novel to the screen.

177

When lost in jungle-like country an elephant is man's best friend.

Any actor signed to play an action-filled hero's role also had to demonstrate a winning technique as a "great lover".

And—for those of you who were too young (or perhaps not yet born) in 1925, here is a glimpse at the cliffhanging thrills we provided for audiences in THE GREAT CIRCUS MYSTERY:

Title—**"The Great Circus Mystery"** A Universal Picture.
Brand—Adventure Picture.
Star—Joe Bonomo.
Types of Story—Circus life and mystery.
Directed by—Jay Marchant.
Story by—Leigh Jacobson.
Photographed by—Howard Oswald.
Footage—Ten two-reel episodes.

Thumbnail theme: Two renegade explorers steal the sacred ruby from the breast of the holy leopard guarding a Hindu temple. One escapes with it, leaving a strange pact, written on a cigarette holder cut in three pieces, with a confederate. The other man is captured by the Hindu priests and held prisoner until the confederate restores the jewel. The scene shifts to America, to a circus. Adams, the owner, is a man under a haunting fear, with the ruby concealed in the heel of his shoe, and one piece of the "Pact of Peril" in his possession. He is in terror of a band of rowdy acrobats who have a pet leopard of uncanny intelligence, and of a "Mystery Man" who incessantly trails him. Landow (Bonomo), the strong man of the circus, is the protector of Trixie Tremaine, Adams' ward, who ever seeks to discover her parentage. The Man of

Mystery tells her she will know all when the Peril Pact is dissolved and the sacred jewel restored. She joins him in the search, with Landow and Dave Darrell, an acrobat, as her allies. Every conceivable mis-adventure is encountered, from runaway autos to runaway elephants, plunges over cliffs, etc. as mystery and excitement crown this remarkable story.

Well, this is what the serial was and its place in our national culture. And the preceding releases cover pretty much what they were with regards to literary content.

But what of the execution of them? How were these serials made? Who were the stars—those idols of millions of kids? Were we Herculean supermen? Certainly we were not! We were actors, playing the scenes, as best we could, making the adventures as realistic as possible, trying always for the more thrilling, more spectacular shot. That countless men were seriously injured, that many were killed, was only incidental to our business of making a living dodging death, to thrill those millions of kids.

The "Next Week" of these dangerous adventures? Simple, when everything went right. The Herculean feats? Nothing to them. It was all make-believe.

I'm reminded of a couple of incidents in PERILS OF THE WILD that might be of special interest. One I like to remember—the other I'd like to forget.

The first was a blood-chilling finish to one of the chapters of the "Perils" serial. I, as the dauntless Frederick Robinson, accompanied by

A break between scenes on "Perils" with director Francis Ford, Laura LaPlante and Arthur Lake, in his youthful pre-"Dagwood" days.

another young fellow, had fallen into a deep lion pit . . . and we were trapped down there with a bunch of hungry lions. The walls of the pit were absolutely vertical and impossible to climb. We were unarmed and at the mercy of those ferocious beasts who were starting to close in. As there was no way out except up those walls our situation seemed utterly hopeless as "See Next Week" appeared on the screen, leaving the audience to ponder, for the next seven days, on how we could possibly extricate ourselves from a certain and horrible death.

What happened "next week?" Very simple. The resourceful and redoubtable Frederick Robinson, just in the nick of time, discovers a rope vine that was hanging down into the pit and, instructing his companion to hang onto his neck, climbs hand over hand up the vine to safety, leaving the lions hungrily yapping at his heels.

Did I say very simple? Well . . . that's how it sounded in the script but actually, it was an utter impossibility. If you've ever done any rope climbing you know there is no living human being, however powerful, who can climb hand over hand up a rope with a man on his back. I argued with the director that it was an impossible stunt, but the sequence would be such a good one he wouldn't give up on it. Then I got a lucky idea. With the other fellow hanging on and the cameras grinding, I seized the vine and LOWERED myself, hand UNDER hand, to the bottom of the pit. Then the film was merely printed BACKWARDS and we had the scene. Even done this way it was as difficult a tax on my strength as I have ever experienced, but we got the sequence, just as we always did.

When it appeared on the screen letters poured in from all over the country, many from famous strongmen who knew the feat was impossible, wanting to know how it was done . . . but we weren't telling.

The incident I'd like to **forget** was the time when, in the same serial, pursued by those same lions, I scrambled up a tree. I was wearing a Tarzan type costume which was practically nothing at all leaving a good four fifths of my anatomy exposed. Ordinarily this would not have been important but this was no ordinary occurrence. The property department had neglected to check the tree and, as I scrambled up and settled myself to outwait the lions, I sat right down on a hill of red ants and all Hades broke loose.

In seconds I had hundreds of angry and vengeful little insects swarming over me and stinging me in every available spot . . . and in that abbreviated costume almost every spot was available. Red ants sting like bees and wasps and each sting felt as though a red-hot needle was being driven into me. Luckily there was a large pond only a few yards away and with a yell that Tarzan would have envied I leaped to the ground and made a wild dash into the water, completely forgetting about the lions who were evidently too astonished to intercept me. The water took care of the ants but once again

In this scene I appeared to climb to safety on a vine with Howard Enstadt on my back— in reality the scene was shot backwards!

90 ft. high "Suicide Cliff" had a reputation that lived up to its name, which made it even a greater challenge for me as a stuntman.

I landed in the hospital and it was days before I got the formic acid poison, from those multiple stings, out of my system. I know having "ants in your pants" sounds funny, but if it happens to you and if they're **red** ants don't stop to giggle —make for the nearest water-hole or you may die laughing.

In other instances I was seriously injured, sometimes almost fatally, making those "cliff-hangers." Many of my friends, some—in all honesty—better men than I, were killed in those corny, faked and phony pictures that thrilled the kids every Saturday afternoon, for some thirty odd years, and, year after year, lured them back with—"See Next Week!"

How did my elevation to serial stardom affect me? It only made me try a little harder. I just wasn't the type to "go Hollywood."

I thanked my lucky star for my good fortune and tried to spread it around a little. When I was riding the highest I never went "high hat" . . . and as long as I remained in Hollywood I was just "Joe" to everyone from the bottom to the top. As I look back on it, I was a lot like a big old St. Bernard dog. I went around wagging a friendly tail and looking upon everyone I met as a friend. That didn't always prove to be the wisest policy, but that was Joe Bonomo. If I'd have been any different I'd have been somebody else.

But no matter how high I climbed I never eased up on the work. I have always been a tough disciplinarian from the first moment I was put in charge of a stunt crew—and I continued to be just as tough, maybe tougher, for I had more pressure on me now. But the first person I disciplined . . . and the one I was REALLY tough on was MYSELF.

I mentioned earlier that stars were not allowed to do their own stunts. Well, I was just stubborn enough to insist the studio make me the exception to that rule. Also that I be permitted to continue with my wrestling and other athletics. They tried to shout me down but stunts and athletics were the frosting on **my** cake and I wasn't prepared to relinquish them for the sake of having a gold star painted on my dressing room door. I said if it was stunts or stardom I'd take stunts . . . and if that meant tearing up my contract, okay . . . it was my neck and if I enjoyed risking it, no one was going to deprive me of that pleasure. I was only twenty-three years old and I didn't want to be just an actor. I'm sure they thought I'd been sitting out in the California sun too long, but by then I was fairly good "boxoffice" so they humored me.

And so I went blithely along, happily risking my neck at every opportunity.

When you stand on the edge of a ninety-seven foot cliff and prepare to dive down into four feet of water between two jutting rocks only fourteen feet apart, you'd better kiss the world goodbye—because there's nothing below you but certain death. No one could do that and live. But suppose you have already observed that the sea comes in in waves . . . and at the precise moment the wave breaks over the rocks, at **that** moment, there is twelve feet of water for you to dive into. It is possible you could do that and live.

The dive you are contemplating is from 'Suicide Cliff' at Laguna Beach, California. It got its name from some half dozen people killing themselves by leaping off it to the rocks below. These tragic figures weren't stuntmen—they were suicides. No stuntman had ever risked it, as survival was deemed impossible. For some reason that fascinates you. It would be like climbing the Matterhorn.

The script of your picture calls for the dive, but at the last moment a dummy is to be substituted to simulate the actual leap. You don't like that—dummies never fool anybody—they always look like what they **are** and you want this sequence to be especially good. It would

of Nature it lets you down, well . . . it will at least be quick!

Now at last the time has arrived—the 'moment of truth' is at hand. You're at the very edge of the cliff—the wave is rolling in—and as you signal the cameras, a great thrill suffuses your body. You poise there for a fraction of a second and the thrill mounts—but watch it! The slightest wrong pressure with a foot, the most trivial miscontrol of your body, even a sudden gust of wind could throw you off enough to head you for the rocks. Every facet of your mind is concentrating—every muscle in your body is coordinating as the wave rushes toward the calculated spot.

NOW!!! . . . off you go—legs gently pushing—your body easing from the cliff. Down through empty air you plunge, holding your breath, the wind rushing past your ears, your eyes staring

be a desperate gamble but so is the Matterhorn. You decide to risk it. You can't explain the thrill you get out of defying death in a stunt where the slightest mistake will mean the end . . . but there's a devilish fascination about it and, say what you will, it's the greatest kick you've ever found in life.

It's two days later. You have stood at the top of 'Suicide Cliff' for hours, stop-watch in hand, computing the speed of the waves as they traveled landward at high tide. And you've dropped rocks and heavy bags of sand down from the cliff and determined exactly how long it will take you to travel the ninety-seven feet down, finally deciding that at this particular point in the movement of the wave, you dive. That certain wave should do as all the waves before it have done, but if, through some sudden freak

down at the spot you have to hit. The slightest deviation and—you plunge on, drawing your arms up close to your face. From the edge of your field of vision—(you **dare** not take your eyes from that one spot in the world that means life to you,)—somehow you see the wave as it begins to break—and the ocean as it swells up to meet you.

Now your hands are out in front of you, breaking the water, and you're IN! Careful not to lose your nerve and make the dive too shallow! You'll break your back!! You've got to finish it naturally—let the water slacken your momentum. In that split second you wonder how close the rocks are below . . . but don't pull up! You've got to let the dive complete itself!

Then—as you feel the water buoy you up, there is that moment of gratitude . . . of wonder

Outside the Universal gate with Jack Kearns (Dempsey's fight manager), Joe Benjamin, Art Acord, Norman Kerry, Louise Lorraine, Teddy Hayes and wrestler Bull Montana.

. . . of giving thanks to God. The surface breaks above you in a spatter of sparkling light and the sun streams down to meet you. You look about. The jutting rocks stand peacefully on either side, like glistening sentinels that have guarded you . . . and you laugh . . . you actually laugh! It was all so easy! And then you swim joyfully to shore, pulling with the strength of your arms and kicking your feet against the caressing water. At that moment you envy no Angel in Heaven!

To show you how crazy a guy can be at twenty-three, I made that dive off "Suicide Cliff," ten more times, just for the thrill I got from it. However, I never did ANY stunt without taking every precaution.

What I'd like to drive home to you future stunters is, if you're going to be careless with your life—BE CAREFUL!

Chapter #21

REALISM FOR THE DIRECTOR

I HAVE MENTIONED BEFORE the ends to which directors will sometimes go in order to get the scene they want, and I've never held it against them. There was never anything but the warmest of personal feelings between directors and myself, for I understood their problems, which often called for desperate measures.

The producer is the man who first conceives the production and who brings together the forces and elements that make the picture possible; the director is the man who stands between the actor and the audience and brings the story to life on the screen. In other words, the audience will see the picture through the director's eyes. He is the one who ultimately creates the illusion and he can make it or break it.

Actually, the director has a triple responsibility. First, he is responsible to the producer. He not only must turn out a good picture but keep the costs down so the film will make money and the producer may produce **another** picture.

Secondly, he must be always conscious of his obligation to the audience. He must assume they have seen almost every picture ever made, that they have been thrilled and emotionally moved by almost every trick possible. So he must devise new tricks or a new presentation of the old ones, to keep the audience fascinated and thrilled. He must produce surprises and new effects that will give them an emotional kick worth more than the admission charged. This he must do so they will accept the invitation to "See Next Week's Feature."

The director's third duty is to his company, including his cast. The entire company from prop boy to star must be made to work as a team. If any one falls down on the job, the entire production will suffer. Thus, whereas every member of the company is dependent upon him, he is equally dependent upon them, for if they aren't efficient or, in the case of an actor, emotionally moving, everyone gets hurt. And he must be quick to recognize talent. On many occasions I have heard a director urge a writer to create a bigger or better role for an actor he thought had greater possibilities than those afforded him. If the director was correct in his judgement, not only the actor, but everyone, from each individual member of the audience to the exhibitor who shows the film . . . from the prop boy to the president of the studio and each stockholder, reaped the benefits. And that is the way stars are born. That is the motion picture business.

Without the producer you would have no production and without the audience you would have no money so the director must turn out the best picture possible and still hold down the budget. That's why he's always trying to cut production time, by squeezing all the spectacular action possible into every scene. Working under such pressure he sometimes loses sight of the risks involved to his actors and stuntmen. Some of the finest, most sensitive men I have ever known were directors, and some of the most successful were those who would stop at almost

A peaceful tree-house set could quickly become a blazing death trap.

nothing to get good film. Producers, directors and audiences you **must** have. Actors and stunt-men are, in a sense, expendable. They can be replaced.

There was one sequence in PERILS OF THE WILD which illustrates this point . . . and the film was well named. I never **saw** so many perils in one film. Fortunately no one was hurt but for a while—my, my!

Let's take the tree-house scene for an example. To be safe from marauding wild animals I had built this hut in a tree, about fifteen feet above the ground. The leading lady, Margaret Quimby and I were up there, hiding from some pirates who were intent upon destroying us. They finally discovered us and set fire to the tree to burn us out.

Before we were called to the scene, Francis Ford, the director, had the prop men soak the tree with kerosene. Whether they accidentally used too much or purposely soaked the heck out of the tree to insure a spectacular blaze, I never did find out, but if they wanted a real conflagration, they got it. After they finished, we arrived and were told to climb up into the hut. They wouldn't use Margaret for the scene —you don't risk female stars in scenes like this, so her understudy was doubling for her. The latter was a budding young actress, ambitious but inexperienced in the rather reckless ways of picture making. We climbed up and pulled the ladder up after us. It seemed there was an awful lot of kerosene in the air, but I have always been very sensitive to smells, so I didn't think much about it. Then Francis Ford called "Action!" and the cameras rolled.

The pirates, lighted torches in hand, sneaked up to the tree, applied the torches and whoosh! In seconds the place was an inferno.

The film being silent in those days, you could talk to the director while the scene was going on and I didn't lose any time.

"Hey, Frank," I yelled, (it would look to the audience as though I was yelling at the pirates) "this whole place is on fire!"

"It's supposed to be, Joe," he yelled back.

"I know, but not like **this** . . . even the ladder's on fire. We won't be able to use it."

"Just keep cool, Joe," he shouted back, "it looks great . . . perfect!"

I looked at the young girl beside me and the poor kid was starting to look pretty scared, I wasn't feeling too good myself, but I didn't want her to know it.

"Don't worry, kid," I said, putting an arm around her, "everything's under control."

"Nice touch," yelled Ford, "now kiss her goodbye."

By now the flames were getting uncomfortably close.

"It'll BE goodbye unless somebody DOES something," I hollered back, "How are we going to get down from here?"

"Stop worrying!" he called back, "We'll get you down."

"Yeah, but WHEN?"

By now I was running around the hut, peering out through the smoke, trying to see if anyone was doing anything to rescue us. (When I saw the scene afterwards it looked terrific.)

"Never mind when," Ford's voice came angrily, "just play the scene! I'll take the responsibility."

I turned back to the girl. Tears were now rolling down her cheeks, but I couldn't tell whether it was hysterics or the heat and smoke.

"It's okay, kid," I said, patting her reassuringly, "they won't let us down." Then I ran back to the edge of the burning hut.

"Hey, Frank, what are we going to **do**?" I wasn't sure he'd hear me over the crackle of the flames, but he did.

"Just keep up what you've BEEN doing, it's sensational!"

I ran back to the girl again and she was in bad shape. The smoke was awful and the fire threatened to cremate us any minute. I figured the only thing to do was jump. I remembered there was a big container of water up there—we used it for cooking in an earlier scene. I poured half of it over the girl and the rest over myself, then I gathered her up in my arms, ran to the edge of the platform and jumped through the flames. We landed pretty hard and we were both shaken up a bit, but by some miracle we weren't hurt.

Now I'm a fairly peaceful guy, but there's a limit. I got to my feet and charged after Ford, who already had the cameras between us.

"What the heck were you trying to do?" I yelled, "Burn us alive!"

"Take it easy, Joe." He still kept the cameras between us. "Wait'll you see the film. This'll make a super star out of you!"

"You darned near made a corpse outta me!" I shouted.

Suddenly he stepped out from behind the cameras.

"Look, Bonomo . . . that was a great scene and that's what we came here to make. We did our job and no one got hurt. You know your business and I know mine and mine is directing. Now do you want to take my direction or do you think, because at last you're rated as a star, you don't need directors any more!"

I didn't have the answer to that one because I knew he was right. No matter how talented you may be, you need good direction to get to be a star—and you need good direction to STAY there. It had taken me a long time to get "star status" written in my contract, but a couple of badly directed pictures that turned into "flops" could cancel it all out. The public doesn't always remember your good pictures, but they never forget or forgive your bad ones. My contract would still be valid—the studio would have to buy it up or let me sit it out, but who wants **that**! If Francis Ford had gambled a bit with my life, it was as much to my advantage as anyone's and, as the picture proved later, the end justified the means.

In serials directors usually burned us alive or sent us to the bottom of the briny deep.

If there was a camera and some water around it always meant another perilous plunge for me.

Water stunts and adventures were always my special dish. As far back as I can remember, I could swim. So if I were chased by pirates, up into the rigging of a ship, and had to dive from the yardarm into the cold and briny deep, that was "duck soup" to me.

It was the "little" accidents aboard ship that could cripple you. Because a ship is so insecure in the water—because it is apt to roll away from you, just as you are pushing off for a jump—because the yardarms are round and always moving—you are really never secure. I often wonder about those "iron men" in the days of wooden ships. Were they really at home in the rigging? Probably they were, because they had spent most of their lives aboard ships. We hadn't, though—and when a bunch of us stuntmen went out on a schooner, anything could happen, but ANYTHING!

Ironically, my roughest experience was with a small boat. We were filming PERILS OF THE WILD, in which Howard Enstadt, then "little Howie," a boy of eleven, was playing my little brother Ernest. The script called for us to capsize our small cat-boat in the Santa Barbara Channel. This was a simple stunt and was to be used in the picture for comedy. It very nearly turned out to be tragedy.

We capsized the boat okay, but not thinking, I had let the sail down without securing it—and when the craft turned over, you can imagine our horror when we found ourselves so entangled in the loose sail and shrouds, we couldn't swim out from under it!

There we were, snarled up in those danged lines, caught under the gunwale. And the canvas sail had filled the space in the center, under the boat, so we couldn't get our heads up where there was air. Also, the shrouds had us caught so we couldn't swim to the outside. Howie got panicky, and as fast as I'd get a line loose, he'd kick another back around us, binding us even tighter with his struggling. I tried to push the sail up with my head and get to the center space where the air was, but I couldn't make that either. We would undoubtedly have drowned but for the quick action of some standby men.

After what seemed an eternity, I saw them swimming down to us. One had a knife in his hand. I expected him to cut us loose, but another of the men tapped him on the shoulder and pointed up, and I saw them all swimming back to the surface. My lungs were about to burst, and I was so weak I couldn't move anymore.

Howie was unconscious beside me now, and those dopes were swimming off! It seemed nothing less than murder!

Then suddenly we were being propelled to the surface—the water broke and that wonderful air was around us again. The men had climbed onto the boat and turned it right-side up again. Tangled as we were in the sail and shrouds, we were turned back into the light and air along with the boat. Howie had to be revived by artificial respiration and I, though still vaguely conscious, gladly submitted to some of the same.

Here was a case of a slight oversight on my part that almost caused our deaths. Only the quick thinking of those other men, our deadly pirate enemies in the picture, saved us. If they had taken the time to cut us loose, it would have cost at least one, if not both our lives.

Another sea experience I will never forget was one we had on a four-masted schooner, the "John Brown." While we were shooting a sea sequence, for BEASTS OF PARADISE, the entire company used to go out on the ship. A tug would tow us about fifteen miles out from Balboa into the Pacific every morning, stay with us all day, and then tow us back in the evening.

On the last day of shooting, the tug burned out a bearing on the way out. Its skipper decided he'd return to port, have the necessary repairs made, and come back late in the afternoon to pick us up again.

Now the "crew" of that big sailing ship consisted of the captain and **one** seaman. We, the actors, made up the rest of it. We knew little or nothing about sailing, but through the guidance of the captain and his "mate"—we managed to get the sails up and down when necessary. Thus we were able to give a real enough impression of being "worthy seamen," to make a credible film sequence, and keep the ship from capsizing, although it was close!

But on this fateful afternoon, we were surprised by a sudden, violent squall. Before we knew it, the ship was caught in rain, lashing high winds and heavy seas—and being under full sail at the time, suddenly took off in the general direction of Tokyo, Japan—with a good chance of getting there if we didn't sink first. We knew we had to get the sails furled fast, but landlubbers that we were, we couldn't execute the orders the excited captain was shouting. He was probably speaking English, but it might as well have been Hindustani for all the good it did us!

"Belay the starboard stun'sle!" "Two-block the foremast guns'le!" "Reeve the lea clew and slack off the larboard mizzen luff, blast ye!" Well, maybe these weren't his exact words, but they might as well have been. And the more the storm mounted, the angrier the old skipper got. "Ye blundering blockheads, belay the stay on the port mizzen top gallant!" The rain was slashing and the waves were breaking over the bow, washing some of us off our feet. We could barely hear him, but he still screamed against the wind and waves. "Ye stupid blunderheads, furl the after mizzen peak to the starboard blabbergrab!" or something like that.

Little by little, however, as we rolled and

Due to an unexpected turn of events, we actors became the actual crew of the schooner John Brown.

pitched and yawed, we managed to get the canvas in. An alert cameraman was getting some fine shots, but that was small comfort as we skidded about the decks. It was well into the night when the storm subsided, and as beautiful a girl as Eileen "Babe" Sedgwick, was a sorry looking heroine when the sea finally calmed. Except for Ruth Royce, the captain and myself, every soul on the "John Brown" was deathly ill with sea-sickness—not excepting the "mate." Everywhere you looked were those gray-faced, green-eyed "zombies", hanging over the rails and wishing they were dead. What a mess!

But that's only part of it. During the day, we had devoured our studio box lunches, and there was nothing aboard but a pound of coffee, some boxes of crackers and some canned soup. And there were twenty eight of us on the ship! The seasickness finally subsided, leaving empty stomachs with short rations aboard . . . barely enough for one light meal. However we weren't worried—we had probably been blown a little off our course, but as soon as it became light again, the tug would find us and take us back to civilization. Hah!

The next morning, after eating the last of the crackers for breakfast, director William Craft announced that, until the tug arrived, we might as well use the time to advantage. So we began shooting again. It would at least take our minds off our stomachs. So up into the rigging we went, to stage fight scenes that would thrill millions.

A couple of the prop men had conceived the idea of fishing. They had spotted sharks in the water and thought they might catch one. But they had nothing for bait and the sharks weren't biting. Undoubtedly waiting for human prey, I thought. I remember even thinking of staging a bona fide shark fight. I'm a pretty big guy, and used to eating well and plenty, and I was getting so hungy I felt I might welcome a shark. I'll fight him teeth to teeth, I thought, to see who will eat whom! Proving that when starvation starts setting in, you get weird ideas.

But by that time I was out on the end of a yardarm, kicking one of the villains in the face. Then the ship took a sudden roll—I fell backwards—and down I went. I missed the ship and landed in the ocean. At that moment I lost all desire to battle those sharks to see who was going to fill whose belly!

Because of the shortage of skilled seamen, it took more than an hour to turn the ship about and pick me up. You can picture my terrors, in that shark infested ocean, without even a knife to protect myself. All I could do was swim around, making as little splash as I could, peering through the water hoping to spot one of the monsters before he struck. I might be able to kick him on his sensitive nose, if I were quick enough. So I watched and I watched and I watched, constantly turning to cover all sides of possible attack. But for some saintly reason the sharks still weren't biting. At last the ship passed close enough for

Bob Hill, one of Hollywood's finest action directors, and the man behind some of Universal's top serial hits.

a line to be tossed to me, and I was pulled out. And would you believe it? Just as I was being dragged out of the water, a gray fin sliced the surface and a shark snapped at me. In two seconds, I was half way up the rope. After that I REALLY hated sharks—especially sneaky ones!

Then another squall struck us and we rocked and tossed worse than ever and a lot of the company got seasick all over again. I was trying to cheer them up and I brought out a lot of dummies we had on board and lined them up leaning over the rail. I thought it would be a good laugh but nobody seemed to think it was very funny. Seasick people are hard to amuse.

By now everyone had lost interest in shooting and we just stretched out in different parts of the ship, hoping we'd fall asleep and dream we were eating, while waiting for help. But no help came that day, nor that night, nor the next day, nor the next night. By then we were like the starving crew of "The Ancient Mariner," ghastly, gaunt and weak from hunger. I wouldn't say thoughts of cannibalism entered anybody's mind, but I've got a lot of meat on my bones and I got some mighty peculiar LOOKS!

Then we suddenly found ourselves in the midst of a school of tuna and with shrieks of joy we managed to pull some aboard. And guess who cooked them? Right! I had inherited Mama's knack with the skillet, in fact, at one time I volunteered to run The Shelter House for the city and such personalities as Pat Rooney and Marian Bent used to drop in for a bowl of "Joe's Clam Chowder" and pronounced it the best in the world . . . so THERE!

Well, I cooked tuna until every tummy aboard was bulging with it and I was so sick of it I thought I'd never eat it again. Then on the morning of the fourth day we were spotted by one of the search planes that Universal had sent out to look for us and, an hour later, we were picked up and transferred to a Coast Guard Cutter, with FOOD aboard! Luckily it wasn't tuna.

Within thirty seconds I was digging into a plate-full of U.S. Navy BEANS... and I hate to be disloyal... but Mama never cooked up **anything** that tasted so good.

Now before I get off the Pacific and back on dry land again, let me relate an incident that happened in that same ocean, just off Santa Cruz Island—and that almost sent me to Davy Jones' Locker.

I was playing a murderous jungle chieftan in one of those eerie South Sea Island fantasies that were so popular at the time. The big scene was where I gathered my native warriors about me and, in six jumbo war canoes, we paddled out and attacked an explorer's ship that had anchored just off the island. It was a fairly large budget picture, the producer had plenty of money to throw around, so he decided to really go to town in this scene.

As he was wondering just how to spend some of the surplus cash, he heard about some sort of musical extravaganza, playing in the East, in one scene of which some Broadway "set man" had devised some elaborate war canoes that the critics had praised as artistic masterpieces. So the producer by-passed the Hollywood set builders and prop men and brought this "genius" on from New York, with a great fanfare of publicity, and commissioned him, at big expense, to build the six jumbo war canoes. He worked on them for weeks and when they were completed I had to admit they were artistic masterpieces, beautiful to behold. I'm sure any cannibal chief would have turned vegetarian to have gotten his hands on one of them.

So they were carefully crated and just as carefully transported to Santa Cruz Island where they were lined up along the beach.

The shooting on the early part of the picture went along very smoothly and the moment finally arrived for the attack on the ship. When we got our cue my "natives" and I picked up those precious canoes, launched them into the surf, clambered into them and started paddling furiously ... but we never made the attack. Unfortunately the genius from the East had built only for the New York stage and had constructed those beautiful canoes out of plaster of Paris, moulded around chicken wire, on a wooden frame. In a matter of seconds the plaster of Paris was absorbing the water and before we were a hundred yards off shore the six canoes suddenly sank like so much lead, leaving a hundred or so "cannibals" floundering about in the ocean, gradually turning white as the make-up washed off.

As my canoe went down it jack-knifed and

caught one of my feet under a cross-board, taking me along with it. Before I could extricate myself I came as close to drowning as I ever shall.

So the producer called in Bob Brandt, one of Hollywood's top scenic and prop men, who should have been called in to begin with. The canoes he built us may not have been quite so noteworthy, but what was important to us, they were seaworthy.

The **HERCULES** of the **SCREEN**

Chapter #22

Perils of the Movies

WE WERE on our most cautious behavior around the big cats. A lion, for instance, is an inherently wild beast. No matter how tame he may seem, you're never sure of what he is planning to do. And follow these statistics: The third most powerful blow, in all the animal kingdom, is the kick of a giraffe. The second most powerful blow is from the tail of a whale. And the first? A blow from the paw of a lion.

Just consider the lion for a moment. A male often runs to four hundred pounds. That's quite a hunk of cat! His paws are huge, deadly weapons, and should he become excited and strike out, his claws protrude from three to four inches. Contrary to popular belief, it is rarely that a lion will bite. That's why the age-old stunt of putting your head in a lion's mouth isn't as hazardous as it may seem—although I don't advise it for beginners. But if you've had experience with an excited house cat, you'll remember how his paw darted out and his claws scratched. Magnify a house cat many times, and you have a lion. Now consider the tremendous power behind those claws when he strikes. Just one lightning slash will rip you often beyond repair.

And those claws are highly poisonous. When a lion is fed meat, he tears it with those claws, and small particles lodge along them and move inside when they return to their inside position. There bacteria forms around them. And who's going to clean a lion's claws? Not me, friend! And nobody else, either. That is why you see so many old time lion trainers–those who are still alive—who have lost an arm working with the big cats. One slash, sharp and deep, and often gangrene will set in immediately, making amputation imperative. All things considered, then, don't think me cowardly when I say I never really enjoyed working with lions.

In PERILS OF THE WILD, I was supposedly attacked at night by a lion, as I lay asleep on my cot. My younger brother had found a lion cub in the jungle and brought it back to our tent. The lion was to enter the tent and, while sniffing out his offspring, start sniffing around **me**. I was to awaken and wrestle hand to claw with him, and in the end, chase him back into the jungle.

For such episodes we kept six lions in the studio zoo. There was one we used just for charging. He was a bad one and the cameramen always shot the charge through the bars of his cage. Another one, a cross old devil, was used for close-up roaring shots. Another was trained in falling, as though shot, and playing dead. Still another, a nice old guy with no teeth and a fine disposition, I used for wrestling, which was done as play, with the old boy enjoying the rolling around on the ground—although on the screen it looked like one of us had to die. The other lions had their specialties, and the bits were shot separately and then spliced together. In this way we could get almost any kind of sequence.

Now I didn't fancy lying, with my eyes closed, and having a lion sniffing at me. You never knew when an unexpected noise or scent would cause him to suddenly revert to type and maybe tear you to pieces. As the scene was being set, that little voice inside me sounded a warning signal. So I said I wouldn't do it—it was too risky.

The lion trainer couldn't understand.

"Look, Joe," he said, pointing to a heavy metal screen, "I'll be right here, behind this screen, controlling him."

"Sure you will," I said, "and the lion will be right here—and I'll be on this cot—and I won't **have** any screen! No thanks."

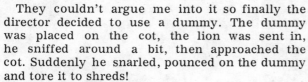

They couldn't argue me into it so finally the director decided to use a dummy. The dummy was placed on the cot, the lion was sent in, he sniffed around a bit, then approached the cot. Suddenly he snarled, pounced on the dummy and tore it to shreds!

When the scene was finally shot, I was on the cot all right, but there was a heavy sheet of plate glass between me and the lion. Then they brought in the old friendly one and I did the wrestling bit with **him**.

Once again I had been saved by a premonition.

It was during the filming of this same serial that I had an experience that shakes me up even now, when I think of it. We were filming another lion sequence and all of us were in the big lion cage in the Universal zoo.

The cage was huge, with rocks, dens and what-not, all within the confines of the bars. There was also a lot of apparatus in there, including several large platforms of different heights, which were used to mount lights for shooting night scenes and as camera mounts. Occasionally you would see a lion on one, sunning himself.

On this particular day I had been working with the lions all morning and I was pretty well bushed. The rest of the crew had a few more shots to make, so I thought I'd relax on one of the platforms for a few minutes, then go to lunch with them. As it turned out, I almost went to lunch with the lions, as the main course!

I stretched out—the sun was warm—my sweater made a soft pillow—and I was tired. I dropped off to sleep.

It was perhaps an hour later when I was awakened by a tickling sensation about my face. I opened my eyes—thank God I didn't jump —to find myself staring at the licking tongue

of a huge male lion! He was standing on his hind legs, with his front paws on this seven foot platform, licking my nose while his whiskers tickled my face. Maybe he was just playing—or perhaps he was after the salt in my perspiration. If that was it—he got plenty!

From the corner of my eye I could see that all six of the lions were in the cage, the other five dozing peacefully in the sun. The two females were more or less tame, but of the four males, Bonnie—named ironically after me—was a really ferocious beast. One called Pluto was fairly tame. The third one, named Willie, was also ferocious as was the fourth one. As I lay there, in inner agony but outward composure, I prayed this might be Pluto.

I dared not lose my composure. I knew any sudden move on my part might startle the beast into action, and perhaps bring the others on me in a flash. Lions gang up like that. I also knew the platform was no protection—a lion could bound up there as easily as a house cat could jump on a kitchen table. There was nothing I could do but lie there and sweat it out.

If I'd had a pencil, even, I might have been able to push it at him. A lion is deathly afraid of any kind of sharp stick. A man can hold a lion at bay with just a sharp-pointed pole. But I had nothing. I was tempted to flick my sweater at him, but thought better of it. Bull-fighting tactics might not go over with lions.

But I had to do something or go mad . . . so I slowly reached out and gently pushed his face away. Wonder of wonders! For some reason he slipped silently to the ground and lay down.

Well, I was on that platform for almost an hour more, locked in the cage with those six lions. I can't recall all my emotions during that time—and I don't want to.

After what seemed years, I heard the welcome sound of the returning motor bus, bringing the others back from lunch. I never accused anyone, but I have often wondered if leaving me there asleep was the work of a practical joker. Everyone seemed to think it was side-splitting except the production manager. He said if I had been killed it would have cost Universal many thousands of dollars—and you shouldn't take chances like that with the studio's money. I agreed with him, though for slightly different reasons.

Lions are as unpredictable as the weather and ten times as dangerous.

196

There was another time when an experience with the big cats didn't turn out so well. There was a prehistoric sequence in which a Cave-Man, in a leopard skin, was to see a lion enter his cave, run in after him, chase him out with his club and drive him away. It was left to an assistant director to shoot this scene. He asked a friend of mine, a member of the ill-fated Black Cat Club—let's call him Al—if he could handle the Cave-Man stunt.

You will recall I mentioned Willie as being a ferocious lion, and he was. But for some unaccountable reason he liked Al. Quite often, in dungarees and sweat-shirt, Al would wrestle with him, and to our amazement, the claws never came out. But Al was the only man beside his trainer who dared go near him, and he prided himself on the fact that he and Willie were such close friends. Al could slap him, pull his tail, ride him, do anything with him—and Willie never resented it. He loved Al—they were buddies. Animals are sometimes like that.

So when the assistant director asked Al if he could do the scene, Al said, "Sure, I'll use Willie. Nothing to it."

The cameras were set up and the scene began. Willie was sent into the cave and Al, now dressed in the leopard skin, went running in after him. Suddenly from inside the cave came several agonized screams—then silence.

Aghast, the trainer and other crew men rushed into the cave with long hooked poles, nets and flashlights. Deep inside was a cowering, quivering Willie—frightened to distraction. And on the cave floor, ripped half apart, lay the dead Al. Willie, in the darkened cave, had become frightened, and not recognizing Al in the leopard skin, had struck him. Or maybe it was the scent of the leopard, a hated natural foe of the lion, that Willie had reacted to.

This was another time when the unforseen had happened. It would have been just as easy to shoot a scene of the lion running into the cave, fire a shot into the cave to frighten him out, and catch him on camera as he made a running exit. They could then have shot Al running into the cave—then running out again, and the film could have been spliced to give the desired continuity. But it had looked so simple. Al and Willie were buddies. How could anything go wrong?!

Willie was never any good after that—he wouldn't work and was eventually sold to a city zoo. In his own dumb way he knew he had killed his best friend and I guess he couldn't forget it.

At its best, working with lions is no picnic for anybody but the audience. It's risky business, not only for the trainers and stuntmen, but for everyone working in the picture. Lions are temperamental and you never know what's going to happen. I'm thinking of one instance where things didn't go according to plan. It was amusing, but it could have turned into a tragedy.

We were shooting a picture in which we were using a full grown African lion named Numa.

In the story, Numa had escaped from a traveling circus and was prowling the city. He was to wander into a street-car, at which the supposedly panic-stricken passengers were to make a break for the front door—all but an old lady who was to let out a wild yell and jump out an open window, outside of which four property men would be waiting to catch her in a blanket, as she came flying through the air.

For the role of the old lady they had picked Harvey Parry who, incidentally, was National Spring Board and High Diving champion, figuring that if anyone could leap through a street-car window, while fending off a lion, he would be the man. However, Harvey was tied up with another sequence and they asked me to step into the breach. They made me up as the old lady, briefed me on the scene, I sat myself down among the other passengers, all actors of course, and everything went according to plan, that is, up to a certain point. The street-car stopped, Numa leaped aboard and started up the aisle. The passengers took one look and fell over each other scrambling out the door . . . all but the old lady who seemed frozen to her seat with terror. (I was playing it right up to the hilt.) I waited until the lion was practically staring me in the face, then I let out a blood curdling yell. Everything had been anticipated except the effect of this yell on Numa. It frightened him so that HE jumped out the window before I had a chance to and the four surprised and unhappy property men had a blanket-full of badly scared, clawing and scratching, full-grown African lion.

Luckily no one was killed· or even badly hurt,

After shooting 90% of my tough PERILS OF THE WILD action scenes without any help, an assist from some piano wire was a bit of relief.

but they could have been, for there's nothing more dangerous than a frightened lion.

Now to a bit of legerdemain we practiced on the audience—the artful trick we always had up our sleeve—piano wire. That was REALLY a fooler and it worked like this:

One story that never seems to die is "The Swiss Family Robinson," that was recently revived again . . . and in PERILS OF THE WILD, which was adapted from it, I was the big muscled Frederick Robinson. I did a lot of astounding things, but there was one sequence in which I was called upon to perform a feat of strength beyond the realm of human possibility. In clearing the space in the jungle, where we were to live for our Island sojourn, you saw me grasp a big tree, give it a jerk and pull it out of the ground, roots and all. Well, that was a pretty good trick and I'd like to meet the superman who could **do** it! Yet you saw me accomplish it with ease and dispatch. How was it done?

First of all, the tree was dug up, care being taken not to sever the roots. Then it was placed back in the hole and loose dirt packed around it. Then Bonomo took over—with the help of a large derrick that was out of camera range. You saw me pull the tree up all right, but what you didn't see were the invisible piano wires fastened to the top of it and attached to the

derrick. The derrick and the piano wires did all the work—I merely took hold of the tree and strained enough to make my muscles bulge.

A little later I had a fight with six murderous, invading pirates, eventually knocking them all out. This done, I draped them over the trunk of the tree, picked the tree up, put it on my shoulder and headed for a nearby cliff. Oops— I had forgotten one of the pirates. Turning, I stooped, with the tree and the other five still over my shoulder, picked up the sixth by the scruff of the neck, and dragged him off, still carrying the tree and the other five. When I reached the edge of the cliff, with one mighty heave, I tossed the tree and the six pirates into the depths below.

A tough assignment? Not if the piano wire held out!

Following the fight the camera filmed me picking up those supposedly unconscious men and draping them over the tree. Then the camera was stopped, the derrick brought in, and the piano wires again attached. The camera was now started again and in a close shot, with the wires invisible and the derrick out of camera range, you saw me pick up the tree, with the five men on it, and toss it over my shoulder like a feather. The distance shot as I threw them all over the cliff? A light, "prop" tree and six dummies.

But there was one close shot where you saw me start to throw the real tree and the real men over the cliff. In this one the derrick was still at work, and the men really went over, but they were only thrown into a shallow ditch. You see even the cliff was a fake—made of papier-mache.

But you wanted thrills and we gave them to you. And after all, we didn't **really** fool you ––**much**!

While I have been filmed countless times making genuine high dives from dizzy heights and performing the most difficult aquatic feats, in many of the shots in which I was filmed **under** water—I was perfectly dry. You would see me apparently swimming among seaweed, darting fish—and menaced by a huge octopus, whose writhing arms were reaching out to entrap me, only—you didn't see this at all. I was there all right—and the seaweed and the water and the fish and the octopus were there—but **they** were in a large transparent glass tank and I was **behind** it, not **in** it. I was suspended in midair, with that old invisible piano wire supporting my center of gravity, while I went through the motions of swimming. Disappointed? So was the octopus!

Of course, this stunt wasn't as easy as it sounds. Holding your body in a horizontal, swimming position, while suspended from a wire, requires about the top limit in muscular control. If any of you youngsters, or oldsters, doubt this, get somebody to suspend you in the air, with a rope about your middle, and see how long you can keep your body stretched out as though you were swimming. You'll be surprised!

I recall another occasion when I was in a twelve foot pit, having a savage fight with four gangsters. In the course of the fight I tossed these fellows, one at a time, twelve feet in the air and out of the pit. Some time later I saw the picture, and it looked so convincing I almost believed it. However, they were really jerked out of the pit by Hollywood piano wire, not tossed out by Joe Bonomo's good right arm.

But helpful as it is at times, if there's anything a stuntman hates it's that darned piano wire, for, when you're dangling in the air, like a puppet on a string, should anything go wrong, like a kink in the wire, there's not a thing you can do to protect yourself. Which takes me to some two reel comedies I made.

In one, I was the heavy—a big-chested bully in a turtle neck sweater, with a watch-spring mustache that snapped and curled back when I pulled it out. I was pursuing the poor little hero, a Chaplinesque type. As I caught him and was about to beat him to a pulp, a mule was to kick me with such force that I'd go sailing through the air and up through the clouds.

In order to get that effect, they decided to put a derrick on a truck, rig a piano wire from the derrick, and fasten the wire to **me**. As the mule kicked I would be jerked in the air where I'd be suspended twelve feet above the ground dangling behind this swiftly moving truck. Two camera cars would be shooting me from the side and below, catching the tops of trees and clouds whizzing by in the background.

The idea didn't appeal to me much, but I let the director talk me into it.

Now a thin, invisible piano wire, only two-thousandths of an inch in diameter, will support a really tremendous weight. However, if it gets the slightest kink in it while under this tension, it will snap like brittle glass. At the time I didn't know this, and if the director knew it he wasn't talking!

Well, the mule kicked and I was jerked into the air . . . and off went the truck at forty miles an hour. I sailed through the air with the greatest of ease, with the camera cars speeding alongside, grinding out film. The director was delighted —it really looked good and I was starting to almost enjoy it. As the clouds and tree tops flew by I blissfully rested my cheek on my hands and closed my eyes like a sleeping baby. But "baby" had a rude awakening. The truck hit a bump, I bounced, the wire kinked and---I don't like to even think about it. When the party came back to pick me up I had two badly sprained wrists and my skin was scraped off in a dozen places.

To this day I still wince when my secretary says, "Mr. Bonomo, I have a WIRE for you."

Many of you will recall the hazardous stunting that used to be done with airplanes. You don't see much of that anymore. The modern planes go much too fast—and those old biplanes are now outdated. But they gave us plenty of thrills in their day, for, because of the light construction, and the speed at which we had to fly them, if anything went wrong it meant "curtains."

It was during an airplane stunt that another of the Black Cats, Jack Connelly, met his death, although, in a way, he was an innocent bystander.

I had to transfer, from an open car in which we were riding, to a fast moving plane. There were four of us in the car, the other three being my "captors." Johnny was in the front seat.

We were speeding down a road and the plane was overtaking us, intent on rescuing me. I jumped to a standing position on the back seat and started to beat off the man who was in the rear with me, as well as Johnny who was reaching at me from the front. The fourth man was concentrating on his driving.

As the plane overtook us, with one hand I caught a rope ladder that was dangling from it. At that moment the car hit a deep rut and

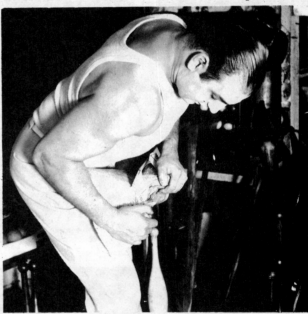

Dividing the population of New York—directory style.

went out of control. The pilot banked the plane sharply to give me a chance to hang on if I could, but the car was doing better than sixty miles an hour and starting to roll over. I knew my weight, on the steeply banking plane, would assuredly cause it to crash—so I let go of the ladder and dove headlong out of the car to the ground, where miraculously I tumbled free and unhurt. But poor Johnny wasn't so lucky. He was pinned under the skidding car and died on the way to the hospital. The Black Cats were getting fewer.

Perhaps the most dangerous work I ever did was those airplane stunts. When I think back on some of the fights I've staged on the wings of those old patched-up biplanes—hundreds of feet in the air—no parachute—and only certain death below me—I wonder what the Lord was saving

Raising a full car with four people in it using my famous harness lift.

A dummy takes over for a stuntman in a fall
that would otherwise only turn into a fatality.

me for! The slightest slip could have spelled disaster. The guy wires and flimsy struts were the only things we had to hang onto and we had to be careful of our footing. Those old, canvas-covered wings were often as slippery as glass. Then, too, those light planes would do a lot of bouncing, and should one of our feet slip off the thin wing ribs upon which we stood, there was a good chance of our going right through the wing. Yet I spent many an hour on those old flying death-traps, and I'm here to tell about it.

To illustrate what the work was like, let me cite one case in point. I was playing a strangler, who was pursuing the fleeing hero. I was to climb out on the wing of a speeding plane in which he was escaping. After a lively fight between the wings, he was to elude me by climbing on top of the upper wing and, catching the landing gear of another plane, easing down on us, make his getaway. I was playing myself and Al Wilson was doubling the hero. The two Franks—Frank Clark and Frank Thomas were flying the two planes.

Well, Al and I put on the fight between the wings, which was ticklish enough, but when we had to climb up onto that upper wing, and stand straight up, with nothing but a foot grip for security, while Al grabbed the landing gear of the second plane as I was grabbing for **him** —well—just put yourself in that situation! A thousand feet in the air on this bouncing, speeding plane—no parachute—and with nothing but your toes stuck under a foot-grip to keep you from pitching out into space. How much would **you** take to do a stunt like that-----huh?

I have made countless parachute jumps, (and this was before chutes were perfected,) and in only one of the jumps did I come close to losing my life. It was in a sequence where two of us were supposed to jump from a high flying plane, with only one parachute. I agreed—somehow I was always agreeing—but no one could be found who would risk making the jump **with** me. After a while I suggested I use a dummy, filled with air, in place of the other chutist. This was okayed, and as it turned out, that dummy saved my life.

We made the jump—Mr. Dummy and I—over the ocean just off Balboa. The wind was unusually strong as I jumped, and I noticed we were being blown quite far from the waiting speedboat that was to pick me up. But not until we hit the water did I realize how strong the wind really was.

The chute, instead of collapsing, billowed— and we darned near went UP again! Then, out to sea we headed! The billowing chute was acting as a sail, pulling us through the choppy water at a terrific clip. I was gasping, gulping and swallowing sea-water and I was getting sick from it. Had it not been for the dummy I'd have surely drowned. He was **behind** me when we hit the water but I gradually worked him around to the front where, holding him before my face, I used him as both a life-preserver and a shield. He broke the water in front of me, sufficiently, to

Each jump I made off a bi-plane could have been the last.

allow me to breathe and remain conscious.

It was almost a half hour before the speedboat could head us off and pick up this very soggy Bonomo and companion. If that seems like making a living the hard way—it WAS. But it at least gave me one distinction. I'm probably the only man in the world who owes his life to a dummy.

But planes and parachutes weren't the only lethal weapons I fooled around with. I used to drive cars off mountain roads and cliffs, wreck them with other cars, drive them in front of speeding trains and flip them over while traveling at "umteen" miles an hour. I don't think there was any hair-raising stunt the most fiendish Hollywood writers could dream up, that I didn't take a stab at. Altogether, I have completely demolished twenty-four cars, eight motorcycles and three trains, not to mention a hundred or more automobiles that I only smashed up a **little**. When I was through wrecking them, they were sold cheap to used car dealers, who patched them up and peddled them to the public as "slightly used cars—only driven weekends by timid old ladies." I hope YOU didn't buy one.

It was while doing daredevil car stunts with another of the Black Cats—Hap, we used to call him—that the Black Cat kissed again. Hap speci-

alized in those "thrill shots" where you see a speeding automobile racing a fast express train to a crossing and making it across the tracks . . . just a foot ahead of the onrushing engine. Hap really enjoyed doing this dangerous stunt and kept trying to cut that foot down to INCHES. Like a good bullfighter, he wanted to see how close he could come without being nicked. He always made it in that hopped-up racing car he drove but one day, he tried it on a motor-cycle—and missed.

I was on the near side of the railroad crossing, watching the stunt, along with the director. Hap waited until the last possible moment and then roared across the tracks just ahead of the engine. But as it flashed by I saw the cowcatcher catch the last few inches of the motorcycle's rear wheel and spin it around. Other than the noise of the crashing bike, there wasn't a sound. Hap, without even time to cry out, had been spun under the wheels of the train. The "Matador" had played it too close, once too often.

While we're on the subject of motorcycles, as the booted and leather-jacketed youth of today will enthusiastically attest to, there's something almost irresistible about them, despite the injuries they cause and the toll of human life they take each year. Several present day Hollywood actors,

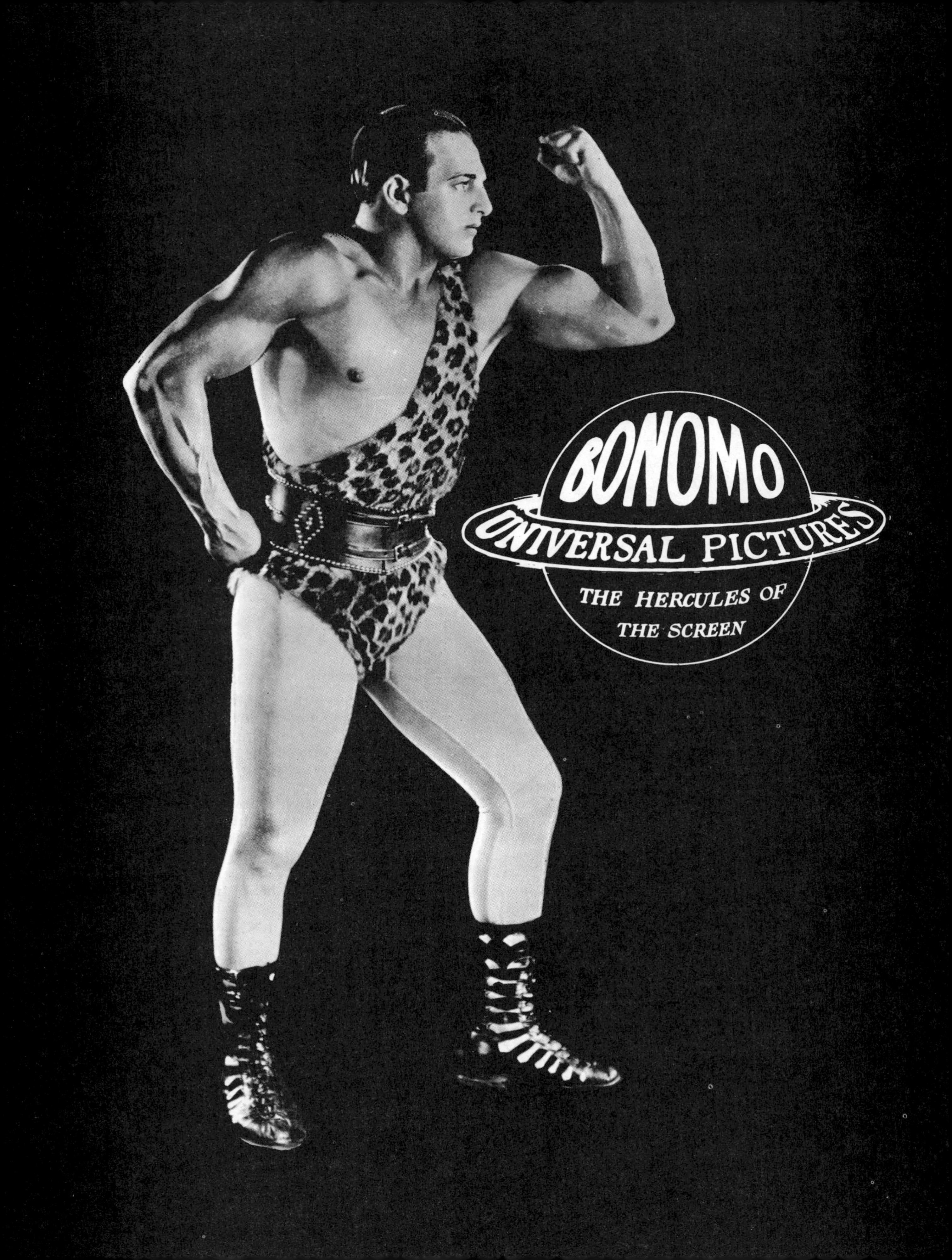

BONOMO

UNIVERSAL PICTURES

THE HERCULES OF
THE SCREEN

whose names are box-office magic, have been motorcycle addicts of the first rank. I put that in the past tense because, after severe smashups and close brushes with death, many of them have a special clause in their contracts, making motorcycle riding strictly off limits to them.

The most ardent motorcycle enthusiast I ever knew was Slim Cole. That wasn't his right name but it was the name we knew him by. He was wealthy, had several college degrees and was a young university professor when the motorcycle bug bit him. Almost overnight he resigned his professorship, put behind him all the luxuries his money could buy and devoted his life to motorcycling. He used to dress entirely in black from helmet to boots and he wore a black cape that, as he picked up speed, would stand straight out behind him. He was really a romantic figure.

Slim had several cycles, all especially made for him and geared differently, which he used for various types of stunts. Nothing was too dangerous for him to try, such as riding, at a hundred miles an hour, over the top of long, fast moving freight trains. He wasn't crazy—he was just one of the refugees from the psychiatrist's couch—who rate the value of a momentary thrill beyond that of their own lives.

I know what you're thinking . . . you're wondering if any psychiatrist ever told me **I** was in that category. Never! You see, I never WENT to a psychiatrist.

The last I heard of Slim he was roving about the country, organizing motorcycle battalions. Then, overnight, he dropped completely from sight. I imagine he, too, tried for one thrill too many.

Changing from a motorcycle to a plane was another good stunt and a cinch when it worked. The only thing you had to remember was to let the plane pull **you** up. Too much sudden

weight on the light plane could pull it down with a crash. A good pilot though, would be able to just ease the plane up as pretty as you please, with you on the rope ladder. Then you just climbed the ladder and that was it. As I say, it was simple when it was executed well. But if something went wrong—?

It was while doing this comparatively easy stunt that the Grim Reaper swung at me with his fatal Scythe—and almost got me. I was zipping merrily along on my motorcycle, doing very close to seventy miles an hour, and the plane with the ladder was settling down on me as gently as a hen on an egg. I used to stand up on the seat of the speeding cycle and balance myself there until I could grab the rope ladder as the plane passed over me.

This time, as usual, I was standing up on the seat with my arms outstretched, but just as I grabbed the ladder my motorcycle hit a bump in the road and swerved. I lost my balance and, still clinging to the ladder, I fell off. Al Wilson, as luck would have it, was piloting the plane and he was one of the best. He was watching very closely—saw me catch the ladder then, a second later, saw the cycle swerve. He gave her the gun and started his pull up but the sudden jerk of my weight, as I fell, started to pull the plane down . . . but Al had anticipated that just in time. Down came the plane with a badly scared Bonomo now hanging onto the ladder with just one hand—and the toes of his shoes dragging along the road for about twenty yards, then the plane began to pick up altitude again.

I scuffed the toes completely off a good pair of shoes but that was the only damage. For a minute, though, both Al and I thought the worst was going to happen and it was a miracle it didn't. The camera got it all—it was a great film shot—but we never repeated it.

The bearded Slim Cole's middle name was danger and I found myself in many a "real" hazardous situation when working with him on a film.

Chapter #23

"NO MARGIN FOR ERROR"

THIS MAY SOUND STRANGE, but of all the stunts I've done, I think driving a car off a cliff is probably the safest. This was the usual procedure:—

Using dummies for passengers, I'd start the machine rolling down a hill at a fast clip. As we neared the drop-off point I'd edge out of the car until I was standing on the running board, steering with my finger tips. (We **had** running boards in those days.) Then, at the crucial moment, I'd turn the wheels sharply toward the cliff's edge and leap clear as the car plunged over. I did that stunt scores of times with hardly a scratch to show for it. But the one time I tried to vary it, something went wrong and I **couldn't** jump.

In that instance I decided it would be a nice change for the audiences if I crashed a car into a speeding truck—head on—and let the truck BUMP it over the cliff. As the camera was to film the scene from the cliff side, a special extension platform was built to get the cameraman out there.

As the stunt was planned, I was to be driving along the narrow cliff road, in an old Model "T" Ford. The truck, apparently out of control, would suddenly round a bend and bear down on me . . . and just a split second before the

collision, I was to jump and let the car plunge off into space.

The off-side door . . . the one away from the camera . . . had been removed so nothing would obstruct my safe exit.

It was so simple I didn't give it a second thought.

At last the camera started—the truck was coming down the road—and I was driving along to meet it, head on. As I glanced down from Mulholland Drive, on that sunny, peaceful mountainside, all seemed sweetness and light. The cliff dropped away, for well over a thousand feet, down to Ventura Boulevard. The drop was pretty steep for the first fifty feet, then there was a ledge, and then it dropped again. I noticed it, but thought no more about it, turning my attention to the oncoming collision.

We were about twenty feet apart when the stuntman, who was driving the truck, jumped . . . and I started to follow suit. As I took my foot off the accelerator and turned to leap out, the car shot **forward!** In that agonizing moment I realized my sleeve had caught on the hand throttle, on the steering wheel, giving the old "Lizzie" the gas! In another moment it hit the speeding truck and I **couldn't** get out without jumping directly into its path. The only thing

206

I could do was go along with the car.

Even as I made this flash decision, we went over the cliff. As we did, my hands shot down to the floor where there were always grip-handles for hanging on in "turnovers." As I grasped them, a post-impression of the cliffside flashed through my mind. I realized that if the car held together to the ledge, I would have perhaps a moment, when I could get away.

Now we were rolling over and over as I hung onto those grip-handles for dear life. After five complete turns I felt the crunching blow of the car hitting the ledge. It bounced without spinning, and even as it teetered for its second descent, I leaped. We both landed on the cliffside, lower down, with the car below me. Then down we both went, the now battered Model "T" a few yards ahead of me as I went tumbling, sliding and sprawling after it.

After a couple of hundred feet of this I was able to stop myself, but the car went all the way to the bottom, a thousand feet below me. They later picked it up in pieces and carted it away for scrap. Fortunately, they picked me up in ONE piece . . . but at the hospital they had to dig an acre or so of the San Fernando Valley out of my hide . . . and brother, that **hurt**.

Incidentally, at Universal City Hospital they had a "Joe Bonomo bed" which they always kept reserved for me . . . and I was never out of it for very long periods. I think that's some sort of a record although a not very enviable one. I sometimes wonder if the head nurse has kept a light burning in the window for me! If so—and you read this book—put it out.

This might be a good time to say something about Movie HORSES. They're a breed by themselves. Trained for Western movies, many of them are veterans of many years experience, and they seem to know they are acting. They work on cue and in many cases do a better job than actors on the regular payroll. I've seen a few, who gave such amazing performances, I caught myself wondering if they had read the script!

Very often, when mounted on one of these veteran equine actors, you had little control over them. Lined up for a chase sequence, they wouldn't budge until the director hollered "Action!" . . . then off they'd go. And there was absolutely no way the rider could stop them, once they got started. Finally, the sequence over, the director would shout "CUT!" and darned if the horses wouldn't stop dead in their tracks! There were certainly times when the studio should have paid the horses and fed **us** the oats!

Some were what they called "cold-jawed", which meant the nerves in their mouths were dead from too much reining. You couldn't steer a cold-jawed horse. Some were half blind. You couldn't steer **them either**—they just followed the pack. Some were "stiff-legged" which meant, that when they heard "Cut!", they'd lock their legs—and if you didn't expect it—over their head you'd go. The studios owned hundreds of physically perfect horses, but they had a reason for

keeping all these misfits, as we shall see later. Some of the specimens they had ME riding should have been stuffed and sold to museums. It's a wonder I'm here to tell about it.

Why did we keep those misfits? For one thing, a trained movie horse is a valuable piece of property. Another reason was because the nature of our work often required a horse with, let us say, limitations. Many times you've seen a horse and rider jump off a high cliff into water. But no horse with an ounce of sense would jump off a cliff. Stuntmen, yes—but stuntmen don't **have** horse sense.

How did we do it? One way was to have a greased-boardslide built into the surface of the cliff. You'd walk your unsuspecting horse onto the slide, he'd hit the grease and before he knew it he was sliding. He'd lock his legs but it wouldn't do him any good. Over the cliff he'd go. It didn't do him any harm but sometimes he'd get mighty indignant.

Or we'd use an almost blind horse. He wouldn't know where he was going until he was in mid-air, then he'd be safe in the river below and wondering how he got there.

If you gave me a car I'd dream up the stunt.

I'll never forget the first time I jumped a horse into water. They had just built an artificial lake on the Universal lot. It was 200 yards long, 200 feet wide, and twelve feet deep at the base of an artificial cliff which we jumped from. This was the first time the lake was used for a horse jump, and Bonomo was to have the honor. I knew a horse could swim faster than a man, and that I'd have to jump to one side before we hit the water, so those sharp hooves wouldn't lacerate me. Well, I jumped and landed clear. I swam to one side of the pool and climbed out, with the horse swimming after me. But can you realize the consternation when we realized there wasn't any place shallow enough for the **horse** to climb out?

Have you ever tried to give a horse a helping hand to get him out of a swimming pool? If you ever do, you'll find it can't be done without a derrick . . . which is how **we** had to do it. It was a neat trick to pass a sling under the belly of that frantic, slashing animal, who had been swimming around for more than an hour . . . but I finally succeeded. And it was a confused and tuckered, but happy animal when he finally got his feet on the ground again. The next day they put a ramp in the pool for horses to climb out on. Who says the picture business has no heart!

Some of the most spectacular Western stunts were the easiest, and many that looked easy were the most difficult to do. How many times have you seen a horse shot from under its rider —yet, have you ever stopped to think how difficult it must be to get a horse to fall, just at the psychological moment? We had two ways of accomplishing this. One was called the "Running W". In this "Running W" a long rope was fastened to each of the horse's hooves, and the ends of these ropes were then tied to a longer rope, which was staked solidly into the ground. The horse would be galloped, and when he got to the end of the slack—a perfect spill.

Another way was to dig a shallow pit, fill it with soft dirt, then smooth it over. When a running horse hit the soft dirt, his feet would sink in unexpectedly, and down he'd go. This method was fairly safe for both horse and rider —but in the "Running W", the horse would be tripped so suddenly, the rider would go shooting ahead through the air. If you studied physics I don't have to tell you why—or if you had studied medicine, you could have made a nice living just · setting all the broken bones suffered by stuntmen in doing that one. Nowadays they use specially trained horses for spills. The rider gives the horse the cue and the animal drops like a stone. It costs a little more for the horse but they save it on hospital bills.

I always thought the most dangerous of all Western work was the chase . . . especially where a number of horses participated. Take the case of a bunch of "bad guys" pursuing our hero. Your sympathies are with "No Gun Cassidy" who's trying to make his escape? WRONG! The fellows to be worrying about are the hard-riding

Rex, King of the Wild Horses—a member of Hollywood's animal royalty.

bunch behind him, for if one of the lead horses steps into a rut or a gopher hole, he'll go down and the others will pile on top of him . . . and the tangle of kicking horses and screaming men will be brutal. Those shots, that never reached the screen, were the real "Horror Pictures."

I used to wonder where all the horses came from, for there were pictures made in which a couple of thousand were used in a single scene. This was always exciting for we never knew what was going to happen—and often it was a good thing we didn't. During my years with Universal, we made one of the early great Western "super-colossals" called THE FLAMING FRONTIER, and to my dying day—heck, I'll let you judge for yourself. You probably won't believe it anyway.

In addition to stunting and doubling and staging the fight scenes, I played the terrifying Indian Chief, Rain-in-the-Face, and when they finished making me up for it I almost scared **myself**. As part of my war paint I wore a coiled snake ("I strike without warning") on one cheek, and a bleeding heart ("I show no mercy") on the other. Add to this, jagged teeth and a painted-on murderous scowl, and you'll start to get the picture.

There was one scene where literally thousands of Indians were lined up on a hillside, readied for a mass charge on the wagon train. We had dug up every horse we could find—cold-jawed, sway-back, anything on four legs that could whinney. And on every horse was a "red-skin." Where did we get all the Indians? The studio merely advertised for "extras," at three dollars a day and a box lunch . . . and it seemed like every man, woman and child in Southern California showed up. There were cowboys, fruit pickers, hoboes, Mexicans, and even a few tourists. And those who had families brought 'em along. The women and children were used for squaws and papooses and the men for the Indian braves.

Costumes? We had thousands of 'em. One-piece dresses and a string of beads for the women . . . loin cloths, feathers and moccasins for the men.

Makeup? We had a dozen drums of our magic "Bolamenia", our Indian stain, to spray them with. Each man on a spray gun would have a line waiting. He'd spray a man up the front, turn him around, spray him down the back, then pass him on to the war-paint man. The war-paint man would make a few quick dabs, working with a brush in each hand, then pass him along to the feather man, who'd glue a feather on his head. If the real Indians had been able to turn out braves that fast, the white man would still be east of the Appalachians! In a few hours we had thousands of "full-blooded," bolamenia-dyed warriors. We gave each of them a horse and a tomahawk, 'til we ran out of horses . . . the rest got bows and arrows and a lesson in war-whooping.

We now go back to the original scene—a couple of thousand horses in a long line across the

Noble Johnson (left) goes into his frantic war dance for THE FLAMING FRONTIER.

hills, each horse with an Indian on its back . . . some perched there rather precariously, but nevertheless they were there. Most of them had never tried to ride bare-back, if indeed they had ridden at all, but that was okay. Those who fell off would be synchronized, in the cutting room, with the frontiersmen's shots, and the film would show another "redskin" biting the dust. To give them "Dutch courage" and perhaps add a bit more ferocity to their war-whoops, jugs of corn-whiskey and tequila had been passed around freely, and a lot of them had reached the stage where they didn't much care whether they fell off or not. They'd try anything! I might add the studio had four ambulances, with doctors and nurses, standing by. They had made pictures like this before.

Now no charge looks good unless all the horses start at once. To insure this, an electric wire was strung the full length of the scene, and the horses backed to the point where it touched their buttocks. At a given signal a sharp electrical charge would be sent through the wire. And to take care of any horses who had worked themselves **away** from the wire, men were placed at intervals who would suddenly don bear's heads. Horses are deathly afraid of bears. Between the two, a fast and even start was practically insured.

My job as Chief Rain-in-the-Face was to lead that wild charge of whooping warriors . . . and I want to tell you I got a chill everytime I thought of that wild horde behind me. Should my horse stumble I'd surely be trampled to death

As Chief Rain-in-the-Face my facial makeup featured a bleeding heart and a coiled snake.

in the on-rush. Rain-in-the-Face was a good name for me, only that wasn't rain; that was cold perspiration!

At last, all was in readiness. The director gave the signal, the electric shock bounced through the wire, the men in the bear's heads leaped up with a yell, and the frightened horses leaped forward as though shot from a catapult, their thundering hooves shaking the ground like an earthquake. Luckily my horse was as scared as the rest of them and managed to stay out in front.

Then the frontiersmen started shooting, the Indians closed in, whooping, and the massacre was on. Between the shooting and the whooping I lost track of the plot but I think the U.S. Cavalry got there just in time.

When the picture was released those "charge scenes" were terrific . . . and as Chief Rain-in-the Face I did one of the best characterizations of my career. I was going to wire Mama and Papa to see it, but I knew what would happen. After Chief Rain-in-the-Face had done his stuff they'd say, "Which one was Joey?"

Incidentally, sixty of the "braves" wound up in the Universal City Hospital, but with the picture a hit, everyone said it was worth it. That is, everyone but the sixty "braves" who wound up in the Universal City Hospital.

Those movie horses were not only smart, but a lot tougher than we sometimes gave them credit for. I recall one western in which Yakima Canutt was doubling John Wayne in a dangerous prairie schooner bit. John would have done the stunt himself if they'd let him—he had plenty of moxie and never side-stepped risking his neck, but by then his neck had become too valuable to take chances with.

As the stunt was set up, the wagon, drawn by six fast horses, had been attacked by several Indians. John, who was driving, had beaten them off in a gun battle, but in so doing had lost the reins and the frightened horses had run away and were galloping along the edge of a high cliff. Unseen by the audience a stuntman is hidden in the boot of the wagon and is driving the horses from there. At a given moment he pulls the king-pin, drops out of the boot and the wagon goes over the cliff, Yakima, as John Wayne, jumping clear at the last possible second. To add to the excitement, at the moment the stuntman in the boot pulled the king-pin, a cable tripped the lead team and the six horses piled up in a squirming, kicking heap.

As this happened, a man from Lone Pine, from whom the horses had been rented, said to the director, "Well, I reckon you just bought yourself six horses. No use lettin' 'em suffer . . . I'll shoot 'em quick and put 'em out of their misery."

"Before you do any shootin'," said Yakima, "let's cut 'em loose and see how bad they're hurt."

The wagon was completely demolished, but when they cut the horses loose they got up, shook themselves and were soon as good as new. Everyone was surprised but Yakima.

"Shucks," he drawled, "them horses is professionals. They knowed what they was doin' . . . they was jes' puttin' on a good act."

We prepare for the savage attack.

Coney Island's big chief whoops up a war party.

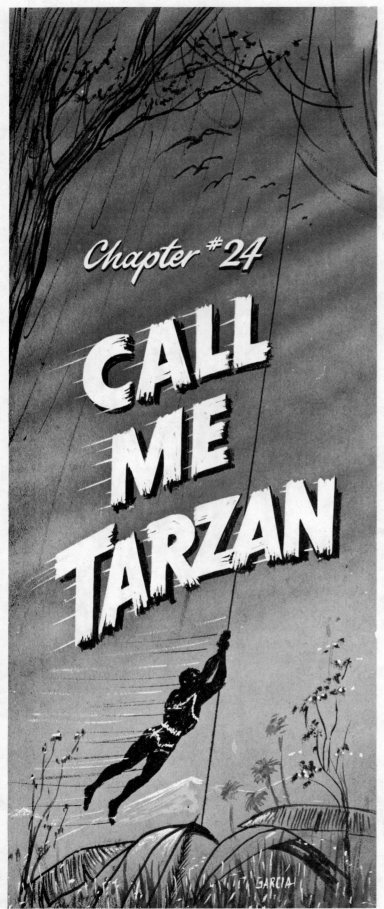

Chapter #24

CALL ME TARZAN

A<small>T</small> THE RISK of boring you a bit, perhaps at this time I should say something about Hollywood contracts.

When you sign your first contract with a Hollywood major studio, you may sign for a period of seven years, with options. This means that during those seven years you work exclusively for that studio at the salary specified in the contract. If the options are for six month periods, they have the option of letting you go at the end of any six months from the date of the original signing. They must RE-HIRE you every six months or you're automatically out . . . but if they DO continue rehiring you, you're theirs for seven years, whether you like it or not.

This may all seem a bit one-sided, in the studio's favor, but remember it is the studio that gave you your first break and if you show promise, it's the studio that will build you up to star stature. This costs them enormous amounts of money, though they'll pick it all up again as you grow in boxoffice popularity.

But if you DO grow big enough—if you really attain stardom—you suddenly are no longer an individual . . . you're a fabulously valuable piece of studio property, no longer permitted to call your soul your own. You have evolved into a money making manikin whose every move is watched and tabulated, to be guarded and protected, not only from the outside world but even from yourself.

In those early bonanza days of picture making the stars were all living the life of Riley. They collected tremendous salaries and, knowing how dependent the studios were on their drawing power at the boxoffice, they took full advantage of the situation—or many of them did. Regardless of shooting schedules they came and went as they pleased. If they felt like working, they worked—if they didn't feel like it the studio could cool its heels 'til they DID. They demanded everything and went into temperamental tantrums if they didn't get it . . . so they usually GOT it. If the color scheme of their dressing room didn't suit them, they screamed for it to be redecorated at once . . . and it was. If they didn't like certain things in the script they brought in their own writers to change it . . . and the studio paid the bill.

Yes . . . for a while the stars got away with murder until several of them, their heads swollen by success and their egos having reached "the King can do no wrong," stage, got themselves involved in some unsavory scandals and then— the merry-go-round ran down! Some smart lawyers stepped in, drew up new iron-bound contracts and the whole picture changed. From then on the studios did the dictating.

First, they inserted a morality clause, for the infraction of which players were penalized in proportion to the gravity of their offense. It read like this:

"The artist agrees to conduct himself with due regard to public conventions and morals and agrees that he will not do or commit any act or thing that will tend to degrade him in society or bring him into public hatred, contempt, scorn or ridicule, or that will tend to shock, insult or offend the community or ridicule public morals or decency, or prejudice the producer or the motion picture industry in general.''

Another clause covered disfigurement and illness, voiding all stars' contracts if they suffered an accident, continued illness, or a facial blemish that destroyed their photographic value. Female stars had to agree to keep sensible hours and lead circumspect lives, abjuring excessive alcoholic indulgence or anything else that might bring on lines to mar their pretty, photogenic faces.

And the male stars were just as carefully guarded. Buck Jones and Tom Mix, who were inclined to be a bit reckless, were forbidden to mount overly spirited horses or even drive their cars through "dangerous traffic" . . . Jack Hoxie and Hoot Gibson were limited to only riding horses which they owned and had personally trained . . . and Reginald Denny and Edmund Lowe, both excellent amateur pilots, were barred from flying any type of airplane, for the term of their contracts. And when Shirley Mason was rumored engaged to a famous automobile race driver, Fox Studios immediately put fast cars on Shirley's taboo list and made her confine her automobiling to taxi-cabs. It all sounds a bit drastic but they were protecting their investment.

Edmund Lowe

Buck Jones

Jack Hoxie

Reginald Denny

Hoot Gibson

Tom Mix

My contract with Universal stipulated that all equipment required for my picture stunts must be specially built according to my specifications. Thus the platforms, body harness and the like, used when the strongman lifted elephants, automobiles etc. and which helped me avoid breaking a bone or pulling a muscle, by distributing the weight over my body, were all constructed under my personal supervision.

They even had clauses covering overweight and underweight—and still retain them. Doctors will tell you they have difficulty getting people to go on diets and STAY on them. Hollywood has no such problems. When a few excess pounds can cost you up to a million dollars, via a cancelled contract, a lamb chop and a piece of lettuce don't look so bad to you. From Nita Naldi, who had to lose her once generous curves, to play

Rudolph Valentino

the vamp opposite Rudolph Valentino, to Gloria Swanson, whose last contract with Paramount stipulated she must retain her slim silhouette, there were no exceptions. To stay under the weight limit permitted by the motion picture camera is easy for some, but to others it is a constant and harassing problem. There are many who believe that too extreme and prolonged dieting cost the beautiful Jean Harlow her life.

If you recall, I also mentioned clauses that covered UNDER-weight. A case in point is that of the rotund cinema star, Walter Hiers. The Christie studios put a clause in his contract that "If he so neglects eating that his rotundity decreases to the point where the scales register less than two hundred and twenty five pounds, the studio reserves the right to cease paying him his weekly check." From that time on, Walter looked upon potatoes and pastry as two of his staunchest allies . . . and never slighted them.

Occasionally stars of sufficient magnitude managed to get a clause of their own inserted, such as Colleen Moore who was permitted to remain in California even though several of the First National production units were moved to New York-----and Lon Chaney who, when he made THE PHANTOM OF THE OPERA, insisted that no photograph, showing him in the startling makeup he wore in that picture, be publicly displayed or reproduced until after the production's release. Also, when the "bobbed hair" craze hit this country and the studios were shearing off the feminine stars' beautiful tresses, Marian Nixon held out for a clause in her Fox contract, permitting her to retain her flowing locks and Dorothy Mackail and Patsy Ruth Miller followed suit. On the other hand, Jobyna Ralston was forced to let her bob grow out before she could appear in Harold Lloyd's productions.

Lastly, the clause that topped the unpopularity poll was the one where the girls had to agree not to marry during the term of their contract. The producer's argument was that motherhood might take them from the screen and the money spent on establishing their personalities would be a total loss. I need not add that this clause is no longer in effect. In those days the per-

215

One of my trademark pictures—taken while on tour on the roof of the RKO Orpheum in Los Angeles. The girls are the original English Tiller dancers and they were responsible for first introducing precision dancing to the United States.

Some action layouts for a proposed new starring vehicle-THE RADIO DETECTIVE, and a shot from a film role it took me years to live down—"Tillie"—the Strong Lady.

Time for reducing with the "Bomo" game at my Hollywood gym-keeping score with Ethel and myself on rotund comedians Hilliard "Fatty" Karr, Bill "Kewpie" Ross & Frank "Fatty" Alexander is director-actor Francis Ford.

formers used to say, "When you sign a contract to play in the movies, you wonder if this is a free country after all." But even as they protested they were reaching for the pen . . . for despite the addition of those prohibitive clauses, a contract with a major studio was something greatly to be desired. If you were talented—really had "Something on the ball"—it was almost a guarantee of seven years of constantly growing fame and prosperity, leading to a real "pot of gold at the end of the rainbow." And the same applies today, only now your fame is more widespread around the world and the pot of gold can reach fantastic proportions . . . even after taxes, if you'll forgive the reference! When the expiration date of my contract rolled around I went into a huddle with Universal. They wanted to renew my contract at the same figure but I demanded a substantial increase and along with it I insisted they add clauses that were outlandish. You see, I actually wanted them NOT to renew my contract for, in view of other offers I had at the time, I had good reason to believe I could make more money free-lancing.

As I look back on it now, Universal was certainly paying me every penny I was worth as an actor—but I was valuable to them in other ways. First, I had a definite value as an idea man. In pictures I might be working on I frequently came up with fresh and different ideas that were often adopted with excellent results . . . and on occasion I made suggestions to the production managers that saved the studio considerable money. Also, when they wanted a stunt figured out or a fight staged, they'd send for Bonomo—and when they were shooting a serial, althouth I wasn't getting paid as a writer, if they hit a snag I could usually straighten them out. Many sequences in those serials were my "brain children." Nobody ever objected as I never asked for writing credits, nor would I accept any.

There were other angles that also added to my value. If the studio had a star who couldn't seem to stay in shape physically, or had a serious weight probelm—both of which are mighty serious when you are constantly before the camera, they'd hustle him or her over to my gymnasium and I'd outline a corrective training or reducing program for them. On two occasions I saved the lives of high salaried stars who were worth millions to the studio at the boxoffice—and I even had a faculty for keeping peace in the Universal "family." When tempers rose I was usually able to butter-up both sides so production could continue with less friction. I realize now I wasn't a Jack Barrymore when it came to acting, but I was certainly a Jack-of-all-trades at Universal —an all-around guy who could do almost anything and never minded when they piled the work on. They were getting their money's worth from me—but for different reasons than I thought.

Carl Laemmle was waiting for the day when I would get my fill of acting and turn to producing, where he felt my natural talent lay. But as men will often bypass their natural talents to pursue that which is beyond them, I rejected producing and lashed my horses in pursuit of a career as a "big" movie star.

I now had only six months more to go on my Universal contract and I notified them I was not renewing it—that I was going free-lancing. Mr. Laemmle, now in Europe, cabled the studio to keep me working and happy—that some arrangements would be made, upon his return, that would be satisfactory to us both. The next week I was assigned the starring role in a new "Tarzan" serial, the publicity released and the production started.

During the third day of shooting, still insisting upon doing my own stunts, I was yodeling my Tarzan cry of defiance, as, grasping rope-vines, I recklessly swung myself, from tree to tree, through the jungle. As I reached the top of one of my long swings, the rope-vine snapped and they picked me up with a compound fracture of the left leg. I also injured my right hip, but that seemed unimportant at the time. Into the old familiar hospital I went . . . this time for seven long weeks.

Ethel came to see me occasionally, but each time with a different fellow carrying the books and the flowers she brought me, so I never had a moment alone with her. I finally bribed one of the prettiest nurses to come in and put on an act before Ethel, pretending she had a violent case on me. I figured this would make Ethel jealous and after that she'd come **alone**. To show you how clever I was—after that she didn't come at **all**!

As for the "Tarzan" serial, the production was shelved. Much later on Universal did make the film and starred Frank Merrill as TARZAN THE MIGHTY, which was finally released in 1928. So that was that!

I left the hospital wishing I could start free-lancing in love as well as in the movies. If only Ethel's eyes hadn't reminded me so much of those blue skies over Coney Island-----.

The word had gotten around that I was leaving Universal and I already had some lucrative free-lance offers; so the day my contract expired I turned a deaf ear to all urgings to sign a new one, and said goodbye. A few minutes later I was driving out under the arch, at the entrance to Universal City. I was on my way out of the hive and into the web—and I didn't even know it.

My tree-swinging "Tarzan" days were numbered by a freak rope-vine accident.

Chapter #25
The BIG FIGHT

I'VE ALWAYS CONSIDERED First National's THE SEA TIGER my best effort in the staging of fights. Milton Sills was the star and I played Sebastiano, the "heavy." (I grew a beard for that one!) We spent eight full days on the fight sequences, for I ran into trouble immediately. Sills kept knocking out my fight men and he gave ME a couple of good ones where they really hurt.

Milton was a big man—even bigger than I— and a nice guy personally, but he either wouldn't or couldn't pull a punch. In every fight he'd flail out with everything he had—and he had plenty. Then, after the man or men he knocked out would be revived, he'd apologize profusely.

"I'm sorry, fellows," he'd plead, "but I just get carried away." It wasn't long before we were wishing he **would** be.

I started working with him on the side, coaching him in the art of movie punching. He'd get it fine in rehearsal, but the moment he got before the cameras again, another man or two would be knocked unconscious. This began to get

aggravating. With that rocking right he knocked out or dazed more than a dozen of us, not counting the ones who got belted two or three times.

Finally, one of my men had a couple of teeth knocked out and we realized, unless something was done about Milton, we'd all wind up on stretchers. I started to wonder if maybe he wasn't secretly enjoying it.

Then came a scene where he was to be hit with a break away chair and fall down in an apparently dazed condition. A break away chair is made of balsa wood and is very light and brittle. You hit a man across the shoulders with it and it will shatter, but do no damage.

But as we shot this scene, unknown to anyone but himself, the man who had had his teeth knocked out, grabbed a real chair, strong and sturdy. When the moment came, he really clobbered Sills with it—and instead of hitting him across the shoulders, he brought it right down on the valuable star's head! He went out like a light and didn't come to for an hour.

When he finally opened his eyes, we all

Milton Sills and I ready ourselves for some rough work ahead as the cameras roll on the spectacular SEA TIGER.

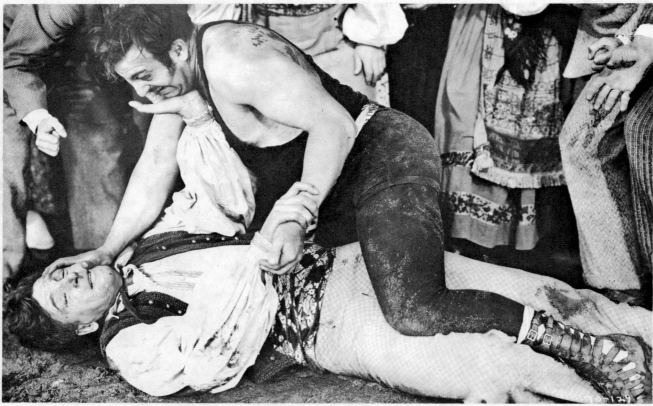

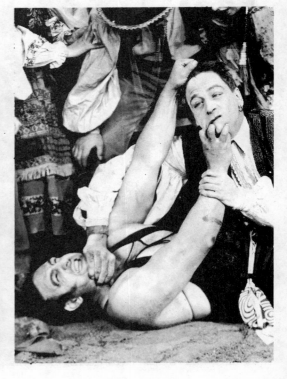

And who said villains never win?

gathered round, apologizing.

"We're sorry, Mr. Sills, but somebody switched the chairs."

He might have been killed, and the picture ruined, and we all got one heck of a bawling out from the executives at First National. As for Milton, you never saw a man learn the art of "pulling punches" so fast in your life!

As I said, the shooting of those "Sea Tiger" fight scenes took eight days, and it was plenty rough. We saved the most spectacular scene, because it was the most dangerous, 'til the last day of shooting. That was the long, crucial fight between Sebastiano and the hero. As Sebastiano, I fought that day for more than seven hours, wearing out not only Sills, but three doubles for him as well. When I dragged my weary bones to the shower, and to get medical treatment, I was a sight. The inside of my mouth was lacerated from the hundred or more punches I had taken . . . my arms, legs and body were rubbed raw in spots, and I needed seventeen stitches to close my wounds. But what a fight scene that was! THE SEA TIGER was another smash hit!

There was a comedy I made for Paramount, in which I played the heavy, opposite El Brendel, the great Swedish comedian. This was before Joe Penner, and Brendel had a trained duck that went through the picture with us, and who used to defend El against my villainous machinations. You think a duck is stupid? I still carry scars from my staged fights with him. He could outfox you every time. Brendel finally sold him and I didn't eat duck for a year or two. I couldn't get over the thought that I just might be nibbling on my old sparring partner.

Now I was slowly getting away from my "Joe Bonomo the Serial King" title. I landed a lead role in a First National feature picture called VAMPING VENUS. The beautiful and tragic Thelma Todd played Venus and I was Hercules, with Charlie Murray, one of the finest comedians in motion picture history, supplying the comedy.

The picture was plotted like this: Thelma and I are playing the leads in a stage play and Charlie, a middle-aged "stage door Johnnie" is trying to get a date with Thelma. I become jealous and konk him with a wine bottle. This puts him to "sleep"—and the rest of the picture is what happens in his dreams. He is transported to ancient Greece, still wearing his twentieth century spats, morning coat and striped trousers —while the rest of us wear the costumes of that ancient period. There the triangle continues, with Hercules now defending Venus from dapper, funny little Charlie.

In one particular sequence I was to pursue Charlie in a chariot, driving my horses at breakneck speed. As I was about to overtake him my chariot wheels were to come off, throwing me out into the street. The scene would be very funny but very dangerous to do. No one could predict exactly when the wheels would come off or into what obstacles I might crash when they did. Furthermore, I was unable to strap

Top: El Brendel
Bottom: A light moment with beautiful Thelma Todd.

As Hercules, I called to "Friends, Romans and Extras", while Thelma Todd comforted a dazed Charlie Murray.

myself up properly because of the scantiness of the Grecian costume. I could be badly hurt . . . but that wasn't what bothered me . . . I was used to being hurt.

My problem was that it was late in the afternoon when the director, Eddie Cline, came to this scene in his shooting schedule—and I had other plans. I was doing professional wrestling, on the side, and had a bout scheduled at the Los Angeles Coliseum for that night. As my contract didn't permit me to wrestle, I had to get out of this scene without telling Eddie WHY.

Doing the scene would not only make me late for the wrestling match, but I might sprain an ankle or even break some bones . . . and the spectators were going to be there—my opponent was going to be there—and with some thousands of dollars involved I **had** to be there . . . and in good condition. I confided in Thelma.

"What can I tell Eddie?" I asked her. "Even if the scene goes fast I can't take a chance on getting hurt today. Tomorrow, all right—but not today!"

Thelma rolled her beautiful eyes and puckered her alabaster forehead, but couldn't suggest any-thing.

When we came to the scene I said, "Let's shoot this one tomorrow, Eddie . . . I've got an upset stomach."

"Yeah?" he said, "That's nothing to what you'll have upset when that chariot turns over."

"But the horses have been working all day—they'll run faster tomorrow." But Eddie wasn't buying it.

"They'll run fast enough right now to bounce **you** out on your noggin. Now come on, let's go! Time's a wastin'."

"But I'm liable to get hurt."

I knew that was the wrong thing to say, but I was desperate.

"You're liable to WHAT?" he exploded. "I thought you were a great stuntman! Now get in that chariot and no more excuses!"

But I wasn't going to drive that chariot no matter **what** he thought of me. I just stood there, a big, hulking, cowardly Hercules. Finally Thelma blurted out, "Joe has to wrestle tonight, Eddie, and can't take a chance on getting hurt."

"Oh, boy," I thought,—"now I'm **really** in

for it.''

"He has to wrestle?" Cline shouted. Then he began to laugh.

"Well, why didn't you say so? To heck with the picture . . . let's all knock off and go down and see the bout."

Some directors are "sweethearts"—and that went double for Eddie Cline.

To me, wrestling has always been an excellent form of muscle building and exercise . . . and, interspersed with my movie chores, I did a lot of it. While with Universal I wrestled under the pseudonym of "Joe Atlas," borrowed from my friend Charles Atlas. My contract forbade any outside activities which might hurt me, either physically or professionally, but as long as I didn't use the Bonomo name, they closed their eyes indulgently, PROVIDED I won my bouts. But they had spent many thousands of dollars publicizing me as "The Hercules of the Screen"

and "The World's Most Perfect Strong Man," and to be out-wrestled would have knocked that into a cocked hat. I just didn't DARE lose!

When I wrestled locally I might as well have used my own name, because everyone knew who I was . . . but it was sort of a little game we were playing. I was wrestling about twice a month and making big money at it, and as long as I kept winning, it wasn't hurting the studio. Besides, it kept me happy and in top condition. Those wrestling bouts are great "workouts."

I remember, for example, wrestling one hot summer night, in Phoenix, Arizona. The temperature must have been around a hundred and twenty. When the bout, which lasted an hour, was over—I had lost fourteen pounds.

Because of my reputation, I always had to be the "hero." My opponent might use every dirty trick, but I had to wrestle in good, clean, All-American fashion. My opponent was usually

Charlie challenges the champion.

Gorgeous Thelma Todd was the ideal choice for the title role in VAMPING VENUS.

a top-name "pro," who wrestled several times a week, while I had only a couple of bouts a month . . . but being the "hero" I always had to carry the fight to him and keep working, hustling every minute I was in there. After an hour of that sort of thing I was about ready to hang on the line.

One of the most amusing bouts I ever had was against Buck Olsen, the Swedish champion, in Kansas City. The bout wasn't amusing but the sequel was. Olsen was an exceptionally strong wrestler who had given the great Gus Sonnenberg one of the toughest matches of his career. This was one the crowd expected me to lose, and when I looked at the huge Olsen, as he bounced into the ring, I wasn't sure but what they were right. He was as tough an adversary as I had ever tangled with, but it must have been my lucky night. To everyone's surprise, including my own, I pinned him to the mat with my spec-

ialty, a terrific body slam, in slightly over twelve minutes.

The amusing sequel was the account of the event, in the Kansas City Times, the following day—which was picked up by many newspapers in the East. That's how Papa happened to see it. It appeared as follows:

CANDY BEATS VITAMIN D

Doctors Get Surprise at Wrestling Match

A strongman who was reared on jelly beans and all-day suckers triumphed last night in a wrestling match with the champion of Sweden, who was reared on cod liver oil.

The victory of the carbohydrate consumer was a distinct surprise to the dozens of delegates to the fall meeting

231

VAMPING VENUS kept me hopping in its jumps back and forth between the modern and ancient eras.

of the Kansas City Southwest Clinical Society who attended the wrestling exhibition . . . The downfall of the Swede, Buck Olsen, all but ruined the doctors' holiday. They had considered it almost axiomatic that a cod-liver oil consumer was superior physically to persons who reached for a sweet instead of a vitamin. And here the whole thing had been disproved in one fall. Joe Bonomo, the candy eater, had conquered.

Viosterol and cod liver oil manufacturers could not hush Mr. Bonomo's dangerous boast with any number of free samples.

"I was brought up on candy from Papa's candy factory," the movie Serial King said in the dressing room after the bout, as he flexed his terrible biceps. "Jelly beans, Turkish taffy, licorice whips, jawbreakers and chocolates made a strongman of me. I used to be an anemic little boy —now look at me. I can tie an iron bar

around my forearm like a ribbon—I can dive over six chairs in a row and light on my back and shoulders on a concrete floor—and I can do a few other things that you can't get out of a cod liver oil bottle."

The article may not have advanced my professional reputation much, but Papa always said it doubled his candy business. Papa was smart. I'm sure if I'd lost that match, he'd have put in a sideline of Cod Liver Oil.

Then one of the worst scourges in wrestling history caused me to retire from the game. This was Trachoma, the dreaded eye disease.

No one seems to know where Trachoma came from. The popular belief that it came from India may or may not be true. No one was even sure just what it was, except it was something like an aggravated case of "pink-eye". But Trachoma could not be cured. Once infected, a victim could do nothing but wait until it disappeared—or blinded him. Strangler Lewis was one of those forced into retirement by this frightful disease which almost cost him his sight. I continued to wrestle for a while, but took every precaution, rinsing my eyes for twenty minutes before and after every bout. But when others, who had taken the same precautions, came down with it—I figured I was tempting Fate and retired from competition.

At the time of my retirement I had had more than a hundred professional bouts, against some of the best men in the game, without suffering a single defeat.

It just goes to show what jelly beans and jaw breakers will do for you.

As wrestler "Joe Atlas" I had to fight 100% clean to remain an All-American hero.

Chapter #26
WESTERN FURY

Before going too much farther along in the recounting of my career, I'd like to philosophize for a moment on the **early** years when Hollywood was young and so was I. Maybe they're more important anyway inasmuch as my movie career was never destined to reach such heights that it alone might justify a biography. You've probably gathered from the preceding pages that I'm not an unduly modest person, but in all honesty, I feel a mere serial star is hardly a figure to show off to the world as "a man of distinction."

The difference between my life and most others was that, through diligent effort and rigid training, I developed my physical skills to a point where they were in demand by millions—for purposes of entertainment. But what, actually, **WAS** Joe Bonomo the celluloid strongman? Paul Bunyan cleared great forests for the benefit of civilization . . . skinny Egyptian slaves, toiling in their ancient, ant-like ways, built the great pyramids to last through the ages—a tribute to man's colossal strength. But, for all my great muscles I never built anything tangible for future generations to marvel at.

No, let's face it. Joe Bonomo was a strongman and entertainer who, along with thousands of other entertainers, brought a few thrills, a few stimulating moments to the people of his own times . . . in a few years to be forgotten . . . and that's probably as it should be.

My story is merely that of a fellow, willing to put his life on the line that this life we live, so often so drab, might be a bit more exciting. That's show business and I was a showman who could move into the jaws of death and skip around in the mouth of Hell and come back again. I just hope the telling of those "round trips to the brink of eternity" are proving as interesting to the reader as they were to me.

A mean villain of the west in HEROES OF THE WILD.

Perhaps, more than any other art form, the movies have been the chief entertainment and inspiration of America. Millions of people who have never seen a ballet and can enumerate, on the fingers of one hand, the stage plays they have witnessed, have seen hundreds—perhaps thousands—of movies. The more fortunate among us who have read many books, attended the legitimate theatre countless times—who, we might say, have a nodding acquaintance with the best in thought that life has to offer—may still admit that those trips to the movies far outnumber all other vicarious experiences combined. This is American culture. Whether we like it or not, this is the American people—this is America—the land of hot dogs, soda pop, candy bars, chewing gum, pop tunes and the movies. Frankly, all things considered, I like it—and I'm proud of the small part I have played in making our country what it is.

In all the thousands of movies we've seen we have witnessed countless deaths or narrow escapes on the screen and, in most of them, there was a stuntman doing the job. There used to be a slogan—"Behind each thrill you'll find a stunt-man," and it was largely true. I can't tell you ALL the things I did—many I myself have for-gotten—but as I stumble along the road of memory I am trying to give the highlights.

Ever hear a "man bites dog" story? V ever **I** hear one I'm reminded of a... I had with Tornado the dog in the Nat Levine-Mascot serial HEROES OF THE WILD. This film was made in 1927, after I left Universal, and starred my good friend Jack Hoxie. I knew the dog well—had played in many scenes with him and we had become good friends. He was intelligent, obedient and as camera-wise as any actor I ever met.

In a certain episode I was playing a villainous character who was out to revenge some fancied wrong by kidnapping the rancher's baby. I approached the ranch-house in the dead of night, noiselessly opened the bedroom window, lifted the baby from its crib and was making off with it when Tornado who had been watching me from the barn loft where he slept, made a spectacular leap to the ground and attacked. I dropped the baby, (a dummy of course), and drew a hunting knife from my belt. Before I could use it the great dog sank his teeth into my arm and bore me to the ground.

Now according to the script he sank his teeth into the protective arm-pad I was wearing, but

Anything went in those old serial fights with Jack Hoxie—even a heel to the villain's chin.

whoever constructed it had miscalculated, for those teeth went right through the pad and buried themselves in my fore-arm, inflicting a wound the scars of which I carry to this day. As I felt his teeth sink into my flesh I let out a yell and jerked my arm to shake him off. The yell had my mouth open and the jerk threw him into the air in a sort of spiral twist that drove his nose into direct contact with the edge of my upper teeth. I'm sure I didn't bite him but the effect was the same, opening a two inch gash across his nose. With a yelp of surprise and pain he released his hold on my arm and took off across the barnyard, yelping all the way—and no amount of coaxing or persuasion could get him to return to complete the scene.

We had to finish it with a French dog who didn't understand a word of English and the cameras were held up for more than an hour until we could find his French trainer who was the only one who could make him understand what was wanted of him. This time I had a double pad put on **both** arms, for I didn't speak a word of French, and if he happened to make a mistake I didn't even know how to holler "Uncle!" so he'd understand me.

As for Tornado—he never trusted me again and would never work in another scene with me.

Hollywood was a strange place in those days—even stranger than it is now. Anything for the

Two of the many moods of adventure in Nat Levine's HEROES OF THE WILD.

Jack Hoxie was a solid citizen and we both knew we'd had it after filming our big barroom brawl.

picture! If a man was seriously hurt . . . or even killed, it was all in the day's work. They would stop the wheels just long enough to carry him out—then the magic cry of "Camera!!" would ring out again. The audiences of millions were insatiable—and there was an increasing demand for more realism—for new and more risky stunts. To give you an idea of what I mean:

We were shooting the Mascot serial THE GOLDEN STALLION with Harry Webb directing.

I was playing the villain with a five days growth of beard and a menacing scowl. In a certain scene I was to take a club and drive away the hero's horse, so said hero couldn't make his getaway. Then my henchmen and I were to surround the cabin and shoot it up. The fact that we were next to a very long, steep hill, practically a cliff, didn't enter my mind.

I picked up the club and started toward the horse. And then I got a surprise! Instead of turning and running, as he was supposed to do, the horse neighed, whinnied angrily, reared up on his hind legs and gave every indication of coming down on me with his sharp front hooves, which could have easily crushed my skull.

Instinctively I dodged aside, right to the edge of the cliff. As I did a couple of feet of earth suddenly crumbled under my weight. I teetered for a moment, arms waving, trying to regain my balance, swinging the club about my head, menacingly, hoping to at least frighten the horse into keeping his distance. But it just seemed to further enrage him. He suddenly charged me again, reared with his hooves flailing the air, obviously intent upon trampling me into lifeless pulp. I remembered the cliff wasn't a sheer drop, but more a steep hill, and with that crazed beast coming at me I had no time for compromise. Over and down I went!

The hill was covered with loose pebbles, and I went sliding down on my back, skinning the seat off my trousers and the skin off what was **under** my trousers. I had a long way to go but I figured I could make it in one piece, if I could keep my speed down. I still had the club, so I used it as a brake, while digging my heels into the dirt whenever I could. I was losing more skin, here and there, but at least I had gotten away from that horse.

Just then I felt a shower of pebbles from above. You can imagine my consternation when I looked around to find myself staring into that horse's face—his eyes wild and his lips peeled back! He had followed me over the edge and was tobogganing down the hill after me. He looked as though he'd bite my ears off if he could, and he was only a few feet behind me.

Now instead of trying to brake myself, all I could think of was how to pick up a little more speed! Whenever my feet would hit something half-way solid, I'd twist my body forward and jump as far as I could. Then I'd land again—

As the villainous Garth, I tried to destroy THE GOLDEN STALLION. The gent behind me in the Mountie hat is not a young Gary Cooper, but Maurice "Lefty" Flynn, the former football star.

JOE BONOMO—BADMAN
IN
"The GOLDEN
STALLION"
WITH
WHITE FURY

THE GOLDEN STALLION bears down on Tom
London, Lefty Flynn and myself.

A surprise change in the script as the wild horse sends me down a steep cliff.

Episode Ten
THE LOST TREASURE

Garth enters the burning shack and rescues Joan. He then orders La Roux to free the mare but to leave the Stallion to die. Garth seizes Joan just as Kendall is spied coming on. As Kendall dashes into the burning shack calling for Joan, La Roux follows and locks the door. As Kendall gropes about he accidentally releases a trap spring in the floor—reaches an opening and hurries to the Stallion, doomed to die, in the stable. He frees the Stallion and mounts him, the first man ever to do it. The Stallion runs furiously after Garth and the captive Joan.

Garth is furious now and tells them he will make them walk the plank at the edge of a precipice if the wampum belt's secret is not read. At the precipice edge, Black Eagle turns to Joan for her final opinion. She is willing to have the secret made known to Garth, if it means the saving of Black Eagle's life. Kendall "steams up" into the group and engages in the toughest bout ever with Garth. The Stallion owes a debt to Kendall and sees his chance to repay, when Garth is about to put a finish to Kendall. The Stallion rears and pounces on the attacking Garth—who falls over the edge of the precipice. La Roux's fate is the same.

Black Eagle discloses the great secret and untold wealth lays in store for Joan and Kendall.

and jump again. But despite my jumping-bean tactics, that darned horse stayed right behind me.

Then, from the top of the cliff, I heard someone shout, "Drop the club! Drop the club!"

By this time I was ready to listen to any suggestions at all, and since I had no further use for the club, I flung it back over my head, hoping a lucky hit might discourage my equine Nemesis. But if I scored it didn't register. Down we both went and the bottom of the hill was getting awfully close . . . and I knew if that big horse landed on me at the bottom, I'd wind up like a fly under a swatter!

So about six feet from the hill's end I dug my heels in hard and went into a diving somersault, twisting and rolling off to one side, just as the horse slid by me in a straight line. Thank Heaven a horse can't somersault!

Without a backward glance I rolled to my feet and lit out for a clump of trees nearby, expecting at any moment to feel sharp hooves in my back. But when at length I **did** look around, there was the horse shaking himself, and walking around for all the world like a happy young colt in a pasture.

And from the top of the cliff, Harry Webb was shouting down, "Good work, Joe! Great—great! This'll make history!" And everyone was lined up along the cliff's edge—cameramen, prop boys, costume people, everybody applauding.

After I had climbed back to the top again, with that horse utterly ignoring me, I got the answer. He had been trained to go into action against anyone with a club in his hand. When you picked up a club it was his cue to go to work. When you dropped it, that was his cue that the scene was finished. It seemed everybody knew but me, and they had purposely maneuvered me next to the cliff and told me to pick up the club, knowing what would happen.

I was pretty sore inside, (to say nothing of my backside) but as everyone was getting such a kick out of it, and as they immediately replaced my pants, I went philosophical. And as it turned out, it was one of the most realistic scenes I ever made. After the serial was released, Webb said, "I've got to admit you're a good actor, Joe. The audiences think you really WERE scared."

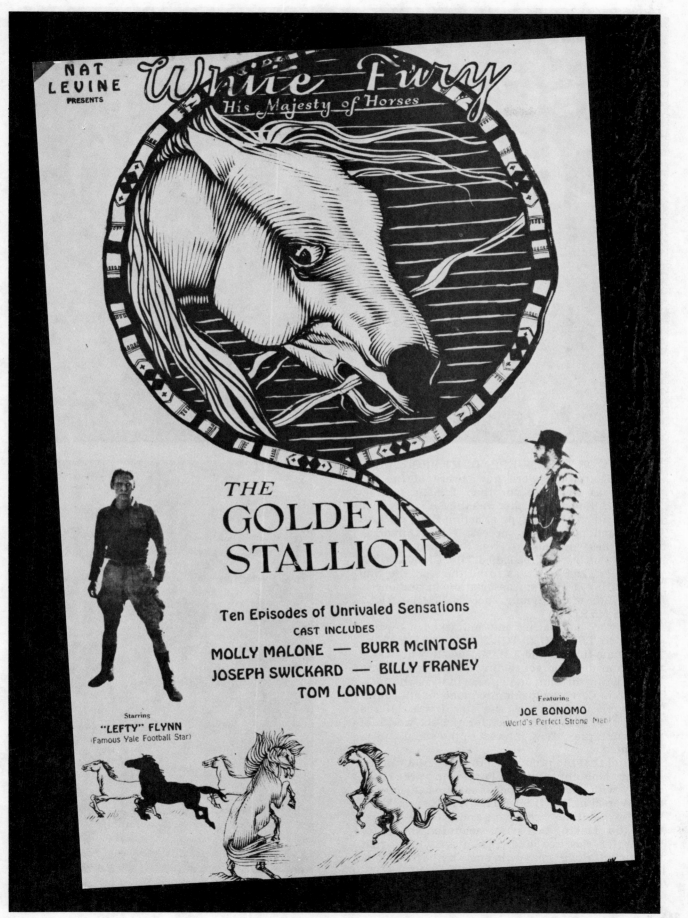

243

Chapter #27
A SECRET AGENT in CHINATOWN

MANY OF THE INDEPENDENT PRODUCERS in Hollywood were now aware of the fact that I was available for their films as a free-lance performer. Since this was the case, they tried to come up with the type of action-filled pictures which had proven so successful for Universal. One of these producers, Trem Carr, had plans for a serial which would be called THE CHINATOWN MYSTERY, and as I was to be the star, the film would bring an instant association in audiences' minds with my previous success, THE GREAT CIRCUS MYSTERY.

Trem Carr approached me and asked if I would like to do THE CHINATOWN MYSTERY for him. He told me that he had J.P. McGowan, who was a top action director, set to direct, and Francis Ford set to write the film and appear in it as the master villain. Carr was looking to make an all around "package" deal, and as the star I was offered a salary of $1250 per week for the six weeks of production plus a 25% interest in the serial, which I accepted.

I found that the production of this serial worked out very smoothly. Francis Ford, who worked very closely with J.P. McGowan, had directed me out at Universal in PERILS OF THE WILD, so he knew what my abilities were and knew all my limitations too. Making this serial meant long hours together for the cast and crew. It was lucky that we all got along well with one another and this friendly spirit helped get THE CHINATOWN MYSTERY finished on schedule.

Little Billy Ford, who played a leading role in

Using an old reliable trick to capture Francis Ford in THE CHINATOWN MYSTERY.

Paul Malvern and I developed quite a few new fight routines for THE CHINATOWN MYSTERY, and we really went to town with them—especially when I threw Paul from the top of a train, knocking Al Baffert off the side of the engine.

In a serial a quick change of plot could take you from modern Chinatown to the old Wild West.

that serial, was actually the son of Francis Ford. He was a real trouper and together with Ruth Hiatt, who was my leading lady, went through numerous fight scenes and train and car chases. Since I had an interest in the picture I felt that the fight scenes and chases should be as exciting as it was humanly possible to make them. I remember one sequence where I threw Paul Malvern (who was playing one of the heavies) bodily at wrestler Al Baffert. In that shot they both fell out of the camera's field of view into a breakaway canvas rigging filled with straw. This was set up with a net on top which the boys fell into. After that was filmed another shot was made of them landing on the ground. This was later cut in to complete the sequence.

THE CHINATOWN MYSTERY was set in Chinatown and featured many beautiful sets and furnishings. But, strange as it may sound, in this very same serial we also had a few chapters which

Trem Carr had a knack for making successful action pictures and eventually helped Paul Malvern rise from stuntman to producer.

took place out West, and I played a type of cowboy hero. The old saying used to be—"**When in doubt use a good horse chase and horseback fighting outdoors!**" While this proved very effective for the audience, it also saved the producer the cost of set construction in the studio.

THE CHINATOWN MYSTERY played to audiences all around the world, but as far as my 25% goes, I never received a penny in cash or an accounting of any kind. More recently, when I acquired ownership of THE CHINATOWN MYSTERY, I felt that after all those years I was finally being paid.

As the film **did** go over well when it was first released, Trem Carr wanted to rush me right into another serial, but now I wanted to do only feature pictures. Doug Fairbanks had the right idea

A gate crasher at the "House of Mystery" I prepare to leap into battle against henchman Paul Malvern (left). My attempts to solve THE CHINATOWN MYSTERY continue on the next few pages—

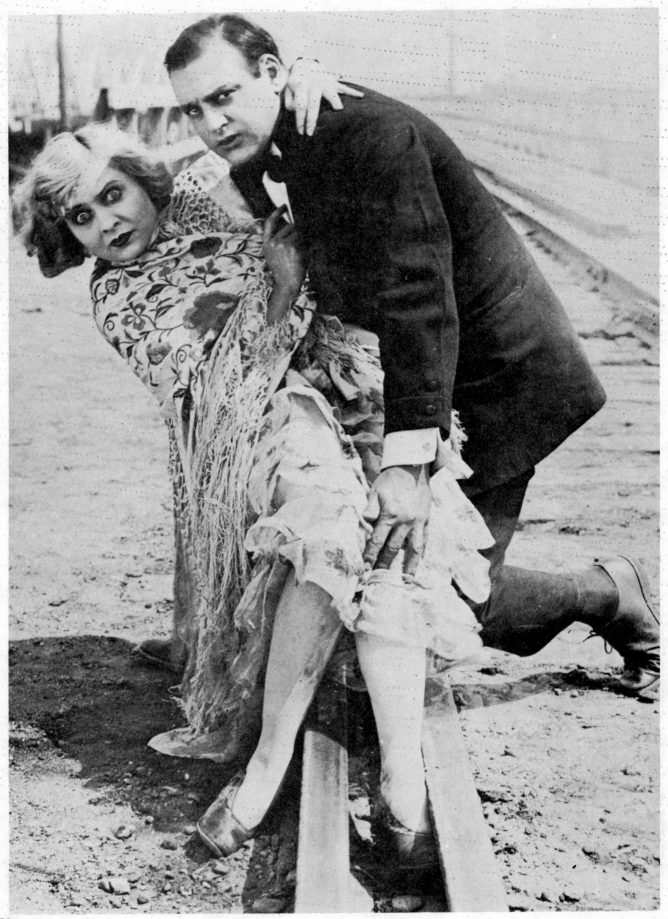

THE STORY

is the Mysterious Order of Thirteen, of which little is known—at least little that is good can be said of them.

Many miles away in Chinatown—shadowy—mysterious—ever interesting Chinatown, we find the home of Lee Chang. Chang is a big power in Chinatown, but a trustworthy, honest character, beloved by all who know him.

A mysterious visitor calls who is identified as Caleb Warren, an American professor of Chemistry at Hong Kong, China, an acquaintance of Lee Chang in days gone by. He is welcomed at the Chang home which is a pretentious affair, furnished in the best of Chinese furniture, rugs and ornaments. Chang thanks Warren for the great charity work he has accomplished among the suffering in China and in return for it presents to him a beautiful piece of priceless jade on which is engraved a secret of great value—in fact worth millions to the owner who can carry out the instructions contained thereon. As he receives it, footsteps are heard approaching from behind him and before the jade can be secreted the lights go out, Professor Warren is shot and the jade is missing, that is, all except a piece that remains clasped in the tight hand of the dead professor. His daughter Sally arrives too late to speak to her father, and Chang asks her to go to his lawyer who will help her solve the mystery of the secret jade.

At the council table of Thirteen two henchmen arrive with the other two pieces of jade but it is useless without the missing part. "The Sphinx"—the leader of the band—is furious and orders it located at once.

Joe, an instructor in athletics, temporarily out of work, is posing for an artist for a painting of "The Gladiator". With him is his adopted pal, little Billy, a Coogan type, a little street urchin of seven and Joe's constant companion. Joe looks out of the window and sees across the court Sally entering the attorney's office. He is attracted by her beauty and cannot keep his eyes from straying in her direction. He sees the attorney reading the instructions from Lee Chang and removes from his safe a paper containing the translation of the message. He tells Sally to memorize it and it is well that he does for as she has finished reading it two slinking figures approach her from the doorway. She hurriedly throws the paper into the fireplace and it goes up in smoke.

Joe seeing this from the window opposite. He quickly routs the villains and is thanked by Sally. The attorney urges Sally to immediately rush to Washington and file the contents of the secret message in the Records. Joe volunteers to do it for her, and leaves to take care of it. On the train, to which he has been pursued by the henchmen, he is attacked. Sally in the meantime to throw the conspirators off Joe's trail has followed in her car, driven by Coco, a comical colored chauffeur. She also finds herself in the hands of the conspirators who are insistent on locating the missing jade.

The engineer and firemen turn to watch the battle between Joe and the conspirators, and in doing so overlook entirely a block signal set against their train, so the Washington Limited dashes madly along the track, while the New York Express is also thundering along the same track running toward them—a slight curve in the road at this point prevents the engineer of the Express from seeing the danger before them. The battle between Joe and the conspirators is becoming furious when a sudden, maddening crash puts it to an end. The Limited and the Express have met in a head-on collision. What a finish for an episode of a serial!

(This is the story of Episode One only.)

In the following chapters, which are filled with not only suspense, mystery and action, but also comedy, we follow the adventures of Sally and Joe in their attempts to solve the mystery of the jade, ever frustrated by the clever master mind—The Sphinx. Mysterious rooms, sliding panels, trap doors, all tend to make their task a difficult one, but the powerful giant Joe gives them many a thrilling battle.

Billy, the little pal of Joe, ever yelling at critical moments "What about some eats?" does not appreciate the seriousness of the situations in which his buddy Joe often finds himself, yet at many times he is a valuable assistant in frustrating the attempts of the conspirators to do Joe harm. Coco, the colored chauffeur for Miss Sally, furnishes many a laugh at most serious moments, and so the serial goes along for ten thrilling, mysterious episodes, with your fans laughing one minute, crying the next, and at all times thrilled and hanging onto the edge of their seats for the next episode to be told. We cannot tell more of the story here in this synopsis, for the reason that it would give away the answers to certain of the questions to be asked those who are interested in following up the thrilling "WHO?" contest arranged by Bonomo.

Francis Ford dreamed up an oriental mystery with all the intrigues of old Chinatown and the film was eventually promoted to the hilt.

A KNOCKOUT NOVELTY HERALD!

The greatest Herald ever prepared for any Serialplay. Obtainable at a price so reasonable you can use them in tremendous quantities. They come packed in lots of 1,000. Use them BIG; they'll bring BIG returns.

Rules For "Who" Contest—Any Boy or Girl Is Eligible to enter.

To the one answering correctly the greatest number of the "WHO" questions, Bonomo will give FREE his three-month course in Physical Culture. With the "CHINATOWN MYSTERY" Serial Bonomo will give away over 100 of his courses in Physical Culture, and also thousands of large Autographed Photographs of himself. Every Boy or Girl filling in the Coupon and sending it to Bonomo at the address given will receive FREE one of his Autographed Photos.

They will also receive a Bonomo Button, a letter telling them how to form a Bonomo Club, and FREE advice on Health and Physical Culture. Every Boy and Girl winning one of the 100 first prizes will be qualified to enter the FREE TRIP TO HOLLYWOOD Contest, meet Picture Stars, have a screen Test taken —all at Bonomo's expense.

HOW TO ENTER THE "WHO" CONTEST. First, you must see the first five episodes of the "CHINATOWN MYSTERY," and then answer the "WHO" questions; the Boys and Girls answering correctly most or all of the questions will then receive FREE the Bonomo Course in Physical Culture.

All winners will also have a chance in the FREE TRIP TO HOLLYWOOD Contest.

Don't Fail to See
JOE BONOMO
in
"THE CHINATOWN MYSTERY"
At This Theatre

9—Who was Little Billy?

10—What was the "Chinatown Mystery"?

11—Whose was the Voice on the Phone?

12—Who finally solved the mystery?

SAVE THIS FOLDER
AS IT IS VALUABLE IN ANSWERING THE "WHO" QUESTIONS

(No. 2)

WHO?

1—Who is the Clutching Claw?

2—What are the Devil's Dice?

3—Who are the Mysterious Thirteen?

4—Who is the Thirteenth Man?

5—What was on the Broken Jade?

6—Was Lee Chang Friend or Foe?

7—Who was behind the door?

8—Who killed Sally's father?

9—Who was Little Billy?

10—What was the "Chinatown Mystery"?

11—Whose was the Voice on the Phone?

12—Who finally solved the mystery?

SAVE THIS FOLDER
AS IT IS VALUABLE IN ANSWERING THE "WHO" QUESTIONS

OATH OF HONESTY

I hereby pledge on my word of honor that I have not seen more than the first five episodes of "THE CHINATOWN MYSTERY" before answering the 12 "WHO" questions printed on this folder:

Signed .... Address ....

(Over)

(No. 1)

CAN YOU ANSWER CORRECTLY THE 12 QUESTIONS ABOUT

"THE CHINATOWN MYSTERY"

If so you can win a 3-months Physical Culture Course—from the Bonomo Institute of Physical Culture—and also be qualified to enter the FREE TRIP TO HOLLYWOOD Contest.

DO YOU WANT AN AUTOGRAPHED PHOTO OF JOE BONOMO?

Do You Want to Form a Bonomo Boy's Club? Each Boy Joining the Bonomo Clubs Gets One of the Membership Buttons FREE!

See JOE BONOMO in his new serial play—10 Thrilling, Mysterious Episodes—Two Big Reels Each Week—Something new to the screen. The World's Strongest Human in new and Daring Death Defying Feats of Strength. Don't miss "THE CHINATOWN MYSTERY"

USE THIS BLANK IN ENTERING THIS CONTEST

JOE BONOMO,
Box M 100,
Hollywood, California

Theatre at which you saw
"CHINATOWN MYSTERY"

☐ Enter me in the "WHO" Contest. Herewith find my answers
☐ Send me an autographed photo of Joe Bonomo
☐ Send me literature on forming a Bonomo Club
☐ Send me a Bonomo Button

Age .... Name ....

Weight .... Address ....

Height .... City .... State ....

(No. 3)

TRIANGLE PRINTING COMPANY, 147 N. 10th Street, Philadelphia, Pa., have prepared a novelty trick-folding herald on "The Chinatown Mystery" that is a wow! Folded it is the size of the standard heralds used on all pictures and you see the Chinese Character as shown in Reproduction No. 2. Turning back the upper half of the herald, we disclose the same design except that the Chinaman is turned into Bonomo, the secret service man, and we see the rules of the "Who" contest being conducted by Bonomo in connection with this Serial (Reproduction No. 1). The back of the herald (reproduction No. 3) when signed entitles the party signing it to an autographed photo of Bonomo, or membership in Bonomo's Boy's Club, etc. A liberal distribution of this herald will build up a great deal of interest in the serial. ORDER THESE FROM TRIANGLE DIRECT.

Above: Sneaking up on one of the heavies, none other than director J.P. McGowan in an unbilled "cameo" role.
Below: Chinatown's undercover ruler, James Leong, and I plot new ways of recovering the "missing jade".

and if he could do it, perhaps **I** could do it. At least I was going to try.

So I retired from serials for a while and started trying to shoulder my way into top features. I knew it would take time, but after all, I didn't need the money. The Bonomo Culture Institute was now a thriving mail-order business.

However, I was never much for just twiddling my thumbs, so while waiting for the right picture offer to come along I contacted Fanchon and Marco, the vaudeville booking agents.

"Certainly we're interested," they said, "that is, if you have the right vehicle."

Well, having **no** vehicle, I sat up for a couple of nights and wrote one. I called it "The Pirate Idea"—and although it was my first serious attempt at writing, they liked it so well they decided to produce it. In a short time it was headlining the stage shows in the biggest movie houses in the West. The audiences never shouted "Author! Author!!!"—but in case they ever should, I had practiced some fancy bows and had my speech all ready.

I also staged the production and engaged four friends of mine, Charlie Schaeffer, Frank Clayton, Jack Nelson and Scotty Lamont—all top acrobatic stuntmen——so the show would have plenty of action. The rest of the cast, including the singers and a singing and dancing girl chorus, were selected by Fanchon and Marco. Gay Foster, their choreographer, (later head choreographer at the famous Roxy theatre in New York), staged the dance numbers. Fanchon and Marco financed the production and paid all salaries, including my $1250 a week.

I tried to get Ethel to join the act but she bowed out, suggesting I use that pretty nurse from the Universal hospital who was so **crazy** about me. Could this be jealousy? My heart skipped a few beats as I looked into her eyes, to

Using a strong-arm approach with Al Baffert.

A leap to a speeding train, a fight for the stolen formula and a porpoise dive to safety.

Joe Bonomo, the strong man of the screen and the holder of many world's championships for feats of strength, has an important role in "Phantoms of the North," which comes to this theatre next week.

How To Score This Picture For Sound

If your theatre is equipped for sound, simply clip out the accompanying musical presentation and take it to your local phonograph dealer, ask him to pick out the necessary records to conform to the action and you've done the trick. This picture can be musically presented on a two turntable device without difficulty, as the scenes are sufficiently long to allow ordinary changes. Try this stunt with "Phantoms of the North." Merely detach your synchronizer from your projector and play the records independently.

This long forgotten silent saga of the northwoods was released in 1929, just as Hollywood was trying to recover from the Wall Street crash and the coming of the "Talkies." The above plan for adding recorded music to the film at the theatre was an attempt to present this picture as a "sound" movie.

BILTMORE PRODUCTIONS, INC.
presents

"PHANTOMS of the NORTH"

DIRECTED BY HARRY WEBB

WITH

EDITH ROBERTS   KATHLEEN KEY
DONALD KEITH   JOSEF SWICKARD
BORIS KARLOFF   JOE BONOMO

and the two pals of the wild

"MURO" *dog marvel*   "ARAB"

DISTRIBUTED BY BILTMORE PRODUCTIONS INC. HOLLYWOOD, CALIFORNIA

PHANTOMS OF THE NORTH was an action picture that prominently starred its animals and adventure angles, while the actors were all given "featured" billing below the title. The chief menaces in this drama of fur smuggling were a then little known Boris Karloff and myself.

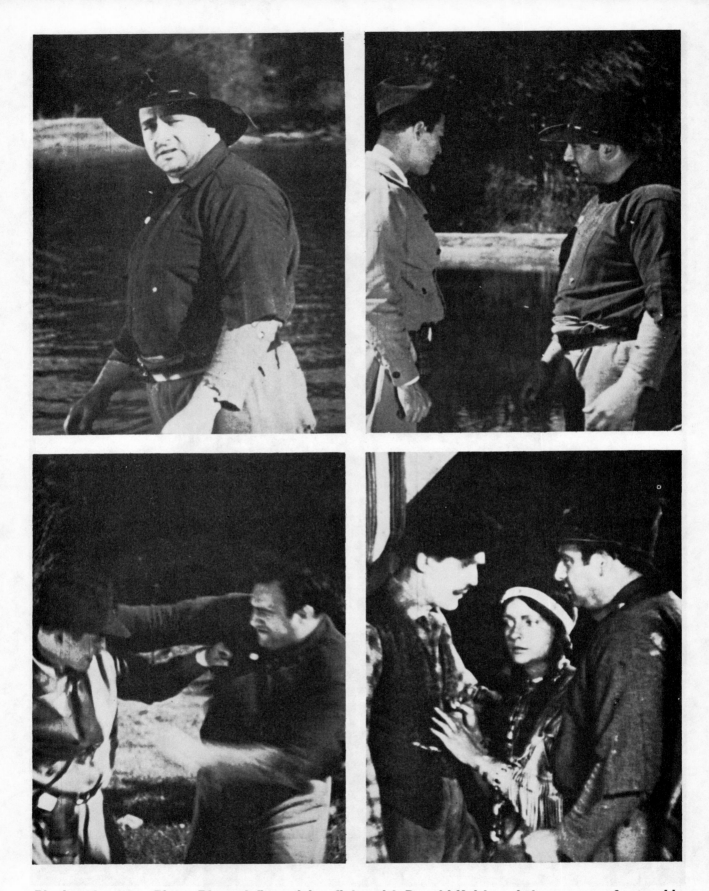

Playing the mean Pierre Blanc, I first pick a fight with Donald Keith and then prepare for trouble with the unscrupulous Jules Gregg (Boris Karloff).

These rare shots of sequences with Boris Karloff and Kathleen Key were enlarged from what is believed to be the only surviving film footage from PHANTOMS OF THE NORTH.

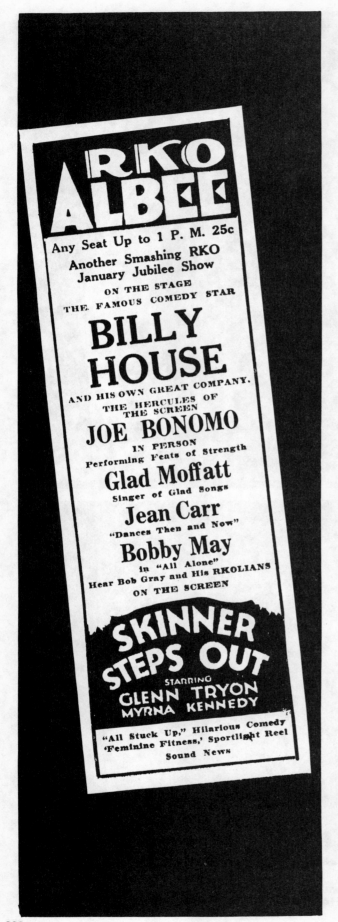
see if they had turned slightly green—but they were never bluer. Who the heck could understand blondes! I wished Papa had raised me in Turkey where they didn't **have** any!

As the act opened, the scene was laid on the deck of an eighteenth century merchant vessel, sailing along the coast of Spain . . . with a couple of singers doing some operatic bragging about the cargo of Spanish gold on board. As they hit their high notes, the audience perceives another ship approaching, flying a Skull and Cross Bones at the masthead. And who should be standing on the foredeck, wearing a pirate costume and an ominous grin, but Buccaneer Bonomo himself! . . . surrounded by his blood-thirsty pirate crew. The blood-thirsty crew consisted of two dozen shapely girls in black tights, pirate boots and bandanas—brandishing shiny tin cutlasses as they chanted a pirate song. It was a bit incongruous but it made good viewing for the bald heads in the front row, and nobody ever complained.

As the pirate chant ends our cannon lets loose with a booming broadside and, with a blood-curdling yell, we board the merchant ship. A short, hectic fight ensues and my pirate girls drag everybody off, leaving me alone on the deck. Then, swinging down from the rigging, come five brave sailors to defend their ship. These were Frank, Jack, Scotty, Charlie and a top tumbler called Turk, two of them with cutlasses and the others with knives. Now we go into a rip-roaring fight scene. The cutlasses are electrified so sparks fly out as we cut and parry. I slash one of the sailors on the head and "blood" comes gushing down his face.

I finally shatter their break-away cutlasses, throw mine away, and tackle them hand-to-hand. A savage brawl follows, during which I throw one of them along the deck and into the footlights . . . Pop! Pop! . . . as he smashes two light bulbs. I pick up another and throw him clear **over** the footlights and into a break-away bass drum in the orchestra pit . . . BOOM! There are shouts and cries of pain as they struggle back to the attack. Just then a scream comes from high up in the rigging and the spotlight picks up Charlie, a dagger between his teeth, as he comes hurtling through the air, headfirst, diving at me from aloft. I catch him in mid-air, swing him down between my legs and skid him completely across the stage where he bowls over two of the sailors who both do spectacular falls. Then, as the fight continues, with the "blood" now flowing freely, I knock them all out—one at a time—and toss them overboard into the sea. There is even a geyser like splash of water as each in turn hits the briny. Then, with a villainous laugh, I exit.

Now, on come the pirate girls again, singing the praises of their victorious captain, as they clamber about the rigging. I then return, lugging a huge chest filled with pieces-of-eight, and we do a super-adagio dance during which, in my

In the middle of those hectic vaudeville touring days I managed time for a part in Warners' biblical epic—NOAH'S ARK.

When NOAH'S ARK was filmed they didn't spare the extras!

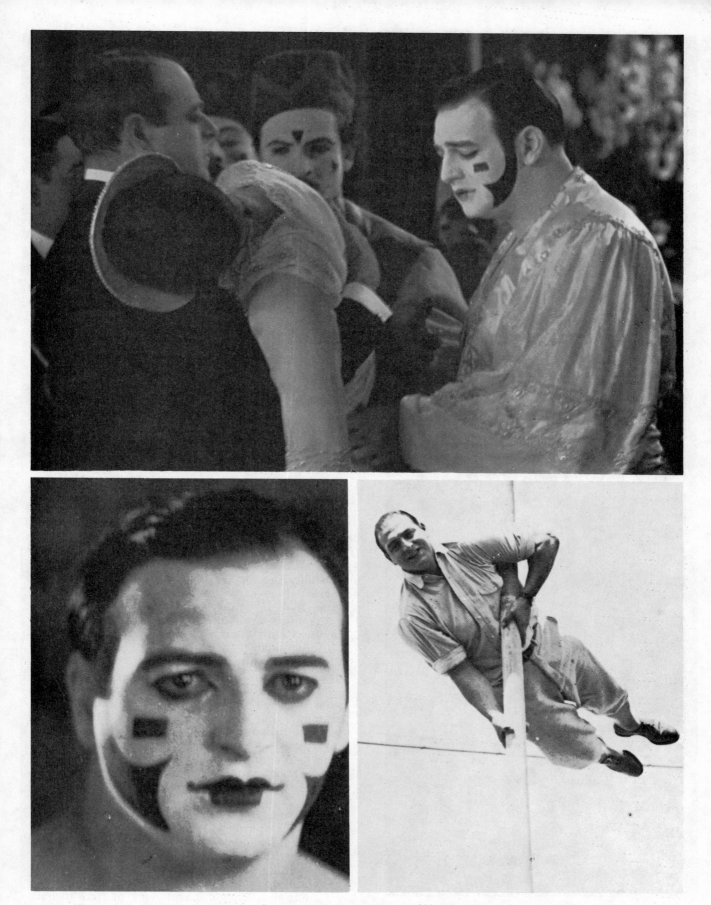

Playing the dramatic role of a sad-faced clown was a great change from action serials, but I always found the time to stay in shape while working on a picture.

On tour with Cecil Whitworth.

glee over my ill-gotten gains, I toss the girls about like Indian Clubs. For a finish, I whirled about the stage to exciting music, with three of the girls suspended in the air from a specially constructed belt I wore.

The act was sensational. The fight scenes were staged with all the viciousness and realism of a movie fight. There were constant screams from the audience and on quite a few occasions, women fainted and had to be carried out.

"The Pirate Idea" got rave reviews and I'm sure we could have played it for a year or two— but after twelve weeks of trying to chaperone those shapely pirates, I hollered "Uncle!" The job of mothering those 24 little beauties was more than Joe Bonomo could handle! Besides, after watching them cavorting around, I couldn't sleep nights wondering what Ethel was doing.

When I got back to Hollywood, I made a bee line for Ethel's **house.** I had to get this thing settled or go out of my mind. I caught her with her hair up in curlers, but she was one girl who could **wear** 'em. She looked more beautiful than I'd ever seen her. I just grabbed her in my arms and blurted out, "I've got to know, Ethel . . . I've got to know right now . . . will you marry me?"

"Of course," she said, pushing me away. "I always **intended** to. I thought you'd never get around to asking me."

What can you do with a girl like that!

"When?" I pleaded, "**When** will you marry me?"

She thought a moment. "The week you play the Palace Theatre in New York."

Where she got **that** I'll never know. I think she was just stalling for time. Although my Pirate act had been a success on the West Coast, the Palace Theatre was the Mecca of all vaudevillians and only the top established headliners ever got there. It was as far out of my reach as the South Pole.

"You can't mean that," I said, "I'm not a **regular** vaudevillian."

"I DO mean it," she said, "the week you play the Palace and that's final. Of course, if you don't want to accept my terms—"

"I accept," I said hastily. At least we were now engaged and that was SOMETHING . . . although that was probably **all** we'd be for the rest of our lives.

I rushed out and bought an engagement ring, with a diamond so large it was vulgar—then wired Mama and Papa I was engaged to the most beautiful dancer in Hollywood. Papa wired back, "A dancer? Come home before it's too late." Then I realized how my wire must have sounded and called them long distance . . . but the harm had been done. Mama wouldn't even come to the phone and all Papa would say was "Come home quick, Joey, and if she sues we'll get you the best lawyer in Coney Island."

I hung up. They'd have loads of time to get to know her and like her, before I ever played the Palace Theatre.

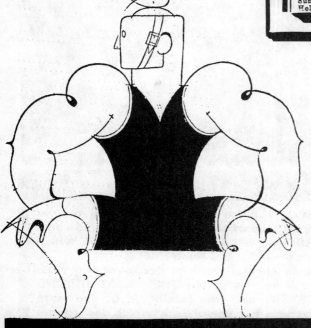

GOLDEN GATE THEATRE

Orpheum Circuit—Golden Gate and Taylor, at Market
VAUDEVILLE — 12:45 — CONTINUOUS — 11:30 — PHOTOPLAY
Always San Francisco's Greatest Continuous Show

NOW PLAYING

ATTRACTION   EXTRAORDINARY

ISHAM JONES

BRUNSWICK RECORDING ORCHESTRA

This Week
A WELL-
BALANCED
BILL OF
UNUSUAL
MERIT AND
EXCEPTIONAL
APPEAL
Attend
THE BARGAIN
MATINEES
ALL
SEATS **30c**
EXCEPT SAT.,
SUN. and HOLS.

PRICES

MATINEES, ALL SEATS Ex. Sat., Sun., 'Hols.	**30c**
Nights ALL Seats **50c**	Sat. Night Sun. & Hol ALL Seats **59c** Plus Tax
Children— Any Seat— Sunday and Holidays	**15c** **25c**

NEAL ABEL
THE MAN WITH THE MOBILE FACE

THE WORLD'S PERFECT
STRONG MAN
BONOMO
THE HERCULES OF THE SCREEN
DIRECT FROM UNIVERSAL CITY

SHELDON & DAILEY
"TOGETHER AGAIN"

CLINTON SISTERS
CARTOONING IN DANCELAND

PERT KELTON

Fables	News	Scenic	Comedy

Claude M. Sweeten's Orchestra

PHOTOPLAY—EXCLUSIVE SHOWING
AGNES AYRES in
"THE AWFUL TRUTH"
with WARNER BAXTER and
PHILLIPS SMALLEY

Above: I returned to Universal as the "strongman of the circus" in Hoot Gibson's COURTIN' WILDCATS, a Western in which Hoot played a shy tenderfoot.
Below: Several years before, Hoot had visited me on the set of THE GREAT CIRCUS MYSTERY and was fascinated by the feats of strength I performed, which led to my playing a similar role in his later film.

Another Universal serial stint as a free lance player—BATTLING WITH BUFFALO BILL. Thanks to my training in tumbling and ability to control my body in motion I always managed to land on top when being jumped off a horse.

Chapter #28
BONOMO PLAYS THE PALACE

T HIS HAS LITTLE TO DO WITH MY STORY, but for those who didn't know the Hollywood of those days, I'd like to go on record as saying that at that time smog was unheard of. We had the occasional earthquake, but that just lent a bit of excitement to the general pattern. I had been urging my agent, Harry Weber, to come out to the coast for a little vacation and, with the ending of the summer heat, Autumn brought not only cooler weather, but also Harry and his charming wife, for a two week stay.

I rolled out the red carpet for them, introduced them to Ethel, and the four of us had a ball. They both liked Ethel immensely and just casually one day Harry asked me when we were planning to marry. I said I was afraid I'd never be able to meet her terms and told him about the ultimatum she had served on me regarding playing the Palace in New York. He laughed, said something about nothing being impossible, and we were soon talking about other things.

The following January, I was almost thrown into a trauma by a telegram from him, asking me how I'd like to open at the Palace in two weeks with my strongman act. How would I like it? Was he kidding? I shot him back a wire and started packing.

I arrived without a "top man" since the one I had used previously had succumbed to the blandishments of the balmy California climate and re-

fused to buck the East in January. But my luck held and I found Arthur Karoli at Bothner's Gym, just recovered from a broken leg and currently available. Arthur was one of the famous Karoli brothers and one of the best high-perch-act men in the business. I made a deal with him and within a half hour we were rehearsing.

That night I strolled over to the Palace Theatre to look over the advance billing and, when I saw the fast company I was going to be in, my heart sank almost to my shoe-tops. I didn't know what strings Harry Weber had pulled to get me in, but these were the headliners that I, with an outdated strongman act, would have to compete with. The then great comedian Phil Baker was doing his famous comedy act and acting as master of ceremonies . . . then came the delightful Ann Pennington . . . Robert Emmett Keane with Claire Whitney and George Sweet, Harry Carroll the songwriter with Maxine Lewis and Eddie Bruce, and that never failing smash hit, Willie, West and McGinty. I was so discouraged I almost called Harry up and cancelled the engagement. What I DID do, after the rehearsal with Karoli the next day, was to take the subway to Coney Island.

No one could feel discouraged after eating one of Mama's famous dinners and, as I pushed back from the table after my second helping of halvah, I got a hot idea. The next day I hunted up Phil Baker and told him about it. Before I'd finished

Issued Weekly to Our Patrons

PROSPECT

Radio-Keith-Orpheum Newsette

REVIEW

9th STREET and 5th AVENUE

Vol. I WEEK OF JANUARY 11th, 1930 No. 75

YOUTH!

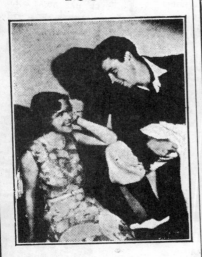

Arthur Lake in "Tanned Legs" with June Clyde

A new slant on the younger generation that will cause many an American parent to both ponder and smile is presented amid dazzling beauty in Radio Picture' "Tanned Legs," scheduled for the screen of this R-K-O theatre.

The screen at last seems to have caught the spirit of twentieth century youth in this effervescent drama which features Ann Pennington, Arthur Lake, Dorothy Revier, Sally Blane, Albert Gran and June Clyde, a refreshingly new and youthful star whose smile and voice promise to carry her far.

Songs, dances, bathing suits and girls are the elements out of which Director Marshall Neilan builds his just-serious-enough drama. There's a thrill or two for variety and enough legs to thrill even a Ziegfeld audience.

BONOMO

The Hercules of the Screen

Seen in "The Iron Man" "The Great Circus Mystery," "The Sea Tiger," "Vamping Venus" and Many Other Pictures

Here in Person

Saturday to Tuesday, January 11, 12, 13 & 14

Turn to Page 2 and Read
BONOMO'S
HEALTH HINTS

IT'S LOVE

"This Thing Called Love," one of Broadway's recent smart comedy hits written by Edwin Burke was, perhaps, one of the most sought for stage productions of the year for motion picture purposes. That the bidding for the rights of this play was very spirited is a matter of history. Pathe, the purchaser of the play, had Constance Bennett, the beautiful blonde star, in mind for the leading role and as a result she is' co-featured with Edmund Lowe, who scored so heavily in "The Cock-Eyed World."

Paul Stein, the Viennese director who has a flare for putting over situations of this kind in a delicate manner, directed the motion picture version of the play which will be seen at this RKO Theatre.

In addition to Constance Bennett and Mr. Lowe, the cast includes Zasu Pitts, Carmelita Geraghty, Ruth Taylor, Roscoe Karns, and John Roche.

BONOMO'S 12 HEALTH HINTS

CONSTANCE
BENNETT

1. Avoid sick people, unless it is your duty to care for them.
2. Drink a lot of water.
3. See that your bowels move at least once every day.
4. Breathe lots of pure, fresh air.
5. Eat regularly, moderately and slowly.
6. Sleep at regular times for 7 or 8 hours.
7. Do not worry.
8. Take lots of exercise. (In accordance with your age and physical condition.)
9. Try to avoid drugs unless prescribed by your physician.
10. Keep clean — physically, mentally and morally.
11. Avoid the bites of insects and vermin.
12. Avoid over-eating, over-drinking and over-smoking.

A chance meeting with Samuel Goldwyn at an Equity dance in New York a few years ago, who recognized in this sixteen-year-old convent girl a personality and a beauty that would mean much to the screen and would carry her far in public esteem, gave her the start she longed for.

Constance succeeded in overcoming parental objection and many were the pictures in which she has appeared on the screen.

Marriage lured her from the screen just as she had achieved stardom, to become the wife of Phil Plant, a wealthy young man who preferred that his wife give up her picture work. During her married life most of her time was spent in her home in Paris, her villas in Biarritz and on the Riviera and traveling throughout Europe.

Then divorce from her husband and her contract with Pathe were responsible for bringing her back to America. Her last Pathe picture appearance was in 'This Thing Called Love.'

BONOMO Will Be On Our Stage Sat. to Tues., January 11, 12, 13, 14

SEE HIM—HE IS THE PERSONIFICATION OF PHYSICAL PERFECTION AND HEALTH

So This is "PARIS"? Yes, the Scene Above is From the Irene Bordoni Picture of That Name

Why You Must See "Paris"—Not the City —Irene's 1st Talk Film

Some of the outstanding scenes of "Paris" are made in Technicolor—the wonderful new process which has finally perfected the art of photography in natural colors.

We see a famous Parisian music-hall during the performance of one of those glittering revues for which the City of Light is so famous. These color effects are not only startlingly realistic—they are utterly beautiful. And in the midst of this chromatic revelation is Bordoni—Bordoni the laughing, the singing, the scintillating—Bordoni at her most inimitable!

She assumes the role of a French actress, a darling of Paris.

"Paris" is an exceptionally clever photoplay. It is saucy and spicy, with a well defined story and it is full of fun.

The dialogue is unusually bright and Miss Bordoni's accent is a delight to the ears.

The supporting cast, including several prominent stage players, is outstanding. Jack Buchanan, famous in London and New York, enacts the chief supporting role of her stage partner. Jason Robards is featured.

Don't miss it. It's as good as a trip to Paris.

From Broadway to you! Here is Vina Delmar's Story "Dance Hall" as it was presented on Broadway — You Will See It Here as One of the January Jubilee Attractions. Arthur Lake, Olive Borden and Joseph Cawthorne are Featured.

THE SIGN OF
A GOOD TIME

ROBERT ARMSTRONG AS "THE RACKETEER" HAS GREAT ROLE

Plays the Part of an Underworld Czar—Ably Supported by Carol Lombard

With Robert Armstrong in the role of the racketeer and Carol Lombard playing the feminine lead, this Pathe production takes its audience into its grip from the opening scene and retains its interest until its highly effective and dramatic finish.

Armstrong is perfectly cast as the racketeer. His suave manner, covering a character that packs dynamite in every swift, dangerous move, keeps the audience on edge with suspense, wondering what will happen next. Yet, the romantic side of his character inspires the hope that he will get the breaks.

Carol Lombard, as the girl who is torn between the love of a dissipated musician and gratitude for this smartly dressed wolf of the underworld, is said to give her finest performance to date. Others in the cast, all of whom acquit themselves as sterling actors are Roland Drew, as the musician; Kit Guard as the racketeer's right hand man; Hedda Hopper, as a society woman; Al Hill, a gangster chauffeur; Jeanette Loff as a society flapper; Paul Hurst as a flapper and John Loder as a rich idler.

he was laughing hard. Sure—he'd be glad to work through my act—and this is how we arranged it.

Preceding my three minute trailer, Phil entered lugging my ''props'' consisting of a telephone book, a long heavy steel chain and a six foot strip of strap-iron. He came on muttering his dissatisfaction over the preposterous business of having a strongman playing on the bill with a star-studded array of talented artists. His grumbled ad libbing went something like this:

''The Hercules of the Screen? Phoney! World's strongest man? PHOOEY!! . . . I've seen some dumb tricks in my time, but where does the booking office get off, putting a gorilla on the stage! If people want to see a gorilla they can go to the Bronx Zoo. Well, I'll show that ape! See this sheet of metal? Bonomo's going to tear up a telephone book? Hah! That's what **he** thinks!'' Saying which he slips the metal sheet between the pages of the book.

''And he's going to snap this chain, eh? And bend this strap-iron into a pretzel, is he? Well, wait'll he sees the surprises I've got for him! So **I didn't** eat spinach on my Wheaties when I was a kid—but I've got the BRAINS!''

Because he was smaller than I the audience began to identify themselves with him. Sure, these big apes were strong, but brains were better than brawn. We'd show Joe Bonomo up, but good—make a dope out of him!

After the trailer I entered, wearing a Tuxedo, and bowed to the audience—and you'd be amazed at the cold reception I got. Things were working out just right! As I bowed again, Phil leaned against the proscenium, with his arms folded, delivering sneering ''asides'' to the patrons—and they howled.

''I will now divide the population of Greater New York, by tearing this huge telephone book in two,'' I announced. Phil smirked and the audience chuckled in expectation. I tugged at the phone book until I was gasping for breath but naturally, with the sheet of metal in there I couldn't make an impression on it. The audience roared. Defeated, I mumbled an embarrassed apology and tossed it aside. The sheet of metal fell out with a clatter. I looked at Phil just in time to see him sneak off. I angrily picked up the phone book and tore it into paper snow.

''I will now snap a chain tested to the breaking strength of six hundred pounds,'' I announced. Supposedly unknown to me, Phil had brought in a trick chain, the links of which were merely held together by black thread. He held up his hand. ''Hold it, Muscle Man,'' he said, ''anybody can do that.'' And taking the chain he snapped it into a half dozen pieces while the audience howled again.

I pretended to be flabbergasted—this guy was ruining my act!

''I will now bend this six-foot length of strap-iron into a pretzel,'' I announced. As I prepared to do the bending, out from the wings came Phil, tottering under the weight of a huge length of

Phil Baker—in a mischievous mood.

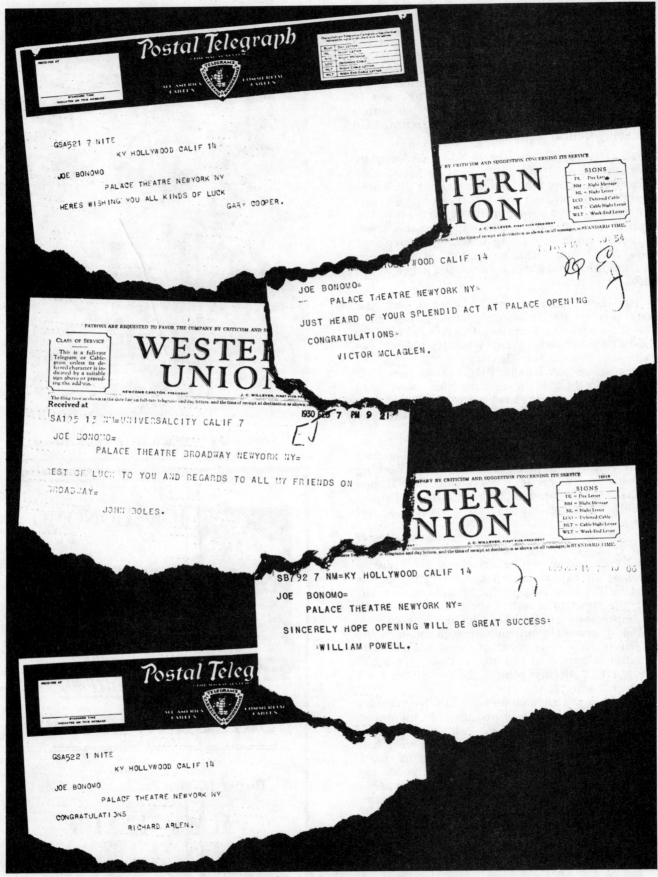

Postal Telegraph

GSA521 7 NITE
    KY HOLLYWOOD CALIF 14

JOE BONOMO
    PALACE THEATRE NEWYORK NY

HERES WISHING YOU ALL KINDS OF LUCK
               GARY COOPER.

WESTERN UNION

JOE BONOMO=
    PALACE THEATRE NEWYORK NY=

JUST HEARD OF YOUR SPLENDID ACT AT PALACE OPENING

CONGRATULATIONS=
         VICTOR MCLAGLEN.

WESTERN UNION

SA125 12 NM=UNIVERSALCITY CALIF 7

JOE BONOMO=
    PALACE THEATRE BROADWAY NEWYORK NY=

BEST OF LUCK TO YOU AND REGARDS TO ALL MY FRIENDS ON
BROADWAY=
        JOHN BOLES.

WESTERN UNION

SB792 7 NM=KY HOLLYWOOD CALIF 14

JOE BONOMO=
    PALACE THEATRE NEWYORK NY=

SINCERELY HOPE OPENING WILL BE GREAT SUCCESS=
     =WILLIAM POWELL.

Postal Telegraph

GSA522 1 NITE
    KY HOLLYWOOD CALIF 14

JOE BONOMO
    PALACE THEATRE NEWYORK NY

CONGRATULATIONS
      RICHARD ARLEN.

It felt great to be remembered by some of my many friends in Hollywood when I headlined at the Palace.

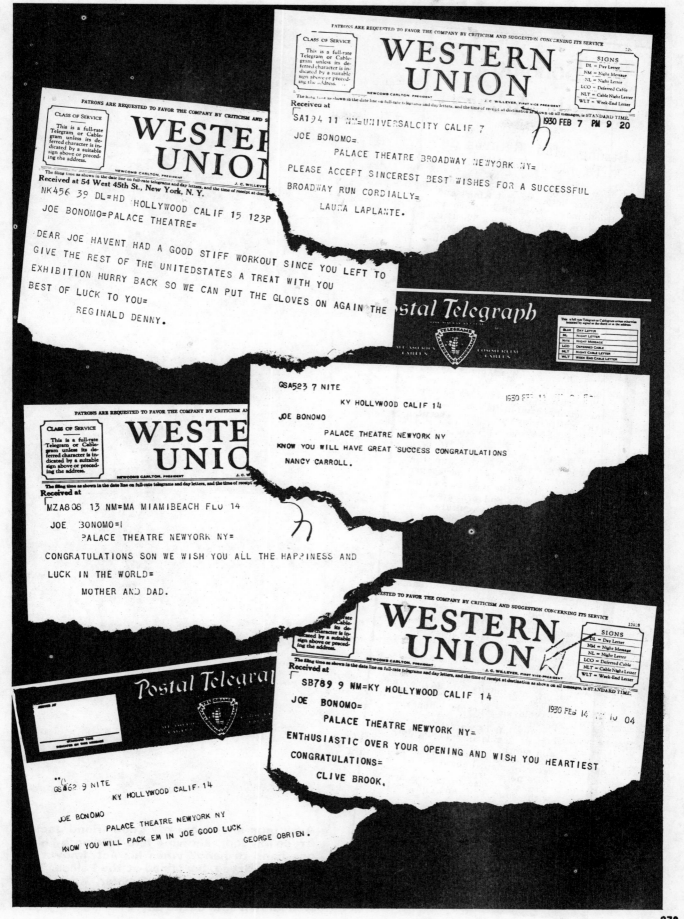

Joe Bonomo's Health Advice

Strong Man Returns to Brooklyn Theatres

Joe Bonomo, motion picture character actor, "Serial King" and strong man, effects his return to Brooklyn, at the Bushwick Theatre, next Wednesday, for a three-day engagement, to be followed with an appearance at the Prospect Theatre for four days. Bonomo, who qualifies as Brooklyn's only professional strong man, is a former athlete of Erasmus High School.

Bonomo was born and raised in Coney Island, where his parents are still engaged in business. He entered Erasmus High in 1919, and was later equally famous as an athlete at the New York Military Academy, in Cornwall, N. Y. His athletic accomplishments take in the entire range of sports except, if it must be told, golf.

His professional career was launched here when he won the title of "Apollo" in a newspaper contest. He is the possessor of innumerable cups and prizes won in popularity, physical culture and health contests, and at present is the head of an extensive correspondence course health school located in Hollywood.

His most recent pictures are "The Chinatown Mystery," "Vamping Venus," "The Sea Tiger," "Noah's Ark," "The Record Breakers" and "Big Time."

Bonomo asserts that excessive weight need not mean excessive clumsiness. He is the possessor of no less than 116 cups won in dance competition.

The rules for health, he declares, are easy. The most important ones can be summed up in a dozen simple statements of advice, as follows:

Avoid sick people whenever possible.

Drink lots of water.

Eat regularly, moderately and slowly.

Sleep at regular times for seven or eight hours.

Do not worry.

Take exercise in accordance with your age and physical condition.

Avoid drugs unless prescribed by a physician.

Keep clean—physically, mentally and morally.

Clean your teeth each morning and night and after meals.

Avoid the bites of insects.

Avoid over-eating, over-drinking and over-smoking.

A vintage shot from my good friend Jackie Bryce (on top), showing him holding a "high one hand to hand" when his act, known as Zarrell & Bryce, headlined at the Palace. The Belclair Bros., Marge & Snyder, Kramer & Patterson and the Dare Bros. were other well known acts of the day.

BONOMO AND BAKER CAVORT AT PALACE

PHIL BAKER is all over the Palace bill again. It's his third week and he's getting better and better each time. And this week, as master of ceremonies, he tries to do a lot of other things besides play his accordion and fire witticisms and what not at that certain party of his in a box. He even tries—only tries—to outdo Joe Bonomo, the screen's handsome Hercules, in the latter's display of strength; a strength that is as graceful as it is powerful. It would take a lot of Phil Bakers to do at one time and with as much ease the stunts Bonomo accomplishes. But because Phil Baker is a comedian, and not a strong man, the result of the two appearing together is a fine comedy situation.

One of the many nice things that can be said about Bonomo is that he probably is the one screen notable who comes to the vaudeville stage showing his audiences exactly the type of entertainment the movies have made him noted for.

Harry Carroll is back in a new revue, the new consisting mostly of one Maxine Lewis and some new settings and a comedian, Eddie Bruce. But Maxine is the little gal that puts the act over big. She has one of the best voices heard hereabouts and knows how to use it to advantage. Mr. Carroll may consider himself in line for credit for having assembled a pretty revue, the type that's just suited for variety.

Vivacious Ann Pennington is doubling between the Palace and the Club Richman for the week. Jack Pettis and a rather good orchestra provide the tunes for Miss Pennington's lively dancing.

Robert Emmett Keane, Claire Whitney and George Sweet amuse in a satire on the so-called wedded bliss. Leslie Strange makes himself resemble to a remarkable degree certain famous figures. The "building blunders" of Willie, West and McGinty are as amusing as ever. Danny Small heads a fast negro act.

Broadway discovers a new song and dance man.

strap-iron, twice the thickness of the one I was using. He let it drop on the stage with a crash.

"Anyone could bend that sliver you've got there, you faker. Let's see what you can do with **this** one!"

I looked at the iron bar—then at the audience—then back to the iron bar. This was impossible. I picked it up and tried to make an impression on it, with Phil ad-libbing all the while. I really sweated over that iron, with the audience convulsed. But you should have heard the burst of applause when, with a sudden mighty heave, I wrapped it around my arm.

But Phil wasn't through yet.

"With the assistance of the famed Arthur Karoli," I announced, "I will now demonstrate how I keep in condition at the studios with my daily dozen." Karoli bounded out, took my hands, and I quickly flipped him up into a high "hand-to-hand." While I had him up, Phil came over and slapped my face a couple of times, hard. He was catching this dumb strongman with his hands full. He then gave me a swift kick in the rear. The audience loved it. I let Arthur drop and turned to face Phil, but he was gone, so I went on with the act. I was now on the floor, with Arthur balancing on my hands. Phil ran out and jumped on my stomach. This was too much. I dropped Arthur again and grabbed Phil. As it looked as though I was going to tear him to pieces, Harry Carroll, who was also on the bill, intervened and suggested we settle it with gloves. That was all right with both of us and Arthur and I finished the tumbling bit.

Then Phil came back in a derby and a turtle-neck sweater with "Phil Baker" across the chest; wearing boxing gloves and smoking a big cigar. I went off for a quick change, while Phil talked about "these big muscled stiffs," and how he,

Phil, had been middle-weight boxing champ at Pocatella U., and was Bonomo due for a surprise! Just then I re-entered in boxing trunks and gloves. I was really in condition and Phil did a triple-take when he saw me.

We started to box, and I let him hit me a few times. Each time he did, his hand bounced back with such force that it almost knocked him off his feet. I just stood there letting him punch himself out. Then Phil's comedy stooge, who always sat in an upper front box, called out "Shinsky! Shinsky!" At this, Phil kicked me in the right shin. "Ow!" I yelled, grabbing the leg. Then he kicked me in the left shin. "Ow!!!" As I grimaced in pretended pain, he grabbed up a huge break-away floral vase, shattered it over my head, and I went out like a light.

"I told you these strongmen were bums!" he announced as the curtains closed.

The act was a smash. I had opened in the closing slot of the bill. The next show I was moved up to the feature spot. Joe Bonomo, with Phil Baker, was headlining at the Palace!

RKO booked me for the balance of Phil's tour and we finally wound up at the Palace in Chicago. Then Phil went to a top radio show and me? I finished my honeymoon.

Yes, that's right. The day I opened at the Palace in New York I got a four word telegram from Hollywood. All it said was "Okay—you win—Ethel." I wired her a ticket and four days later I paid two dollars for the privilege of supporting her for the rest of her life.

WILL FERRY THE FROG

Something odd from the wacky world of vaudeville: a "human frog" contortion act— he stopped the show every time.

Rags Ragland: from baggy pants days in Burlesque to the major Hollywood studios. (Right) With Red Skelton at MGM.

But I know now it was the best thing that evei happened to me. She even won Mama and Papa over. You see, Ethel had a way about her—and she still has!

Now Harry Weber suggested that if I would get a musical revue act together, he could get me all the bookings I wanted. I'd need a good comedian, so I went down to 42nd Street where the burlesque boys hang out. They were the best comics in the business. I ran into Phil Silvers, who was later to become a big star himself. He was writing material for the burlesque shows and told me Rags Ragland was the pick of the crop. Rags was looking for an opportunity to get out of burlesque and he gladly signed up with me. The revue featured both Rags and Ethel. The comedy high-spot was a ''broken ankle'' dance done by Rags, which never failed to bring down the house. He got rave notices and it wasn't long before he was offered twice what I was paying him, to join another act.

''Sorry,'' he said, ''but I've **got** a job—with the man who gave me my first real break.''

A year later I was able to get him another break, introducing him to several influential men in the picture business, and he was on his way. When he suddenly died, at the peak of his ca-

reer, it was a real loss to both the industry and the public. But they had only lost a great comedian—I had lost a valued friend.

But to go back . . . about the middle of the fourth week that Rags was with us he had a fall which broke one of his big toes and we lost our comedy star. He tried to go on despite the injury, actually struggled through a few performances, but the pain was too severe and he had to quit.

We had to lay off while we scouted around trying to find someone who could take Rags' place. I wanted to hold the act together so I kept everyone on full salary. However, my search for an adequate substitute was fruitless and, with the salaries continuing, it wasn't long before we had lost most of the profits we had accumulated. Well, what the heck, that was show business.

But regardless of that I realized I was growing restless in vaudeville and was secretly hankering for the movie cameras and Hollywood activity again.

Pictures were in my blood and I couldn't wait to get back. I called my little vaudeville company together for a confab and broke the news to them. We had had a lot of fun together, we had all picked up a little do-re-mi and now the best of

The display that was used in connection with all my vaudeville appearances.

friends must part. I gave them an extra week's salary and we said goodbye. I then advertised for a driver to go west with me, got one, and we were off.

Ethel was to follow me out by train. My driver and I would be traveling day and night, as fast as we could go, and as much as I loved Ethel, in this case, she'd be excess baggage.

Today, a cross continent motor trip can be made in three or four days, but in those days neither the cars nor the roads were that good— especially the roads. But we pushed my big white Locomobile, one of those long, low jobs with a rumble seat, as fast as it would go. The story of that trip could almost fill a book by itself, but I'll just touch on a couple of the high spots, approaching the first one in a rather round-about manner.

One mighty good reason for developing your muscles is that life is unpredictable; you never know when a little extra "horse-power" will stand you in good stead. I think this incident will bring that out very vividly.

The first part of our dash westward was uneventful. We were making excellent time, zipping along at from 70 to 80 miles an hour, even over

those bad roads which were a far cry from our highways of today. We were somewhere in Ohio . . . I recall it was Ohio because, in those days, as a grim warning to speeders, that state used to erect a white cross at each point where a fatal accident had occurred.

We were taking turns at the wheel, one driving while the other slept and, as night came on, I took over again. I was starting to be concerned as we had run into heavy rain and the mud was thick on the roads now and especially on the shoulders. I had just entered a narrow strip of highway when a speeding truck suddenly came around a curve and, to avoid a head-on collision, I had to pull sharply to the right. I struck a soft shoulder and the car ploughed into the wet mud and sand up to the hub caps. I tried to pull ahead, then I tried to back out, but it was no use . . . my wheels just spun in that sandy quagmire. It certainly looked as though we were stuck there with no possibility of getting back on the road. As far as I could see there wasn't a house or a sign of life, which meant no place to phone for a tow-truck to pull us out, even if we'd had the time to wait for one, which we didn't. The rain had slowed us down and we were already be-

hind our schedule.

My driver was awake now but proved to be of little help. We had a jack with us but it was useless in all that soft mud; with each effort we seemed to be settling a little more firmly. There was no use hailing passing cars as a push wouldn't have helped even if we could have gotten it. I surveyed the situation and decided there was just one thing to do. Time was passing and time was what we didn't have to squander.

I remembered that in our emergency tool kit there was an axe and, without further ado, figuring that once again the end justified the means, I proceeded to chop down a roadside telephone pole. By the time I got it down a couple of cars

had stopped and the drivers were curiously watching the highly unusual proceedings. Now I shoved one end of the pole under the car, wrapped my arms about the other end and, with a couple of healthy heaves I lifted the car out of the mud and back on the road again. As my "audience" looked on in open-mouthed astonishment, I hopped back in the driver's seat and we were once more on our way.

Later, when I paid the telephone company for the expense of putting up a new pole, they told me the one I had chopped down supported high voltage wires and if one of them had snapped and fallen on me I, undoubtedly, would have been electrocuted. It was a neat stunt but it could have

NAT LEVINE presents "THE PHANTOM OF THE WEST"

Tom Tyler, also a wrestler and strongman, and I had a real opportunity for some outstanding rough and tumble fights in this Mascot serial.

Ready to lick my weight in wildcats.

had dire consequences.

From then on the trip was again fairly uneventful until we started approaching the famous Raton Pass in northwestern New Mexico. A few miles back we had picked up a couple of Boy Scout hitchhikers. They were sitting in the rumble seat, happily busy with a box of Bonomo candy I'd happened to bring along and we were whizzing merrily across the landscape trying to make up as much time as possible.

My driver had the wheel and I had one eye on the kids and the other on the road which was, it seemed to me, too narrow and winding for the high speed at which we were traveling. I was just wondering what might happen if we missed one of the sharp turns and the car suddenly plunged off that mountain road when, with a sound like a pistol shot, our left front tire blew out. Before I could realize what had happened the car had gone into a crazy, whirling skid. We turned completely around, facing the direction from which we had come, but still skidding, then over the side of the road we went, in a rolling plunge down the bank of a deep ravine.

But Saint of all Saints that protects this crazy Bonomo! We had rolled over twice in the space of about twenty feet when we were abruptly stopped by crashing broadside into a tree. As we hung there I reached over instinctively and snapped off the ignition. All we'd need now would be to burst into flames! In our downward plunge I remembered the jack coming up from the floor behind the seat and hitting me in the back of the neck and my head crashing against the roof

Above: Twirling Charlie Schaefer through the air without missing a shot, as Charlie tries his best to keep his hat on.
Below: Bob Kortman has the drop on Charlie Schaefer, Philo McCullough and myself in the Nat Levine-Mascot serial THE VANISHING LEGION.

Harry Carey, the veteran Western Star, was a New York born cowboy like myself. (From THE VAN-ISHING LEGION).

of the car which, half the time, was actually UNDER us as we rolled. I was groggy and there was a sticky trickle of blood down my back, but I didn't think much about it at the time.

Then I looked down through the window and beyond the tree against which we were precariously balanced and my heart almost stopped. The ground fell away in what must have been a three million foot drop! Well, maybe it was only about three **thousand** feet, but that's still a good drop. And in all that long stretch, for hundreds of yards on either side of us, THIS was the only tree anywhere that was big enough to have halted our downward progress!

So there we hung on the steep side of that ravine, almost afraid to breathe for fear we might disturb the delicate balance that was holding us there, and cause the car to break loose and continue its plunge to the bottom.

Within minutes, which seemed hours to us, our plight was discovered by passing motorists who summoned help and my driver and I were hauled back up to safety, without disturbing the balance of the car. Miraculously my driver was only shaken up. We got a lift to the nearest town,

found a doctor and I had four stitches taken in the back of my neck. Then we located a garage and, with the use of a couple of derricks, the car was pulled back up to the road. It was badly dented but, to our surprise, it was still in running order, so we drove back to town and decided to take a room for the night while the dents were being hammered out. We felt we had pushed our luck far enough for one day and, since it was now late afternoon, we'd best get some sleep before moving on.

After showering and getting into bed, I was just dropping off to sleep when a thought flashed through my mind. My God! The Boy Scouts! Unbelieveable as it may seem, in all the excitement, we had forgotten all about them!

No words could describe my terror as I leaped out of bed and started pulling on my clothes. Had those two kids been thrown out of the rumble seat and down into the ravine? Or if not, had they been crushed, mangled, suffocated—if the seat had closed up on them? No sound had come from them if they were alive . . . no tapping . . . nothing. Still only half dressed I dashed down the street to the garage. There was the car . . . they

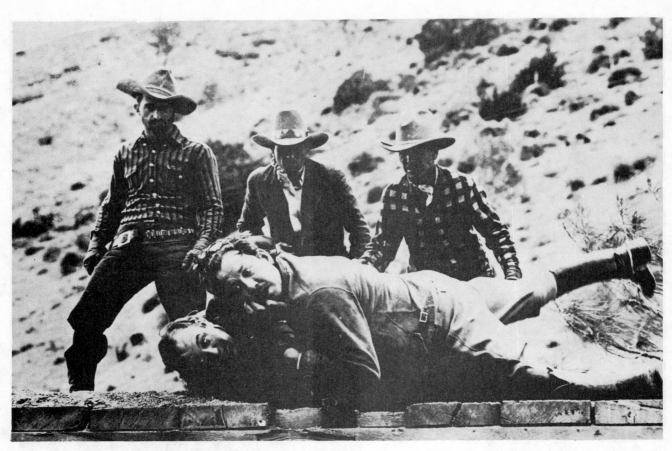

Above: A fight to the finish with Philo McCullough.
Below: Another serial slug fest—Rex Lease (left) and I in action in THE SIGN OF THE WOLF.

As Kit Gordon, a rugged pioneer character, in the RKO serial THE LAST FRONTIER. My good friend Fred J. McConnell, formerly with Universal, served as associate producer on this one.

Settling another argument in THE SIGN OF THE WOLF.

hadn't started working on it yet . . . and the rumble seat was closed. I opened it with trembling fingers, fully expecting to find it empty, which would mean those poor kids had been thrown to their death. But as I raised the lid, there they were, lying motionless on the floor.

It had been about two hours since the accident and I feared they were dead. But the kids were pretty tough. A little first aid, skillfully applied and, except for a couple of good-sized eggs on their pates, where they had bumped their heads together, they were just about as good as new. How it was they were not thrown out as the car rolled and how the rumble seat luckily closed on them and how, even in the excitement of the accident we could have forgotten about them, are three things that will always remain a mystery.

The kids only lived in the next town, so we drove them home. I explained the accident to their parents who, fortunately, were very understanding people, and everything turned out okay in the end. I later sent them autographed copies of my body-building courses and promised to show them around Hollywood if they ever came out. They never did though, perhaps figuring I played a little rough!

We reached Balboa late on the fifth night and I went to work for Nat Levine on a new Mascot serial in the morning. In the course of the next couple of years those serials he made were to make him a millionaire. I got little more than a very good salary from them, but that wasn't bad either.

Young Frank Albertson's disastrous fate was to be "continued next week" as I flexed my muscles for the Universal serial THE LOST SPECIAL.

More villainy from THE LOST SPECIAL—
Above: Tom London, George Magrill and I form an unbeatable gangland trio.
Below: When you're on the wrong side of the law you always surprise your victims.

Chapter #29

"A GOLD PIECE FROM DeMILLE"

GARCIA

As a stock player, I was often called upon to play animals—and because of my size and strength it was frequently a huge gorilla or large ape. One gorilla suit I wore cost more than a thousand dollars. It was made of real gorilla hide with a mouth I could open and shut. I wore large fang-like teeth over my own and developed a snarling growl that would have scared a **real** gorilla out of a year's growth. That suit was like wearing a fur coat in the middle of August, and if I wasn't the **best** gorilla you ever saw I was certainly the **hottest**. Yet I wore it countless times in circus films, comedies and in hunting pictures made in "Africa." I never told Papa about those gorilla parts I played. I was afraid he'd sell his business and go back to Turkey. Papa was a proud man.

But I wonder how many people realize the care and artistry it takes to make a good gorilla. The torso is built low, to create an illusion of a long body with short legs. When the camera is not too close, you wear foot long extensions on your arms, like hand-stilts, so you can touch them along the ground as you amble about. In close shots, where you must use your hands for "business"—they are either heavily made up or you wear big, hairy gloves. The eyes and inside of the mouth are yours . . . the rest is sponge padding and monkey hide.

A gorilla suit is about the most uncomfortable costume a performer can wear.

Acting like an aggressive ape with Leon Ames and Bela Lugosi in MURDERS IN THE RUE MORGUE.

I have played many animal parts. In ISLAND OF LOST SOULS, which starred Charles Laughton, I was several of those terrifying creatures, part human and part animal. I recall it took me three hours to put on the make-up for the Tiger-Man. All of us who played beasts in that picture wore animal suits, constructed with the torso built down nearly to the knees, with a fifty pound sack of sand in the crotch, making any effort to walk exceedingly clumsy and grotesque. There were Lion-Men, Tiger-Men, Leopard-Men, Gorilla-Men—every type of animal-man they could devise a costume for. I never made so many quick changes. At the end of the picture the hero had to capture an Ape-Man and bring him back alive. You guessed it—I was also the Ape-Man. It's hard to get away from type-casting.

During the shooting of the homeward bound ship sequences, while waiting around in my "monkey-suit" 'til time for my entrance, I got fooling around with some of the boys on the ship's fantail . . . and in the course of the shenanigans, I slipped and fell overboard. Down I went and I thought I'd never stop. The sponge rubber in the ape suit filled with water immediately, and I had that fifty pound sand bag in my pants as well. What a way for Bonomo, the swimming champ, to go! I fought like mad and luckily, the boys on deck realized my dilemma and dove in after me. It took three men and two life-rings, to keep me afloat, and it finally took a windlass to get me back on board. As I look back on it, it was quite an amusing situation—as I look **back** on it.

Then one day I met Cecil B. De Mille. He and I got along fine and he would use me in his "spectaculars." I later played in CLEOPATRA, and I had several big scenes in THE SIGN OF

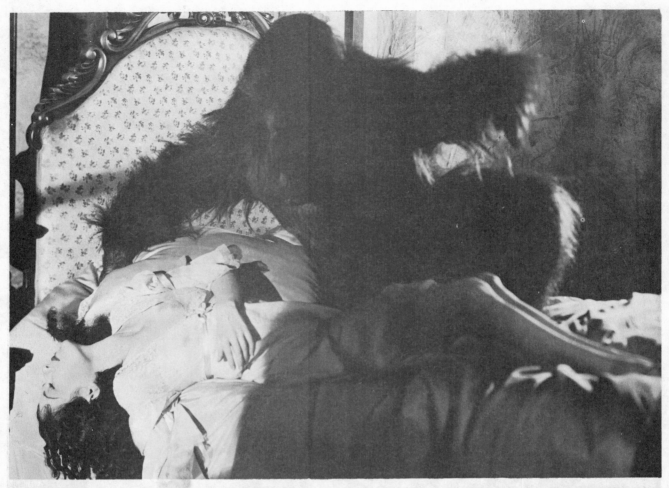

In this picture the ape was the central character and the part required a great use of strength and stunting skill.

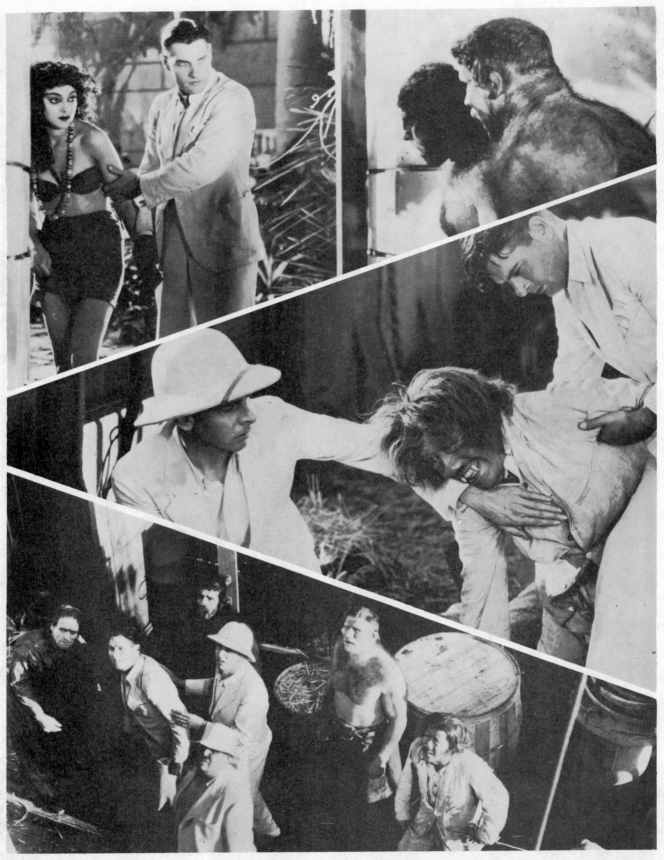

ISLAND OF LOST SOULS gave me the opportunity to play several of the terrifying part-human creatures that menaced Charles Laughton, Richard Arlen and Leila Hyams. In recent years I have met many people who fondly remember this picture and regard it as one of Hollywood's best off-beat productions.

Above: The arrow indicates Tiger-man Bonomo, one of the jungle animals Charles Laughton transformed into a semi-human creature.

Below: A rare makeup shot of one of several fiendish characters I played in Paramount's ISLAND OF LOST SOULS. My wig was originally the one worn by Fredric March at Paramount as Mr. Hyde, in his Academy Award performance in DR. JEKYLL AND MR. HYDE.

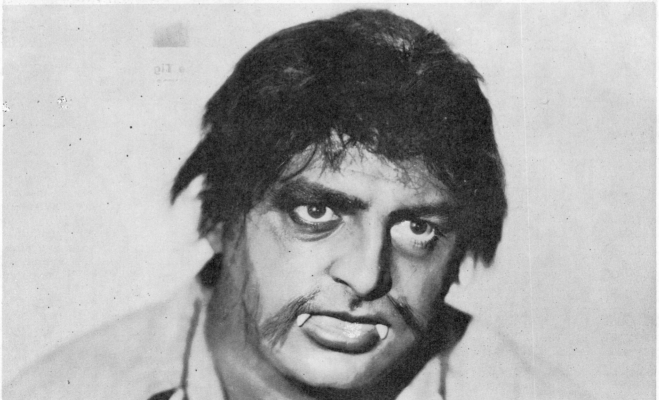

THE CROSS. While this picture was shooting he sent for me one day. "Joe, I've got to do something my regular stuntmen are backing away from. They just say, 'Get Bonomo. He'll try **anything.**'"

Flattered, I assured him I **would**, but I almost weakened when he told me what "anything" **was**. I was to play a Christian martyr, be thrown into a pit of hungry crocodiles and be devoured before the eyes of the Roman spectators. Now I **ask** you!

Before I could answer yes or no, he said, "Figure it out, Joe, and make it look good." . . . gave me a pat on the back and was gone, leaving me standing there, wishing I was back

My makeup as the Tiger-man in ISLAND OF LOST SOULS took many hours to apply.

Cast again as a rough customer—the mute keeper of the torture chamber in THE SIGN OF THE CROSS.

in Coney Island. It happened I knew about crocodiles.

The crocodile has a double-hinged jaw—that is—both the upper and the lower jaw can move, either together or independently. In addition, it is smaller, much faster and far more vicious than the cumbersome, more complacent alligator. All of which means that if you get within reach of a crocodile, you'd better have your insurance paid up and your affairs in order, for you practically haven't a chance. Crocodiles have taken a greater toll of human life than any other reptile or animal in the world.

After a night filled with nightmares, in which hungry crocodiles were snapping at me from all sides, I awakened with two ideas. The first, and I was sure the better one, was to go into hiding until the picture was finished. The other idea was to substitute alligators for the crocodiles. I decided if Mr. De Mille didn't go for the second idea, **I'd** go for the **first**.

THE SIGN OF THE CROSS was a DeMille historical spectacle all the way, and he didn't hold us stunt-men back when it came to the more gruesome scenes with the elephants and alligators.

Not too many people in Hollywood were ever anxious to be filmed in a pit with these snapping babies!

To my surprise he agreed immediately. Alligators were bigger and **looked** more ferocious, whether they were or not.

"But just remember this was your decision, Joe, and if an alligator gets you, the studio won't be responsible." And with those comforting words he gave me another pat on the back and was gone again.

The reason for my choosing alligators was that a 'gator is built all along one vertabrae, from the tip of his nose to the end of his tail. Though the tail is flexible, the forward end of him is fairly rigid. He lacks the double-hinged jaw the crocodile possesses. Only his lower jaw moves and that hinges down. If you can catch this lower jaw when it is open, you can **hold** it open, unless he twists away. Of course, there is always the danger of being knocked senseless, perhaps having your head smashed by his powerful, thrashing tail, but I'd have to risk that. Then too, being thrown in a pit with six of them, I'd have his buddies to contend with. I just hoped they wouldn't gang up. What I needed, instead of the flimsy Christian martyr outfit I'd be wearing, was a suit of armor!

The following day they set up for the shot . . . and in the pit they had six of the ugliest, most vicious looking alligators I had ever seen. As I walked toward them I wondered how many legs I'd have left to walk **back** on—if any! I had taken one precaution—just out of camera range I had stationed five men with long poles with big cloth wads on the ends of them. They had instructions to watch the other five 'gators and shove the wads into their mouths if they started to mix in. Meanwhile the make-up man sprayed both me and the 'gators with oil, to make everything glisten ominously, not realizing

an oily alligator would be twice as hard to wrestle with and pin down.

But it was too late now—the cameras were set—we waited until my particular alligator was a little apart from the rest—then two husky Roman soldiers threw me in beside him. As I hit the mud I grabbed him by a front leg—the one away from the side where the cameras were going to shoot the death scene. We wrestled for a moment, and he opened his big lower jaw. I grabbed it with my left hand, held it open and half put my head in his mouth, but from the side away from the cameras. From the camera side it looked as though my head was IN his mouth, then I slammed it shut and held it shut. Had my head actually **been** in that mouth, I would have been decapitated.

I quickly pulled him down on top of me, kicking my legs in the air so it looked as though the 'gator had me down. I kicked my legs violently just once, then stiffened them out suddenly as though he **had** gobbled off my head—then I slowly relaxed and fell "lifeless." As the cameras stopped shooting I slowly got up and walked away. I did WHAT?? I lit out of there as though the Devil himself was on my coat-tail!

Actually, the death scene was so realistic that for a moment De Mille, the cameramen, and everyone else thought the world had seen the last of Joe Bonomo. De Mille was torn between delight over having captured a sensational scene —what he should wire my family—and what he would tell the newspapers. What publicity it would make! Then, when I came up alive and smiling, I'm sure he was pleased—that is—I'm **reasonably** sure.

He used to carry a few twenty dollar gold pieces with him in those days, and when he was particularly thrilled by a performance, he

Delivering my latest torture victim to Fredric March and Ian Keith in DeMille's THE SIGN OF THE CROSS.

One of the many unusual animal actors I have worked with—a python!

would give one to the actor or actress. To possess a De Mille gold piece was a mark of distinction —much like an Academy "Oscar" is today. I got one for that alligator sequence.

Everyone said it was great footage. As a matter of fact, it was too great. At the preview women fainted at the horrible sight. It was too macabre for public viewing. So one of the greatest alligator-gobbles-man scenes in the history of motion pictures, wound up on the cutting room floor.

In another picture I did a scene so starkly terrifying it, too, had to be deleted. I was supposedly asleep in bed, when a giant python—a huge constrictor snake, 28 feet long—was sent slithering in through my window, to squeeze my life out, in one of the most horrible forms of death. And he very nearly did just that!

I had a hunch not to do this scene, as I didn't savvy pythons, but everyone assured me it would be a breeze. They said a constrictor couldn't constrict without using his tail for leverage, and they were lashing his tail to a stake, driven into the ground, outside the window. As a double precaution, on the underside of the bed was a series of sharp steel spikes—and no python would tighten his coils in the face of anything like that. What's more, he was a tame python, practically a pet, used in snake charmer scenes. And if that weren't enough, in case anything **should** go wrong, there'd be a crew of six men standing by to handle the monster. What they **should** have had standing by, was the snake charmer!

The precautions complete, I lay down on the bed, feigning sleep, and this huge "crusher snake" was pointed my way and thrust in through the window.

From beneath my lashes I could see his ugly head coming toward me, his evil beady eyes riveted on me. On he came, and with all his huge bulk, he moved as silently as a shadow. Then I felt him slither over me, and before I realized what was happening, he had completed a loop around Bonomo and the bed, and was starting to squeeze. If the spikes under the bed bothered him, he didn't show it . . . he just kept putting on the pressure as he coiled tighter and tighter.

After a few seconds of this it felt as though the boys would have to dig me out of the mattress to bury me. With my arms pinned to my sides, I was completely helpless and I began to get a little nervous. This was no place for Joe Bonomo, even if the director and cameraman **were** nodding their heads in approval.

"Hey," I gasped. "This baby's really doing a job on me. Get him OFF!"

"Hold it just a little longer, Joe," the director was saying, "the scene is terrific!"

"To heck with the scene!" I gasped, really sucking air now. "He's cracking my ribs!!"

The director's voice came over as from a distance.

—"Just another thirty seconds, Joe."

As though he understood the time was short the python reared that hideous head, his evil, greedy eyes fastened hypnotically on mine, and once again tightened his coils. The pressure became unbearable . . . I felt as though the veins in my head were bursting.

"Another—thirty—seconds—and—" But the breath was all gone out of me . . . I was passing out. Then, from miles away, I heard the director yell something—a man ran forward with a blow torch and five other men started pulling. In a few seconds they had me loose; shaken, blue in the face and panting for air like an English bulldog. That was the last time I mixed with a constrictor. Some of my ribs WERE cracked and, after I came out of the hospital, the director joked, "You must be a lovable guy, Joe . . . that big snake sure had a **crush** on you." Luckily for him my muscles were still hurting too much to toss him under a passing truck!

I now continued with my wrestling, the Bonomo Culture Institute, more serials and some feature pictures. Ethel and I were enjoying a happy married life except she used to worry terribly about me, with all the stunts I was doing, especially after she was carrying our child. But I kept assuring her nothing could go wrong— this was one Black Cat who **really** had nine lives.

But soon something happened that quieted all Ethel's fears and put the sparkle back in her eyes again—Cecil B. De Mille selected me for the role of Marc Antony in one of his first big epics for the new "talking pictures." When I romped home with the great news she was overjoyed . . . not so much because it was my golden opportunity to move up to top rank, but because as co-star of the picture I would not be permitted to do any stunts . . . I would no longer be expendable. Furthermore, if I delivered an outstanding performance, my membership in the ranks of Hollywood stardom would be firmly established. It could well mean that my days of constantly risking my life were all behind me now. This could be the break that would lead us out of the Wilderness.

C.B. DeMille always tried to get the most exciting effects possible on the screen—but I still feel I would rather wrestle men than alligators!

The studios knew that I was always prepared for either the grisly or the glamorous. And, it's really a big jump from fighting alligators to appearing with Garbo in AS YOU DESIRE ME.

Chapter #30

WATERLOO

LIFE IS HARD TO FIGURE. I have always considered myself primarily an athlete and a stuntman . . . yet most of whatever fame and fortune I garnered in Hollywood, came to me as an actor. I played featured or starring roles in numerous serials and full length pictures—and at times my salary reached enviable proportions. Why does acting pay so handsomely? Well . . . I doubt many people realize the skill and highly specialized training required of an actor. Just get in front of a camera and make faces, people think. Just say the lines—the directors, makeup men, costumers and cutting room editors will do the rest. Anybody, if they're good looking and halfway intelligent can be a star if they get the right breaks!

It DOES happen occasionally. There are a few actors and actresses in Hollywood who made stardom with little training and in some cases, with very little talent. The hundreds of technicians—the real artists of the motion picture industry—were able, through countless clever tricks, to build them up and sell them to the public.

But these are rare exceptions. When I was a so-called star I wasn't bad I guess, but that was in the days of **silent** films, before the advent of the "talkies." Acting then was strictly visual —and visually, I was a good actor. I had the physique . . . I was photogenic and I had spent many years before the cameras. I had learned my craft the hard way—and I had learned it well.

I had worked with De Mille in THE SIGN OF THE CROSS and we had become warm friends. Also, his casting director, Joe Egli, was almost like a brother to me. So no one was too surprised when I was selected to play Antony, opposite

Claudette Colbert, in De Mille's new spectacular —a "talkie" version of CLEOPATRA. I wasn't surprised either . . . but I knew they had made a mistake. Maybe in some way I could bluff it through but—

I said nothing to anyone regarding my misgivings. I reported to the studio and was made up, costumed and screen tested—(in those early days of talkies many of the tests were made silently)—and was pronounced perfect for the part. The director told me to report the following Monday morning to begin work on the picture. I said, "Sure—all right," but even as I said it I knew, deep down inside me, that it was all **wrong**. This was a "talkie" . . . and I had no training as a speaking actor. I knew next to nothing about the art of reading lines.

Because I had always been a good talker socially, no one had stopped to think that I might not be able to talk before a camera, especially in the highly stylized manner a picture such as "Cleopatra" called for. And I had only until the following Monday to master this new technique.

In desperation I phoned a good friend—one of Hollywood's better actors and a Shakespearean performer of considerable acclaim. I pleaded with him to come to my rescue and, if possible, help me over the hump. He said he'd do what he could, gladly, and within an hour we were headed for Big Bear, a mountain resort a few hours from the film city.

We labored Friday, Saturday and Sunday—all day and most of each night. He was a wonderful coach, encouraging me, drilling me and showing me his many technical tricks with the voice. After a while I began to feel that maybe, miracle of miracles, I might be able to pull it off. We

DeMille had plenty of stunts to be done in CLEOPATRA, but I figured this time I could forget all about that.

were about exhausted but we kept going until the last minute. If he was pessimistic as to the outcome he didn't let me know it.

When we started back to Hollywood, on Monday morning, it was almost day-break. I was driving and he was dozing beside me. I was feeling pretty good over all the work we had done.

"You sure gave it the old college try for me," I said. "I'll bet you never worked THAT hard for an **Oscar**."

"Relax boy," he said sleepily. "Save your voice for tomorrow."

"Tomorrow's already here," I said. "Isn't that dawn breaking over there?"

He laboriously opened one eye and squinted at the landscape.

"Aye," he said, "'tis the East . . . and Juliet is the sun . . ." and dropped off to sleep.

By nine o'clock I was on the set, in costume. No cameras yet—this was just to run through our lines and get the feel of the scene. De Mille and his staff were sitting around, watching, and my sleepy-eyed coach was also there, to give me courage I guess. I sure needed it.

Claudette Colbert, playing the "Queen of the Nile," as directed by the almost legendary C.B. himself.

Miss Colbert, as Cleopatra, had a scene with a servant and then Antony was to enter. I glanced over at my friend and he forced a smile and gave me the thumbs up sign. I made my entrance and went into my first long speech. After a few lines I stole a look at De Mille. I was just in time to see him throw back his head in anguish. Then he emitted a suppressed groan and covered his tortured face with his hands. I stopped dead.

"What's the matter, C.B.?" I asked. "It can't be **that** bad."

He uncovered his face and regarded me sadly for a moment, then he nodded his head.

"But it is, Joe," he said, "it is."

I wasn't getting a De Mille gold piece this time.

Without another word I turned and started for my dressing room. Before I had gone ten feet my friend's lean arm was across my shoulders.

"Don't take it too hard, Joe," he was saying, "No one can do EVERYTHING. Look at **me** —could I lift two thousand pounds or let someone break rocks on my chest? See what I mean?"

But I couldn't have seen anything just then . . . What was I going to tell Ethel? Just the plain truth I guess. For the first time in his life The Mighty Bonomo had struck out.

Henry Wilcoxon played the part and the picture was outstanding. I did the stunt work and played a few bits. Then I went back to being the Serial King of the "silents"—where I belonged.

I couldn't believe that I had failed in my bid for a leading role in CLEOPATRA. DeMille eventually filmed it with Henry Wilcoxon and I let time heal my wounded pride.

CLEOPATRA had plenty of action and stunt scenes to be done, so I gave it my usual all in the work it provided.

Al Wilson, the screen's famed stunt pilot, met the death he had cheated so many times before as the result of a flying accident.

The Black Cats were going fast now. Harry, who tried that rope slide, unsuccessfully, in "The Hunchback," was killed in a Western. A runaway stagecoach hit a boulder just as he was starting his escape-leap, and he was thrown against a tree. He died of a broken neck.

The one we called "Noodles" was cremated, crashing a plane into a flaming barn.

Another one got his in a war picture. He was running across "no man's land" and, as a shell burst in the air, he dove to the ground—right on a spot where a charge was buried. He took the explosion squarely in his face.

And then Al Wilson went to Stuntman's Heaven trying to outsmart Death at an Air Carnival. Poor Al—we had worked so much together— many times each had held the other's life in his hands. It hit me hard. In a new serial for Nat Levine, I was doing more dangerous stunts than ever, as we invented new thrills for a jaded public. How long before my luck would run out!!

Ethel didn't talk about it anymore, but every morning, when I'd leave for the studio, her good-bye kiss would last a moment longer—and her arms would cling as though to never let me go. And there was dread clouding those formerly happy blue eyes. Yet this was my profession— my life—I couldn't turn back now. We both knew that only one thing would ever stop me.

Around this time I had a really close call, although not the type I might have expected. I almost killed Columbia's famous Western star, Buck Jones. In a staged fight scene I hurled a chair at him and, being left handed, he instinctively ducked to the left instead of to the right as we had rehearsed it. The chair hit him head-on, and he went down with a sickening thud, with a fractured skull and bad internal injuries—for when I throw I throw **hard**. When I visited him in the hospital he wouldn't even let me apologize.

"Forget it, Joe," he said. "It was my fault . . . and besides, I needed a vacation. And when I get to Chicago I'm going to talk to some baseball people I know there. You should be pitching in the National League!"

He got to Chicago all right, and then went on to Boston, where in 1942 he was burned to death in the terrible Cocoanut Grove fire.

BUCK JONES SLOW TO DUCK; HURT

Buck Jones, cowboy film star, suffered two broken ribs and possible injuries to his spine yesterday while filming a fight scene at Columbia Studios.

In the sequence, Joe Bonomo, movie strong man and "heavy," was supposed to throw a chair at Jones which the latter was to duck.

He didn't duck soon enough.

Jones was taken to Hollywood Hospital. Doctors said that unless subsequent observation reveals more serious spinal hurts, Jones will be able to resume his work in a week or ten days.

Little Joan's arrival gave me a real family of my own and I started her right out on her own physical fitness program.

Then one day our child was born.

As I paced the hospital corridor outside the delivery room, my pockets bulging with cigars, I was already making plans for him. He'd never be a stuntman . . . I'd see to that . . . but I'd build him into a physical marvel such as the world had never seen. And he'd go to college—and he'd be an All American football star and—a door opened and a nurse was coming toward me—and from beyond the door I could hear the first cries of a new-born baby. The nurse was smiling.

"Congratulations, Mr. Bonomo," she said. "They're both doing fine and you're now the proud father of—"

"You don't have to tell me," I grinned, "it's a boy and his name is Joe Junior. Have a cigar —have TWO cigars!"

"Thanks," she laughed, taking them, "I'll smoke them after dinner . . . or the doctor will." She walked back through the door . . . started to close it . . . then looked back at me with a twinkle.

"As for Joe Junior," she said, "take my advice and call him Josephine. I'm sure she'll be happier that way." And she closed the door on my dreams. At that moment you could have stirred my knees with a spoon! I had to sit down. Fate had double-crossed me. My son had turned out to be a daughter!

We named her Joan—and even though she WAS a girl I wasn't planning to be completely frustrated. Male or female, I was going to have another "Joe Bonomo" in the family.

So even before she could walk I had her doing exercises and working out on a little trapeze I built for her. She'd have probably turned out to be a Strong Woman in a circus, if Ethel hadn't stepped in and put her foot down.

"Look, Joe," she said, "enough is enough. Keep this up and you'll have muscles coming out of her ears. I want to raise a daughter— not an Amazon!"

So I sadly packed away the little trapeze for the day the Stork would bring us a boy. But he must have lost our address. He never came our way again.

However, soon I was too busy to do much ranting against Fate. My "Bonomo Boys' Clubs" had grown to more than a million membership throughout the country; my mail order business had thrived to the point where I had to take a large suite of offices in the Warner Brothers' Building in Hollywood; and I was getting more picture offers than I could accept.

Furthermore, I was beginning to forgive little Joanie for being a girl. After all, didn't everybody say "She sure is the spitting image of you, Joe!"

Phone Gr. 1850 ~   Res. H.E. 8944

P.S. — Just Moved The Whole Works To Warner Bros. Theatre Bldg. Joe Bonomo.

My good friend Ted Eshbaugh, director of many major studio film cartoons, caricatured me in this manner when I moved to new offices.

The Bonomo Boys Clubs were spreading out all over and I never missed an available chance to meet the gang in person.

Through advertising such as this comic strip sequence, the Bonomo mail order business was really on the move.

Two of the early publications which were part of my physical culture enterprises.

And then—the blow fell. While doing an auto stunt bit for a picture, in some way I got my signals crossed, and went over the same cliff and bounced on the same ledge that had been my Nemesis years before. This time they picked me up with a broken right hip. But once again I had survived the Black Cat's kiss—or so I thought at the time.

The next day, in the hospital, I questioned the surgeon who did the work on me.

"How serious is this one, Doc? How long?"

"The break? Oh, about five weeks or so."

"After that I'll be okay, huh?"

He didn't answer for a moment, then—

"Ever have any trouble with that hip before?"

"I never **broke** it before."

"But has it ever bothered you? Ever have any pain there?"

I told him about a dull pain that had annoyed me intermittently for the past couple of years.

"Umm-hm," he said thoughtfully, then he looked away. "Joe, I'm afraid you have a worn-out hip joint."

"A what??" I had never heard of such a thing.

"Don't look so tragic," he said. "You'll be okay as long as you avoid all forms of strenuous exercise."

"And if I don't?"

"You'd better," he said grimly, "or you'll be crippled for life."

Avoid all forms of strenuous exercise? That's how I made my living—that's what I was trained for—what I had become famous for. He must be wrong . . . he HAD to be. I was still a young man, with most of my life ahead of me. I had already survived 36 broken bones . . . I wasn't going to let the 37th ruin my career. Why I knew acrobats and strong-men who had had plenty of accidents, and they were still top performers at sixty. I couldn't be finished at **MY** age—it didn't make sense. I'd show that saw-bones as soon as I got out of the hospital. Joe Bonomo wasn't washed up yet . . . not yet he wasn't!

During the ensuing six months I went to the best bone specialists in the country . . . I spent a week at the famous Mayo Brothers clinic in Minnesota . . . but everywhere the diagnosis was the same. There was no operation that could help me . . . as a professional athlete, strongman, stuntman, and actor, I was grounded for life . . . the third act curtain had come down!

Chapter #31
The One Shot King

IN THE SIX MONTHS following my accident I also did a heap of thinking. I kept trying to convince myself that THIS time the doctors had slipped up on their diagnoses, but my better judgment told me this was only wishful thinking. I knew my ship had foundered and from then on I'd have to steer a different course, so I started checking on the possibilities for building a new career.

While I had been recuperating from my accident, telegrams and letters from well-wishers had flooded in from all parts of the country and with them, many business and professional offers. Now Harry Zehner, my old friend and an executive at Universal, dropped in on me to say that Mr. Laemmle and Universal Studios wanted me as a producer. Today I know that offer was strictly business, but at that time I felt it was prompted by a feeling of pity. I was always a pretty proud guy and if there was anything I didn't want it was pity, so I said "No thanks." I wanted to make it on my own; I had done it before and I could do it again. The question was where and how??

I talked it over at great length with Ethel . . . I wanted her advice . . . but her answer was always the same. "You decide it, Joe, I'm sure you'll do the right thing."

It was while I was in this period of indecision that Fate stepped in and took over. Papa became suddenly ill and wired me to come home and help Victor with the candy business.

It wasn't easy to leave Hollywood. Roots can sink deep in eleven years . . . and Hollywood had

been good to me. It had paid me off with a lavish hand and it had made me famous. So it was with a heavy heart that I said good-bye I knew I'd always carry with me the happy memories of those years of make-believe—the many warm friends I had made and my association with those wonderful guys who had dodged death with me, most of whom hadn't made it the last time out. Now I was leaving it all behind me, going back home to Mama, Papa and the candy business. This was farewell to all the excitement and thrills. But I was soon to learn that there was a lot more excitement still to come!

Back in New York, Ethel, Joanie and I got a nice apartment on Central Park West and I settled down to what I expected would be a more or less routine life of business—dividing my time between the big city and Coney Island. Mama and Papa were delighted to have Joey back again and there was a warm feeling of family unity in our work and in our lives. Papa wanted to retire and he did, more or less, just as I was made sales and promotion manager. Papa's guidance came from the side and all went along quietly and happily. It wasn't until the following year that we were to realize why Papa had retired.

Maybe I had had a premonition or perhaps there were a couple of Turkish rug peddlers among my ancestors, but during my Hollywood days and while I was out on my vaudeville tours and personal appearances, I used to spend many hours in variety chain stores. I'd walk in, introduce myself to the manager and we'd have a chat. This was a kind of hobby with me—a

Back on the east coast with the winning cup from a summer resort dance contest.

funny sort of hobby maybe, but I enjoyed it. I'd examine the merchandise, think about the psychology and economics behind the items and just generally keep track of the fads and fashions. I'm sure a lot of the managers thought I was nuts, but they all knew me from the movies . . . I was too big to throw out . . . so they good naturedly went along with me and quite often we became friends. Incidentally, there's nothing like a few tours through a five-and-ten to show you what the mass of our population is thinking about and how they live.

As luck would have it, this turned out to be some of the most fruitful work I did during those movie-making years, for, now back in New York and the candy business, I found many of these variety store managers had been promoted to buyers in the New York offices. Almost everywhere I went I ran into them and they were only too glad to help me when they could. Now our business was growing steadily, Mama and Papa were happy and Ethel wasn't worrying any more.

Then Papa died. He had been retired for less than a year, but he had lived to see his sons together again and his business in good hands. Shortly after that my old friend Charles Ludwig passed on and Mrs. Ludwig turned the mail-order business back to me, including August Leidy, who had been their general manager . . . and the Bonomo Culture Institute began to flourish anew. I didn't neglect the candy business but I put every spare moment into the Institute work. It was something more in my line. Perhaps this is the way Joe Bonomo would come back, I thought. What I now couldn't do myself I could teach others to do. And I was suddenly finding real excitement in the business world. Heck, this wasn't routine! Business could be as much fun as making movies!

With this new lease on life the whole world began to change again. A new cycle had begun for me and I was on the upswing now. By the next fall the Bonomo Culture Institute had blown up to a size that necessitated larger offices, so I moved into the Times Square area in New York. With this better location I could not only push the Institute farther but I was also better situated to sell the Bonomo candy line. And although I didn't realize it at the time, Fate was planning to move me into still another field . . . publishing.

My new offices were on Forty-second Street, just across from Bothner's Gym—and I could work at the business, spend a little time with the show people who frequented that section and also get into the gym every day, for a light workout and a steam bath.

Then I met Tony Bruno again. Tony had been an assistant cameraman and "still" photographer at Universal and I knew his work well. Back east now, Tony wanted to set up a studio of his own called "Bruno of Hollywood." I helped him, loaning him part of the money he needed and making him the Director of Photography for the Bonomo Culture Institute as well.

Then one day, while in the steam baths at Bothner's, I got talking to another friend, Sam Golden. Sam owned a printing shop and wondered why I hadn't gone into publishing, like Bernarr MacFadden. MacFadden and I were close friends, he had published several stories of mine, but the idea had never entered my head until Sam brought it up.

"You ought to bring out a 'One-Shot,' Joe, and see how it goes."

"A 'One-Shot?'" I had never even heard of such a thing.

"That's a book in magazine form," Sam explained. "About the size of **Cosmopolitan** maybe. Only there's no recurring issues. One shot, and that's all, see?"

Well, we discussed it some more and Sam said he could print up maybe ten thousand for around a nickel apiece. If I could sell them for half the twenty-five cent retail price there'd be a nice profit in it.

I talked it over with Bruno and August Leidy and we decided the idea had possibilities. So, just like that, I became a publisher. August and I did the writing and Tony the photography, as the Bonomo Culture Institute prepared its first one-shot . . . "Beautify Your Figure." For the cover we needed a really beautiful female figure so I contacted Gypsy Rose Lee. Gypsy said she wouldn't be interested but suggested her kid sister, June Havoc. I'm sure Gypsy would have done it but she wanted to give her, as yet unknown sister, the break. So we got June and the girl was truly an inspiration for Tony. He got some of the best stills of the feminine figure I've ever seen. (Sorry, fellows, no copies left!)

"Beautify Your Figure" was at last completed and I had Sam print ten thousand copies to be sold at twenty-five cents. Through my contacts with the local chain stores I had no trouble getting it spotted in a few Woolworth stores as well as other chain drug and variety stores. Another friend, Julius Schwartz, the manager of the Rexall-Liggett Grand Central Station drugstore, gave me a feature counter and a large window display. We placed "Beautify Your Figure" on the counters on a Wednesday morning and then . . . the fireworks started!

With the help of the photographic talents of Tony Bruno, BEAUTIFY YOUR FIGURE started off my long line of one-shot publications. The cover girl was June Havoc, who later became a quite talented and successful actress.

With Mama after my farewell to Hollywood.

315

With each new one-shot I planned a publicity campaign which drew heavily upon promotional experience I gained during my years in show business.

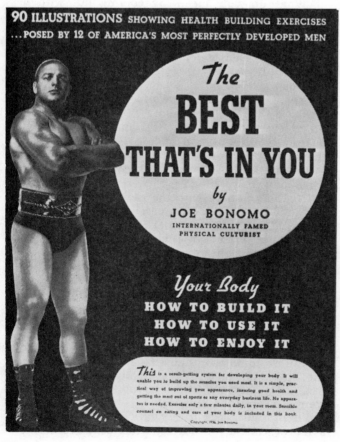

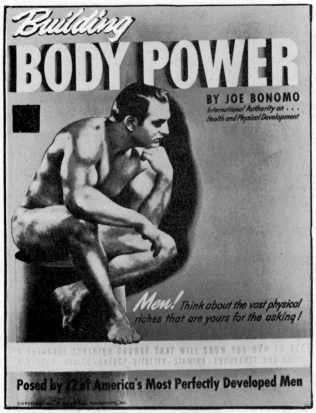

As sales grew so did my publishing business, and I kept trying to think ahead to new topics the buying public would be interested in.

We kept making more deliveries all day long on Thursday and Friday and by Saturday afternoon every one of the ten thousand copies had been sold. The superintendent at Grand Central Station reported to the Union News Company that it was the first time he had ever seen women fighting to get a magazine!

I was flabbergasted. I knew it had happened but I couldn't believe it. But I didn't have much time to think about it because, the first thing Monday morning, I got a call from the Union News Company to see their Mr. Boyd at once. He was an executive buyer and one of my best customers for the Bonomo candy line.

Anticipating another nice candy order I hustled right over. As I hurried into his office I noticed a copy of my One-Shot on his desk.

"You wanted to see me, Mr. Boyd?"

He picked up the copy of "Beautify Your Figure" and there was a nasty look in his eyes.

"Is this your book?" he asked, waving it at me.

"It sure is," I said with a proud grin, "only don't ask me for an extra copy . . . it's completely sold out."

Then my smile froze as he just sat there and glared at me. I couldn't understand it, but I didn't have long to wait.

"Bonomo," he barked, "don't we buy a lot of candy from you?"

"You sure do. The Union News is one of my biggest and best clients."

"It was!" he snapped. "You just lost us!"

What's all this, I thought. What did I do wrong? But Boyd wasn't finished yet.

"What do you mean by coming out with a book like this and not letting us in on it!" he exploded. "You've been doing business with us for years! Who's handling this?!"

"I am," I said, defensively. His anger changed to incredulity.

"**You** are?!"

"Yes," I stammered. "Wait a minute, will you? If I made a mistake, I'm sorry. But I just printed up a few thousand of these, and I didn't know if they were any good or not. I was just trying them out. I only printed a few thousand!"

He was appeased, and pressed a button, and somebody answered, "Yes?"

"Bonomo is here with me now, Mr. Morrisey," Boyd said. I almost fell over. Mike Morrisey was president of the huge **American** News Company. "He says he's handling it himself."

"Bring him right up here," Morrissey said.

The elevator shot up a couple of floors to the American News Company, and we went in to Morrisey's office. There were about six big wheels in there, and they all began shooting questions at me. What could I tell them? I was new at this publishing business, but I assured them I was honest, that I'd have the answers to their questions tomorrow, and that nobody would get the jump on them. They finally let me go. It was a mighty confused young publisher who went out through that door!

When I got back to my office there had been a lot of calls from other outlets as well. In all,

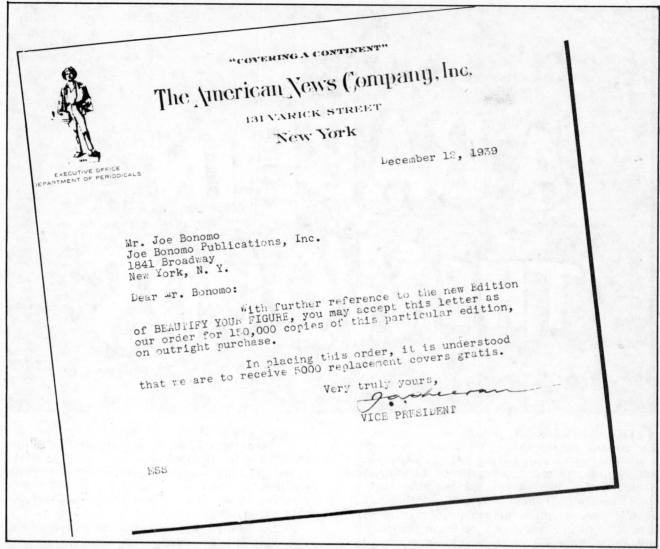

The letter reads:

"COVERING A CONTINENT"

The American News Company, Inc.

131 VARICK STREET

New York

EXECUTIVE OFFICE
DEPARTMENT OF PERIODICALS

December 12, 1939

Mr. Joe Bonomo
Joe Bonomo Publications, Inc.
1841 Broadway
New York, N. Y.

Dear Mr. Bonomo:

With further reference to the new Edition of BEAUTIFY YOUR FIGURE, you may accept this letter as our order for 150,000 copies of this particular edition, on outright purchase.

In placing this order, it is understood that we are to receive 5000 replacement covers gratis.

Very truly yours,

VICE PRESIDENT

ESS

A photostat from my files of an original order I received from American News. All together I sold them over one million copies of my one-shots on an outright sale basis—an unheard of practice to this day.

before noon on Monday, I had orders for my "Beautify Your Figure" totalling about two hundred thousand copies!

I tied up Sam's presses completely for the next two months, then finally he pulled me aside.

"Joe," he said, "I've got a pretty good sized printing shop here, but I can't handle this. Besides, I've got to think of my other accounts. You need a **big** printer; you're in the big leagues now!"

Well, Sam introduced me by telephone to C.S. Ruttle of the Cuneo Press. Cuneo is the largest magazine printing press in the world, turning out those millions of weekly copies of **Life**, as well as other magazines. When I went to Philadelphia to see their presses, I realized what Sam had meant. I thought Golden's shop was a pretty good sized one, but it compared, without exaggeration, as a rowboat might compare to a battleship. This **was** the big league!

Halfway through the second year of my publishing ventures, I had come out with six more One-Shots. "Beautify Your Figure" had sold more

than 400,000 copies! The others followed with corresponding success. "The Best That's In You," the male counterpart of the first, was the second of these One-Shots. Then followed "A Healthy Start In Life For Your Baby"; "Improve Your Dancing"; another edition of "Beautify Your Figure"; "Building Body Power," and "Make Up and Live."

By the end of that second year, I had sold more than a million of the different One-Shots to the American News Company **alone**, and had sold more than **two-and-one-half** million through all outlets! The success these books had was phenomenal; unprecedented in the history of One-Shot publishing!

From the Serial King of the movies, Joe Bonomo had become known in the publishing world as the "One-Shot King"!

Little did I realize how soon the bubble was to burst . . . that even then Fate was rolling up its sleeve, preparing to slug me with its best Sunday punch.

Chapter #32
"A BABE IN THE WOODS"

ONE AFTERNOON, a little more than two years after my first One-Shot hit the stands, I bumped into Roger Barrows again. Remember Roger, the promoter's promoter of the Bonomo Health Camp, located on the beautiful shores of a reservoir? I had always liked Roger . . . he had one of those personalities that it was hard NOT to like. He was a genius at promoting and could have charmed an oyster out of its last pearl. I'm sure he could have been an outstanding success if only he could have turned his mind to something beside crooked deals! Of course, had I known about his shady past I'd have been on my guard, but he had been honest in his dealings with me and I had no reason to suspect him, and I was sure glad to see him again.

We went in for a sandwich and a cup of coffee and to renew old acquaintance. Yes, Roger had been busy over the years. (I later found out that part of those years had been spent behind bars—but I didn't find it out in time.) He said he'd been working with a law firm in St. Louis and "a good lawyer is always busy." (It turned out he wasn't a lawyer, either, but he did know a lot about law, which he had picked up trying to stay out of the calaboose.) Yes, he was working in New York now as legal adviser to several Wall Street brokerage firms. "A fascinating place, Wall Street. Those fellows really know how to make money." Then the conversation got around to me.

"Joe, m'boy," Roger said, "I was sure glad to hear about your success with the One-Shots. It couldn't have happened to a nicer guy."

"Mostly luck," I acknowledged.

"Luck nothing!" Roger was tapping his temple. "You've got BRAINS, Joe—and IDEAS! Heck, I realized that way back when you were with Universal . . . and Laemmle and a lot of others did, too. You were the fair-haired boy around THAT studio."

I must admit I was enjoying the conversation. That kind of talk is mighty easy to take.

"How come you didn't stick with them?"

"Oh, you know how it goes, after my accident I—

"I sure was sorry to hear about that," he cut in, "but it all worked out for the best, proving, you can't keep a good man down. How's the hip now?"

"It could be lots worse . . . I can still get around all right."

"It must have hit you awfully hard, though." His mood had suddenly changed . . . he was shaking his head sadly and there were actually tears in his eyes. "What a tough break! You'd have been a top star by now."

"Aw, Roger, I couldn't have made it in the talkies. You know that," I said.

"What're you talking about, Joe," he protested, "a good coach could have gotten you ready in three months. Look at—" he flipped out a couple of names of top stars, men we both knew personally. "You remember them in the silent days —real stiffs. You were better than either of 'em, but THEY made it."

In both cases, these men weren't so hot and I had to concede the point. Also, I'm only human and I was beginning to like Roger Barrows more and more.

"The trouble with you, Joe," he was saying, "is that you were a fine actor and a **great** idea man, but when it came to plain business sense, tch, tch, tch . . .! You never should have gone back to stunting. You know that, don't you?"

I had to concede another point.

"The only thing you needed then was a smart manager." Roger snapped his fingers in frustration. "What a dunce I was! If I'd taken you in hand you'd never have had the accident and we'd both be top men in Hollywood today! Boy, was I a dope!"

Now I was starting to feel sorry for Roger.

"Don't blame yourself," I said, "neither of us could tell what the future held." But Roger wasn't to be comforted.

"No, Joe, let's face it. I was just a blind fool. What you needed then was a manager—just as you do NOW."

"What do you mean?" I asked, puzzled.

"Oh, don't misunderstand me, Joe . . . you're doing well enough I guess, just as you did in Hollywood. But why be satisfied with well enough! You've sold more than two and a half million One-Shots and what have you got to show for it? A million dollars? Not by a long shot!" He

seemed to know my business better than I did myself. "Why you should be another MacFadden —another Bernarr MacFadden!"

Here he whipped out a pencil and proceeded to show me, in mighty convincing figures, scribbled on the tablecloth, how I COULD be another Bernarr MacFadden and, in the next two years, definitely rake in a million and a quarter dollars—and in the next five years TEN million. I know this sounds preposterous but Roger SHOWED me! It was all there in black and white. Well, to make a long story a little shorter, I went for it like a little kid for a lollipop.

Then Roger told me to leave everything to him. For the extra capital, which of course we'd need to swing it, he'd dig up the backers among his Wall Street pals. A couple of days later he called to tell me he had a brokerage firm that was definitely interested in us—it was **us** now —and if we could show them we could produce, they'd back us to the tune of one hundred thousand dollars. We would become a regular publishing house, "Joe Bonomo Publications, Inc." and turn out a bi-monthly magazine. In a year we'd have three magazines and be rolling. Roger, genius that he was, had drawn up a complete prospectus covering the next two years.

Being congratulated by Tony Bruno outside the Wall Street broker's office where the ill-fated Joe Bonomo Publications Inc. was formed.

My staff and business kept growing as American News went to bat for us with our new magazine.

He took me down to Wall Street, to a brokerage firm. They had a beautiful suite of offices and I was greatly impressed. They said THEY were impressed by Roger's prospectus and my One-Shot record and saw no reason why they couldn't sell a hundred thousand dollars worth of stock almost immediately. The success of the venture lay squarely in my hands. Could I get out a bi-monthly health and beauty magazine comparable to the best on the market at the time? I was sure I could. All right then, they would guarantee me five thousand a month to operate on, from the sale of the stock. Yes, they could start selling it right away. It all sounded okay to me. A corporation would be formed with me as president. Management (me) would retain 50% of the corporation stock and capital (the brokers) would retain the other 50%.

What about Roger? For bringing the deal about we would each give him 5% of our holdings. So the contracts were drawn up. I had 45% — the brokers had 45% and Roger 10%. This was all to the good Roger told me in confidence, because, in an eventuality, he and I, with our combined 55%, would have the controlling vote.

So we moved into an impressive suite of offices at 1841 Broadway, occupying the entire third floor. (I have these same offices today—have **two** floors, as a matter of fact—but there was a lot of water to flow under the bridge from that time to this.)

All of the functioning offices of an enterprising publisher were set up, posts filled etc. and we were in business. Roger was retained as Legal Adviser, Secretary and Business Manager. It was a few weeks before we actually got up a full head of steam—then I came out with a couple of One-Shots and brought out the first issue of our bi-monthly magazine. "Good Healthkeeping." It included feature articles by Lowell Thomas, Jack Dempsey, several eminent physicians and myself, among others, and the fiction was by the top story writers of the day. "Good Health-keeping" was a truly beautiful slick paper magazine and an instantaneous click. It was a pity that the first issue was to prove to be the last!

At the end of the first three months the brokers had sold only $15,000 worth of stock, but with the One-Shots and the anticipated revenue from "Good Healthkeeping" I knew I could bring in well over $40,000. This, in a new publishing enterprise, was exceptional. We were moving a lot faster than we had anticipated and those brokers couldn't control themselves. A meeting was called and they proposed we declare a dividend, call back the stock and re-issue new stock. This refinancing was to be to the tune of a MILLION DOLLARS!

Mine was the only dissenting voice.

"Wait a minute," I protested, "you're way out in left field! Let's first get the rest of the hundred thousand. With the profits we're now showing we'll have more than enough to do everything we need to do. Let's keep to the prospectus!"

I looked to Roger for support but he was intently studying the pattern in the rug. A heated argument followed, with everyone yapping at me, telling me I had no vision and didn't know anything about stock manipulation, which was true enough. But I **did** know sound business and I flatly told them how things were going to **be**. With that the meeting broke up and they went out for a drink, taking Roger with them.

I don't know what went on after they left but I can pretty well guess. The next morning I got a registered letter informing me that another meeting had been held, a vote had been taken and I had been relieved of my duties as president of the corporation. Roger had voted his 10 shares on **their** side! I was still a director but I was no longer an officer and I'd have to do what the majority decided was for the good of the corporation.

Now, as I remarked once before, I'm a fairly peaceful guy. What the heck, I HAVE to be. With my strength, if I weren't, society would have to lock me up in the zoo with the OTHER gorillas. But when I got that letter, just as I was sitting down to breakfast, I felt a sudden surge of blood to my head and literally turned purple with rage. I had never known the "killer instinct" but I was feeling a touch of it then. Ethel told me later that in all the years she'd known me, she had never seen me like that.

I didn't storm out of the house...I even went through the motions of eating breakfast. I was trying to think . . . trying to think calmly. For God's sake, Joe, keep control of yourself or you'll do something you'll be sorry for. I kept looking at Ethel and Joanie and thinking about Roger—and looking at Ethel and Joanie again and thinking about Roger and the others. I finished my coffee and put the cup back in the saucer. Then I looked down and saw that both the cup and saucer were broken. Ethel was watching me and was now really alarmed.

"Joe—what IS it?"

"Nothing I can't take care of," I spoke as calmly as I could.

All the way to the office I fought to control my anger. I had a feeling Bonomo was once again going to stage one of his famous fight scenes—only this time for REAL!

The first and last copy of our new magazine.

They were there when I arrived and suddenly all my pent up rage exploded. I was fighting myself not to hurl them bodily through the office windows and they knew it. Roger and the others ran behind the desks, got all kinds of obstacles between me and them, did everything but climb up the walls. There is nothing more pitiful to me than a frightened man and they were terrified. They talked fast and, in a half hour or so, had me calmed down enough to talk rationally.

They said they still wanted to use the name Joe Bonomo, which they couldn't do without my permission . . . and they were prepared to take a one year option, for $45,000, on my 45% of the stock. They also agreed to pay me $200 a week for life, for the use of my name. I finally agreed to all this and the papers were drawn up . . . which I had no less than four different lawyers examine before signing. They'd never take me again!

When a man's down in the dumps it's good to have his family around.

The following week I left with Ethel and Joanie to visit Ethel's family in Los Angeles for a month. I needed a vacation now!

After my first week out on the coast the $200 checks stopped coming. In all, I had received only two of them. I wasn't worried though, because my contract was **fool-proof**.

When I got back to New York I immediately went over to 1841 Broadway to see about the over-due checks. You can imagine my feelings when I found the offices completely empty— stripped bare of everything. Even the lighting fixtures had been removed. I looked around in a daze—I couldn't believe my eyes.

Investigation showed they simply had not paid the bills against Joe Bonomo Publications, Inc. and thus had forced judgments to be taken. There was no judgment against **me**, just against the corporation and I had already resigned from that, but a marshal had been called in and had taken physical possession of the assets of the corporation. Then, at the private (and pre-arranged) marshal's sale that followed, my crooked associates had bought up the entire assets of Joe Bonomo Publications, Inc. for a few hundred dollars and moved everything to a new address down on Fifth Avenue. Forming a new corporation, HEALTHKEEPING, INC., they were a brand new outfit and didn't have to pay me a cent. In short, I had been very neatly manipulated out of the way. The maddening part of it was that everything was legal. Roger Barrows may not have been

a bona fide lawyer, but the buzzard certainly knew his law! The guy was a genius!

What happed to HEALTHKEEPING, INC.? Like most shady operators, my former partners had overlooked one thing in their haste to close me out and take over. They had forgotten that I was the only IDEA man in the crowd—the only one who had the basic ideas to make a successful venture of it. Now, unable to use my name, they got another strongman to front it, who went along for the $100 a week they paid him. They used him on the cover as a substitute for me, but the public had never heard of him and he meant nothing. And that's about what they had inside the cover—nothing! The second issue of the magazine never hit the stands and in a short time HEALTHKEEPING, INC. was bankrupt.

In the years that followed, several of them, including Roger Barrows had their pictures on display in U.S. Post Offices marked "Wanted." However, the knowledge that they had not succeeded was of small consolation to me. I was fighting now for my very existence, for a big slump had hit the candy business and our candy factory, dangerously over-expanded, hit the skids and it, too, went into bankruptcy. All of which goes to show how Fate, sometimes, piles it on.

Well, there I was or rather, where was I? I didn't know any more. ALL I DID know was that I was back down at the foot of the ladder and I wasn't sure I'd ever be able to climb back up to the top.

Chapter #33
THE STRANGE ROAD BACK

IT WAS AN AUTUMN DAY when Roger Barrows and the others nudged me out into the street . . . and left me stripped of everything but grim determination. I'd make a comeback —I HAD to—but how? I had no office to go to so I just sat around the apartment, racking my brain for a solution. What about going back into publishing? Maybe that would be barking up the wrong tree, though. Perhaps that cycle had completed itself. And with such a fiasco behind me where would I get enough backing to do it right?

How about Hollywood? Sure, I could probably get started again out there. Ethel's family was there. Perhaps that's where we belonged. But no, that didn't seem to be the answer either. After all my success I couldn't go back a failure. Here was where I'd lost it and here was where I'd have to make it back. All I needed was one good idea, something I could get my teeth into, something that would point the direction in which to go. So I moped around the house and nothing happened.

One day Ethel said, "Why don't you take a run down to the gym, Joe? You'll stagnate just sitting around doing nothing."

"Yeah," I said, "maybe I will." But I didn't move.

"Joe," Ethel persisted, "you can't let this get you down so. This is simply the way Fate is pushing you. Something better is going to come out of it—I can feel it."

"Okay, maybe I will go down to the gym." I put my coat on and started out.

"What time do you want dinner?" Ethel called after me.

"Don't bother with dinner for ME, honey. I'll eat at Lindy's with some of the boys."

"Good," said Ethel, "that sounds more like you."

I stepped out of the apartment building into one of those clear, brisk October afternoons. I stood there under the marquee for a minute or so, then started for my car that Ethel, after shopping, had parked at the curb. It was tightly sandwiched in between two other cars and I considered for a moment as to how to get it out. Then I noticed the autumnal colors of the foliage across the street. I crossed over and started walking through Central Park.

I walked for a bit, then sat down on a bench, lost in the old indecisive thoughts. Maybe if I looked up Tony Bruno or August Leidy, they might have an idea. Or maybe if I phoned Hollywood and talked to—

"Hi, fella!" I looked up to see a tall, good-looking man standing in front of me. "Got a cigarette?"

He was a few years older than I, with sandy hair and a warm smile. I noticed he was pretty well dressed and wondered why he didn't have his **own** cigarettes.

"No, I'm sorry, buddy, I haven't." I answered truthfully.

"Then maybe you'd like one of MINE," he grinned, producing a package from his pocket.

If I could just work up the old Bonomo spirit and interest—I'd be back in business in no time.

What the heck is this guy's angle, I thought . . . so I asked him.

"I just wondered if all that stuff about you not smoking was true. You're Joe Bonomo, aren't you?"

I admitted I was. I guess I was sort of pleased that he'd recognized me. It wasn't too often that strangers did, anymore. So I grinned back at him and asked him what the pitch was.

"No pitch," he laughed. "I just felt like talking —I recognized you and I thought you might be an interesting guy to talk to. It's as simple as that."

Then we both laughed and I asked him to sit down. He asked me about Hollywood and some of the pictures he had seen me in and I learned that his name was Bill Ashline and that he was sales manager for a big toy manufacturer. Things were pretty tight, he'd made all the calls he could, so he figured he'd just take the rest of the day off.

"Business doesn't sound too good," I said.

"Oh, it's all right," he replied, "only we're not doing the volume we should."

"Have you tried selling the syndicates?" I asked.

"No, our sales are to jobbers . . . jobbers and the big department stores."

"But surely you realize the tremendous volume the syndicates represent? Why those chain stores do a business of—"

"Oh, we realize it all right, but with no connections I haven't been able to get a foot in the door."

So I told him about my work since I left Hollywood—and about the candy business—and about the contacts I had with the chain store buyers. One thing led to another and Bill suggested that perhaps we could do some business together —perhaps I might represent them with the variety chains.

So we talked some more. He told me about his company and what they made. He had brochures with him on some of the merchandise and right there, on that bench in Central Park, practically in the shadow of my apartment, "J.B.A. —Joe Bonomo Associates—Manufacturer's Representative," was conceived.

We had been talking for more than an hour and I began to grow restless again. But this time it was with that wonderful, tingling feeling that used to come over me as I got ready to do a stunt. I knew then that I was off the hook— that this was the break I'd been waiting for. I had to get into action. I suggested we get my car and go for a drive.

"I'd like to," said Bill, "but I've got to get back to the plant and sign my mail. Why not take a run over there with me and meet the big boss?"

"Nothing would suit me better. Where's the plant?"

"Just over the George Washington Bridge, in Jersey. We can grab a cab and—"

"Heck, I live just across the street," I said. "My car's right in front of the door. Come on, I'll run you out there."

When we got back to my apartment house my car wasn't sandwiched in anymore. It seemed a good omen.

Over at the plant Bill introduced me to the president of the company. He was impressed with my background and I was able to convince him of the syndicate store potential, through my connections. I showed him how he could easily repack and reprice his products to make them attractive to the chain stores and I was given exclusive representation to the variety chains.

It was just getting dark when Bill and I left the plant to return to New York. We were driving along the Palisades when Bill suggested stopping for something to eat.

"How about going over to Lindy's?" I said. "Do you like the food there?"

"Who **doesn't**," he grinned. "Is their cheesecake still as good as ever?"

"It's better," I said. We were both working

up an appetite, just thinking about dinner, as we headed toward the bridge. Darkness came on fast, the way it does on those autumn days. We could see the George Washington Bridge in the distance now, with the lights strung out along the big suspension cables. If I live to be a thousand, that's a sight that will always give me a thrill.

Then we turned onto the approach to the bridge and started across. I was telling Bill about the dives I made from Suicide Cliff when I suddenly spotted a man standing upright on the bridge outer rail, with his hand on one of the suspension cables. I guess my mind was still on stunting and I thought, for a moment, that there was a pretty good shot. It would make a great scene. In the next second I realized there were no movie cameras around. That guy was for real and he wasn't ACTING! I jammed on the brakes—I had already gone a little past him—and threw the car into reverse.

"Yell at that guy," I shouted to Bill as we started back.

"What guy?" Bill must have thought my mind had snapped the switch. But by then I was out of the car and running.

"Hey!" I yelled, "Hey, YOU!"

There, blinking dazedly in the edge of the headlight beams, this pathetic figure stood, in suspended action at that fine edge of indecision between living or dying. I skidded to a quick stop.

"Hiya, buddy," I said in a matter of fact tone,

"What're you looking for? Lose something down there?"

"What?" He started to edge away along the rail.

"I said what did you lose down there . . . maybe I can help you find it."

I knew I had to be quiet with this fellow, just as I had to be quiet that time, long ago, when I was locked in the cage with those lions. I knew if I alarmed him he'd let go and plunge to his death.

"I'll bet if we **both** looked we could find it." I edged a step closer to him. He just stood there, sort of transfixed.

"What was it, buddy? You can trust ME."

By this time I was close enough. I lunged forward, caught him above the knees and pulled him off the rail. He started to struggle but I clamped an arm-lock on him as Bill came running up to us. When he realized he couldn't get away he suddenly went limp and started to cry. There was no use trying to talk to him then, so we put him in the car and drove on across the bridge. We parked on the other side and Bill and I went to work on him.

I won't go through the details of the next half hour . . . they're not important anyway. What IS important is that he wasn't out of his mind as I had first thought—just at the end of his rope. We got his story in bits and pieces.

I'll just call him Jerry, because he's a fairly well known man today. If HE ever wants to tell his story to the world, well, that's HIS bus-

Things began to take a turn for the better.

In the role of manufacturer's representative I got back on the showmanship bandwagon by starting off Marlon Confections in a big Walgreen—"Marlon Girl" promotion.

iness. Meanwhile let's keep him anonymous. He was a writer, a college graduate, married and, at the age of thirty-three, considered himself the all time All-American failure. His wife had proven to be one of those gold digging gals and Jerry just couldn't keep up with her demands, so she'd left him for another guy. Jerry was still in love with her but there wasn't much he could do about it. He was lonely, mixed up, frustrated and dead broke. The only solution seemed to be the bridge.

"Look, buddy," I said, "there are three billion people in this crazy old world and half of them are women. Do you mean to say that out of all those gals you can't find one to take the place of that doll who walked away? You want to end your life—the only one you'll ever have, probably—on account of you picked a Lemon in the Garden of Love? Aw, come off it—there's a million opportunities—and a million jobs—and a jillion women."

Then Bill chipped in with his two cents and it wasn't long before Jerry was feeling a lot better. By now Bill and I were starving, so we dragged Jerry along with us to Lindy's . . . and after he got a good meal under his belt the world didn't seem such a bad place after all.

The next morning I went back to 1841 Broadway. Although I was about as welcome, to the landlord, as the Black Plague, I explained that Roger Barrows incident to him and I guess he felt sorry for me, for he rented me a small office on the second floor for twenty-five dollars a month. And by that same afternoon I was hustling from one buyer's office to the next, as a manufacturer's

representative. Within a few weeks I had the exclusive variety chain representation for Marlon Confections—I had Bill's toy line in the chain stores from coast to coast and I had started work on another One-Shot.

Jerry? Oh, he went to work for me as a publication editor, mail answerer and general all-round assistant. He worked for me for more than a year and got a new lease on life. Since then he has been off to war, came back a decorated Naval officer, worked successfully in advertising in New York for a while then, through a contact I was able to make for him, got a good job on the west coast in the picture industry. And he finally found that other girl in the jillion. Yes, he's happily married this time and has a wonderful little family. And while Jerry was rebuilding HIS life, I was rebuilding MINE. I soon had an enviable list of clients and had even gone into the manufacturing end myself. A new door had opened for me and the future was filled with promise.

It's strange how Fate sometimes uses a seemingly insignificant detail as a keystone. If my car had not been sandwiched in that afternoon, I'd never have gone to the park. If I hadn't gone to the park I wouldn't have met Bill Ashline who, unknowingly held the key to my problem. And if I hadn't met Bill I wouldn't have been driving back from Jersey that evening and Jerry would have gone off the bridge! Was it merely chance . . . a lucky coincidence . . . or is it possible that, mysteriously operating between heaven and earth, there really IS "a destiny that shapes our ends?" What do YOU think?

Chapter #34
"The GLORIFIED PEDDLER"

In the world of business it's usually a crazy mixture of ingredients that makes a man successful. Call it luck, experience or the knack of outsmarting the other guys—your competitors—and you have it all. I guess my own career covers this ground, but somehow my experiences in the world of commerce have at times turned out as humorous and fantastic as many of the movies I appeared in out in Hollywood.

I do know that I have something going for me in the areas that I specialize in and having confidence in myself and my decisions is an important link in the chain. When a person comes into my office and puts a piece of merchandise down on my desk, somehow I have that sixth sense of knowing what will and will not sell. This is actually half the battle. I will never take on a product which isn't a volume seller—but, when something has promise I go to work on it. My first thought is to try to improve the quality, price it properly and package it in a colorful way. This then gives me a stronger item to sell when I present it to one of the large chain store organizations.

I found that the best way to get real promotions for my big chain store buyers was to watch the better department stores and see what they were featuring. One store might be having a run on lamps selling for $12.50 or so. We would buy a sample and have our factories come up with what we called a real "knock off". In other words, by cutting all corners we would produce a duplicate of that very lamp, which could retail for $6.95, and then we would promote them to the hilt.

This procedure worked on all kinds of merchandise and was a successful way of selling high priced articles to the mass buying public at popular chain store prices. Today this practice is a billion dollar business and the Japanese have taken over as the world's leading "knock off" artists. Their trade with this country alone in copy goods half the price of the original is tremendous.

I have always been fascinated by what compels people to buy. In the old days at Coney Island it was the spieler at the sideshow—that amusing man who had the wonderful way with words. Why he could talk you into seeing any show—almost! Being a super salesman the spieler always had some extra ways of tricking the public into buying that ticket. He would bring along two or three shills—people who became quickly enthused with his talk and were the first ones to buy. (They were of course on his payroll.) This had a funny effect on the crowd and many of the people standing around in the crowd would also rush up to buy tickets. As wacky as it sounds, products of all kinds are still sold today with the help of shills.

I'm sure that many times you've seen someone demonstrating kitchen gadgets in one of the big chain stores. These demonstrators may be

Discussing a new product line with Howard Hawkins, electrical buyer for a big national chain store organization.

actors, regular product salesmen or just individuals who enjoy the art of selling—and it is an art! Well, as you watch the demonstrator's deft hands peel a potato into the Venus de Milo, or something close, you get hooked. This man is an expert at his trade and you feel you can duplicate his feats on the spud at home. Suddenly, several of the people watching this demonstration rush up to buy potato peelers. Here's where the shills come in—and, you feel that burst of inner exuberance, that voice inside telling you to buy. When you get home somehow you're "all thumbs" and unable to cut rings around ordinary vegetables as the expert at the store did. Well, this is how millions of those unused gadgets in almost every average home's kitchen get there.

Selling is a strange business and sometimes the most attractive counter display of a product will fall on its face. On the other hand , another counter may be set up as a "dump display" and sell out. This is when everything is thrown on the counter and piled up high. Above this a boldly lettered sign proclaims: BARGAIN SALE—TODAY ONLY. Once again the people buying are mesmerized by the atmosphere created. Everybody seems to be buying a great bargain and each person wants to get his before somebody else does. This is what we call "Mass Hysteria Buying"—and many times pretty good panics over ladies' lingerie do result.

If items are shown off to their best advantage or not usually decides how they will sell. In the candy business it was originally a great problem to promote peanut brittle in an attractive display. It just didn't have "eye appeal". So we figured out a way of making special wire frames to display the peanut brittle and then poured it hot on these frames. What we came up with was very impressive little buildings and huts, which never

failed to attract attention when they were used in the windows of the big chain stores. The trick paid off well—it sold tons and tons of peanut brittle.

In selling candy we would also make a "dump display" counter of salt water taffy, putting a heater near an exhaust vent that led out into the street. Then we would boil hot water with several ounces of peppermint in it and a fan would blow the aroma out through the exhaust vent onto the street. This would go down the street for blocks and it never failed to bring crowds into the store to buy peppermint taffy. This was pre-selling.

When our candy company bought out an outfit specializing in roasted and salted nuts I called on Alan Crane, the senior buyer for Liggett-Rexall, to sound him out on the subject. He was all ready for me and quietly tried to find out if this salesman knew what he was talking about.

"Joe, what's the best new up and coming nut line today?" (As if he didn't know at that time.)

Well, I thought a bit, knowing it could be any one of a couple of items. And, using a salesman's imagination, felt I'd play it safe.

"Mixed nuts are always very popular and should be the top seller nationally." Well, I couldn't be too far wrong as mixed nuts combined most of the other popular nuts in one product.

Mr. Crane looked at me hesitatingly for a moment, not sure of how to take the answer and then showed me his sales charts. Mixed nuts **were** popular, but a new item **was** coming up strong—cashews.

"As you know Joe, these are comparatively new over here and quite expensive, but they're

Sponsoring a promotional meeting with Mrs. Henri Sedacca, wife of the president of Noma Electric. At this gathering the then new Christmas tree "bubble lights" were introduced.

I sold my Self Improvement mail order courses to the hilt with ads in many national magazines. We had a special diploma for all students completing the course and a medal for outstanding achievement.

How 'BLACK BEAUTY' TURNS AN ALSO-RAN *into* "VIDEO VIC!"

Some of the top comic strip artists of the day produced my physical culture advertising over 20 years ago. So great was the reader interest in these courses that our *Strongmen's Club of America* had over 350,000 members, while our women's *Charm Circle* boasted over 860,000 members.

building a following all their own. The only problem is that cashews are too expensive for the average family. Come up with a popular price for us and we can sell tons of cashews."

For a week I worked on "Operation Cashew" and figured that if I didn't wind up as a "nut expert" I would at least be considered to be a "nut". I checked with every importer and firm having anything at all to do with cashews. In my researching I found out that cashews were not a nut at all, but a fruit which grew in a type of shell. They were originally from the East & West Indies and their background, for some unknown reason, was not highly publicized. The importers of cashews sold the shelled whole nuts at a high price to outfits like ours which roasted and salted them for over the counter sales. The nuts that were broken in half became pieces called "splits" and the ends that were broken off were called "butts". These were sold at a much lower price to outfits that chopped them up for use in candy and bakery goods.

Here was where I saw an idea for an exceptional cashew promotion. Returning to Alan Crane I told him of my discovery.

"We can mix 'splits' and 'butts' with whole nuts, which won't affect the taste, and give you a deal that will let you cut the market price by twenty cents a pound." His surprised reaction was clear and quick.

"Joe, if you can successfully put this across, we'll take all the cashews you can supply."

And that's just what happened—by this one little trick cashews came down in price, making them available to all and leading to the great popularity they enjoy today. To help sell them we came up with an elaborate disply on "cashews", their background and featured samples of the whole nut, the uncooked "inside" nut and the final ready to eat product. I even had a huge cooker brought in to one of the stores as a demonstration of how cashews were freshly cooked. Just another deal out of the frying pan and into the nut roaster.

In this crazy life of ours so many strange things go on that we know nothing about. This couldn't be more true in the commercial world. Tricks and stunts are constantly used in selling and production in an attempt to get a bigger profit at the end of the year. At the candy factory one such method was very successfully employed to the company's benefit.

We were the first to put out a low priced assorted box of miniature chocolates for the chain stores. To speed up this work the factory had a system of automatic conveyor belts. There were thirty two different types of candy to go in each box and lined up by the conveyor belt thirty two girls performed the task of placing the correct chocolates in the box. The candy box would start on one end of the belt and as it passed each girl she would put one piece of candy in it. At the end the box went into an automatic cellophane wrapping machine and was finished.

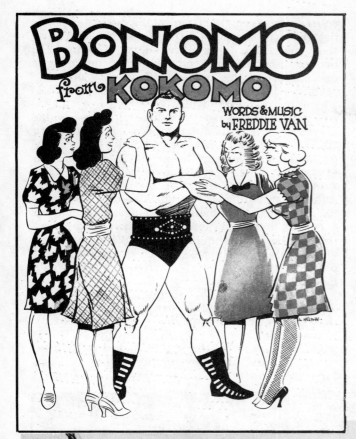

(Above) During World War II I was flattered to have a song about me written & published.

(Below) Both Ethel and Joan graced the cover of my BEAUTY FAIR magazine—and, our glamor policy included tie-ins with the Hollywood studios, like this cover girl promotion on Republic Pictures' actress Adele Mara.

Our belt ran on three speeds, but the girls never knew it. In the early morning we'd run at low speed, changing into a brisker pace at 11:00 as the girls were hitting their stride. When they came back from lunch the faster third speed was used. In this way we got a higher amount of finished boxes off each conveyor belt without anybody being a bit the wiser.

Throughout my years in the game of selling I continued to publish my courses and one-shots in the fields of health and self-improvement. After the start of World War II the entire publishing business was put on a system of paper allotments, which hurt many of the publications that were not printed and sold on a regular schedule. This was so because you could get only as much paper for printing as you had used in your previous consumption.

Once again another obstacle to overcome and with it success or failure for my publishing operation. If I had ceased publication it would have been difficult to start up later on as a "known" publisher. On the other hand, putting out publications on a regular basis could also prove disastrous, if they didn't catch on.

I decided to take the gamble and almost literally "go for broke". I took all my one-shots and courses, updated them and along with new, similar subjects started to bring them out as a quarterly magazine. This gave me all the paper I needed, and as luck would have it, they caught on. As part of this operation I brought out four revised editions of BEAUTIFY YOUR FIGURE, which became established as a quarterly magazine. After the war I introduced it as a regular magazine, which had its name soon changed to BEAUTY FAIR. It was a successful bi-monthly for well over five years with a certified circulation of 250,000 copies each issue. In this manner the Audit Bureau of Circulations guarantees the magazine's exact number of copies sold to its advertisers. When I published the magazine I had an excellent staff and personally supervised everything done. My formula was to have many different articles in each issue, which covered different parts of the world of female beauty. The gals loved it.

Now what could be further away from the world of action and adventure that I love so much than a specialized woman's magazine—actually nothing! You see, I was close to this in Hollywood and many of the studios' glamorous little secrets wound up right in my books. Anyone for horror movie makeup?

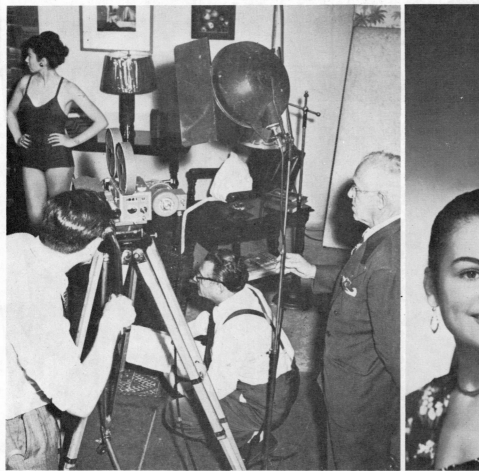

My old boss, former Universal serial chief Fred J. McConnell (right), supervised the production of my filmed health & beauty series, which was the first show of its kind in the early days of television. I also managed some time away from the office to visit on the set with Joan, in the days when she was a professional model and dancer.

Chapter #35
STUNTING IS FOR PROFESSIONALS

A few years ago I was having lunch with Harvey Parry in Hollywood and he surprised me by presenting me with an honorary membership in the Stuntmen's Association of Motion Pictures. Later on he took me over to meet some of today's top stuntmen. I was really amazed. The more that I study the stunt business today, I see that it is just that—a **business!** The Association helps to protect the stuntmen so that they get properly paid for each stunt they do. The payment is according to the difficulty of the stunt plus the risk involved.

Each man is listed at the Association for his own specialites—the stunts he does best. In the old days we had to do everything—even if it hadn't been done before. We found out the best way to do the stunt and then we did it. All the tricks and stuntman's devices that we came up with years ago the stunters of today can use and improve on. The safety belts, wires and padding are still there, but stunting still must have men who are top athletes as its first prerequisite.

What makes a stuntman? Why do people do stunts? First of all, performing a stunt is like participating in every sport—there's a basic thrill involved while taking part in the activity. Secondly, there's a bigger thrill still when the stunt is accomplished. Where do stuntmen come from? Years ago many stuntmen came from the circus. Top men like Paul Malvern and Richard Talmadge had strong acrobatic backgrounds as their families brought them up as circus performers. Dick Talmadge, in many cases with the help of his famous brothers (the Metzettis), accomplished some of the most sensational acrobatic stunts and jumps ever seen in the business. A lot of stuntmen, like myself, were and are good all around athletes, although they do not have a circus or similar background.

Harvey Parry, seen here risking his neck in an early silent comedy, is still active today and one of the few stuntmen on Medicare.

(Left) Harvey Parry does a high comedy fall into a net.
(Above) Retired motorcycle stunter Allen Pomeroy in action & Harvey Parry becomes a flaming inferno while wearing a special face mask to make him look like the actor he's doubling.
(Below) Troy Melton, Harvey Parry and Joe Yrigoyen were all injured by hitting hard ground in this spectacular 38 ft. tower fall.

(Clockwise from Left) Paul Malvern leaps onto a speeding train—An unexpected shift in heavy logs on a railroad flatcar almost costs stuntman Bob Morgan his life—Cliff Lyons, Harvey Parry and Duke Green stage a daring three man fall in a big western fight—Harvey Parry crashes through a saloon window.

(Above) Two great pals of mine — Paul Malvern and Harvey Parry.
(Below) Hollywood's car crash specialists—Harvey Parry, Carey Loftin and Dale Van Sickel.

A good stuntman is a strong, muscular fellow who has developed superior coordination of his muscles. He has stamina, is cool-headed and doesn't panic in a situation that goes wrong. Stunting also requires the utmost confidence in the people you work with, who **must** be dependable—your director, your fellow stunters and your crew.

Dick Talmadge, who is now directing, was great and even starred in many of his own films. But,

for years he was Douglas Fairbanks' stuntman, which was quite a task. Not that Doug couldn't do most of the stunts himself, but because of the risk to a big star, he couldn't take **all** the chances. As we all know, Fairbanks was one of the greatest athletic stars of his day and he always had enough money to hire the best talent to teach him exactly what he had to do for a film. In one instance he wanted to know how to do some fancy whip tricks. He hired the top whip expert in the business and for two or three weeks this man was Fairbanks' guest at a terrific salary. Every single day they went out and practiced the various whip snapping tricks and stunts until Doug was an expert at it. Whenever he wanted to learn about shooting, archery or fencing there too he hired experts to teach him. As in the case of fencing, Fairbanks would use the person who taught him in the movie and they would get a great sequence shot.

I knew Doug when I was working for Universal and he used to be fascinated by the tricks I did with trampolines. Sure enough, he quickly took to using trampolines for trick jumps, being trained by one of the top circus acts. In three or four weeks he was as good on the trampoline as anybody. Of course, being a natural born athlete helped.

In the 1920's and 1930's a lot of working cowboys who were good riders were hired by Hollywood studios to do stunts. Unfortunately, many of these cowboys depended on good old rye whiskey for the confidence needed to do a stunt. Many a time I'd see one of these boys take a few slugs before trying a horse fall or running "W". This was because he was insecure and unsure of what he was doing. To professionals like former rodeo champ Yakima Canutt and Cliff Lyons, who both specialized in horse stunts, a fall was an easy everyday performance and men like this always knew exactly what to do, they didn't need confidence from a bottle.

Floyd Criswell used to specialize in motorcycle stunts, but before doing a stunt he'd warm up for at least a half hour. This was to be sure that his circulation was good, his muscles limber, his mind clear and his body in generally good shape. He warmed up to the point where an ordinary fall would not cause a broken bone, as his bones were somewhat pliable and he was prepared for the rough work he was going into.

A long time ago I developed **VIBRO POWER** and five great principles of exercising: **COSMIC BREATHING, VIBRO PRESSURE, RHYTHMIC PROGRESSION, PSYCHO POWER** AND **TONIC RELAXATION**. These varied principles have been more recently adapted by others and called Isometrics, Isotonics and other fancy names.

On these pages I have outlined a series of suggested exercise combinations which cover my five principles for body building and body conditioning. Whether you're a professional athlete, stuntman or business man, physical fitness is a must. Out of this illustrated group you can pick out twelve series and do these exercises at least fifteen times each (**more if you can**) daily and every week go back and pick a different combination of twelve. These exercises are designed to strengthen your heart, your breathing and will tone up every muscle in **your body.** This type of routine is essential for physical well being and should be done every day of the week.

Keeping in good condition is as important to the average man as to the movie stuntman. Good health always pays great dividends.

(Above) Harvey barely survives a flaming wreck.
(Below) An old-time "awning jump" escape.

343

JOE BONOMO'S "GOLDEN DOZEN" BODY CONDITIONERS

Proper Exercise and **Proper Breathing** are a daily must for good health. The Human Body is divided into 10 systems: 1—**Skeletal**, 2—**Muscular**, 3—**Nervous**, 4—**Circulatory**, 5—**Tegumentary**, 6—**Respiratory**, 7—**Alimentary**, 8—**Excretory**, 9—**Endocrine** and 10—**Reproductive**. Here is a series of exercises that have been especially chosen to aid the functioning of these systems as they work out the 45 important muscle groups, which include the hundreds of muscles in your body.

Pick out a series of 12 different Exercises each week. Do each one at least 15 times daily, for a full week. At the end of the week select a new series of 12 to make up your weekly "Golden Dozen". Exercise at any time of the day that suits you best, but always **allow at least one hour after**

EXERCISE 1—Stand comfortably erect, hands at sides. Inhale slowly, and at the same time, draw in the muscles of the abdomen, raising arms slowly at side. In other words, pull in your stomach and push up the chest as you fill your lungs to their capacity. Relax the stomach muscles as you exhale.

EXERCISE 2—A variation of Abdominal Breathing to develop the lower sections of the lungs. Breathe in deeply and then press the air down and out as far as you can go. With practice you should easily simulate a "pot belly".

EXERCISE 3—This exercise to depress the abdominal wall is the reverse of #2. First, breathe out and, while doing so, try to draw up your innards as if trying to turn yourself inside-out. Master this and alternately combine it with #2 so that you can keep up an undulating movement with your Abdominal muscles.

EXERCISE 4—This will combine the isolation of your Abdominal muscles with deep breathing control. First, breathe in deeply, then exhale slowly. When your lungs are a little more than half empty, contract your Abdominal muscles and hold this for a moment. Then relax and repeat.

EXERCISE 5—Here's another variation of a combined isolation and breathing exercise. After you have learned how completely to depress the Abdominal wall, as in #3, contract the Abdominal muscles until the contraction demonstrated has been secured. Relax, and repeat a few times more.

EXERCISE 6—Take a standard size newspaper sheet of four pages and hold it up by one corner. Crumple it into a ball in one hand, without the assistance of the other hand. Do this until your hand and forearm begin to feel tired, then repeat with other hand.

EXERCISE 13—Do this one cautiously for it is harder than it looks. Lie flat on your stomach, arms and legs outstretched, with arms stiffened and legs stiffened, raise both the arms and legs off the floor until you are resting only on your abdomen. Now, try to rock back and forth on your stomach. Continue until you are pleasantly tired.

EXERCISE 14—Lie on your right side with your legs held about 6 inches off the floor. Swing the left leg out and the right leg back; then reverse these leg swings, performing the exercise in rhythmic scissors fashion. Then lie on your left side and repeat. Start doing this exercise 8 counts on each side, work to a maximum of 15 times.

EXERCISE 15—Lie down flat on your back, keeping arms straight and on the floor with palms and hands on hips. Bring your legs up and above your head while supporting yourself with your shoulders and elbows. After attaining this position, lower the right leg until it touches the floor, keeping the left leg erect as illustrated; then raise the right leg to original position and simultaneously lower the left leg. Stop when tired.

EXERCISE 16—Lie flat with your chin and backs of hands on the floor. Press your toes as far back as they will go. Now raise one leg, pointing toe hard upwards, pull head back. Internally resist upward movement. Lower head and foot back to starting position, apply internal pressure against downward movement. Repeat with other leg. Do 15 times with each leg.

EXERCISE 17—Lie flat on your stomach and then raise yourself until you are resting on your palms and toes. Lift one foot clear off the floor, resisting the upward movement all the way. Now raise and lower your entire body with your arms, without sagging. Repeat and alternate this exercise, raising the other foot off the floor.

EXERCISE 18—Lie flat on your stomach with your legs straight out behind you. Place the palms of your hands flat on the floor and push yourself up with your arms. On the downward movement, flex at the elbows. Return slowly to the floor and repeat until you are slightly tired.

EXERCISE 25—Seated in a chair, as per the illustration, bring up the right foot and grasp it with both hands. Turn and twist in every direction, resisting with hands. Stop as soon as you feel that you are actually tired and repeat this procedure exactly with the other foot.

EXERCISE 26—Rest your left hand on a stool or wooden box of the approximate size shown in the illustration. Now, resting your left hand in this manner, lift your left leg from the floor, and sink down on your right leg. Raise yourself to an upright standing position using only the muscles of your right leg to do so.

EXERCISE 27—Sit on a stool and grasp the inside of your ankles. Pull up as hard as you can, resisting the upward movement by pushing down with your feet. Make hard work of the resistance for the maximum benefit to be gained from this exercise.

EXERCISE 28—This exercise is a variation of exercise #27 and will benefit other muscles. Grasp the "outside" of your ankles, and pull up as hard as you can, pushing down with your feet. Again, pull real hard, gripping the ankles firmly. Relax, and repeat at least ten times.

EXERCISE 29—To properly start this exercise stand erect with your feet placed slightly apart. Bend over and then partially squat, reaching through your legs and putting your knuckles as far back as can possibly be done. Press back hard and then relax.

EXERCISE 30—This exercise movement builds up the thighs and rounds out the knees, helping the pectorals, shoulders and back. Squat with hands outside knees, with knees together. Pull knees apart, resisting all the way with your hands. Push knees together with your hands, resisting all the way.

eating. These few Exercises should take you only 15 minutes a day to do.

Exercise in a well ventilated room, wearing shorts only. Try to do this in front of a mirror to be sure of the proper movements—this will also help you to note improvement and muscle development. **Proper Breathing** is important—upon starting take a big, deep breath. As you do the Exercise exhale through your teeth making a hissing sound. Remember, you can add years to your life through doing the **Proper Exercise.** Don't forget to get a complete **medical checkup** at least once a year. If you have any physical ailment or infirmity . . . or have any doubt about the advisability of applying any of these Exercises to your particular case, be sure to submit them to your doctor first. **Attention Ladies:** Look over these **Body Conditioning Exercises** as there are many of them you can pick out to do. They will positively not make you muscular, but will help to tone up your body and **Beautify Your Figure.**

EXERCISE 7—Lie flat on your back with your hands under your head. Bring the legs and lower body upward, overhead in a slow arc, and try to touch the toes on the floor behind you. The weight of your legs will offer all the resistance necessary at first. You may assist this movement with your hands—later try to do it with palms under your head.

EXERCISE 8—Lie flat on your back, palms on floor. Press toes hard away from you. Now raise your thighs slowly, resisting the upward movement until your knees are pressed as close to your chest as possible. Then return to the starting position, resisting the backward movement.

EXERCISE 9—Lie flat on your back, hands beneath your hips. Press toes away from you. Gradually raise legs, and spread them at the same time. When legs are raised as far as they can go, they should also be as wide apart as possible. Lower legs bringing them slowly together to starting position. Apply internal resistance to both upward and downward movement.

EXERCISE 10—Sit on a chair and clasp your hands behind your neck. Pull your head down between your knees, resisting this movement all the way. Rise to a normal sitting position, pause and then repeat. Stop before completely tired.

EXERCISE 11—Stand erect. Lower your chin as much as possible. Put the butt of your hand against your chin and push slowly back, resisting all the way with the muscles of your neck. Return to original position, alternate and repeat about ten times.

EXERCISE 12—Stand erect. One hand on hip. Place other hand against ear and push over as hard as you can, resisting all the way. Both the neck muscles and side muscles should come into play here. Return to starting position, resisting the return movement. Repeat each side about 10 times.

EXERCISE 19—Stand erect, with your feet spread slightly apart. Extend your arms straight out in front of you. Bend down until your fingers touch the floor between your feet, then rise, swinging the arms upward and backward overhead as far as they will go. Stop when tired.

EXERCISE 20-21—Stand bent over with arms outstretched as illustrated, with the feet wide apart, the knees rigid. Swing forward until you touch left toe with the finger tips of the right hand, at the same time swinging the left arm to over-head position. Continue this pendulum action, alternating from right to left. Start with ten counts and increase to a maximum of twenty. Be sure your legs are kept rigid. If your hips and mid-section are heavy, work fairly fast on this exercise.

EXERCISE 22—Sit on the floor, legs straight and slightly parted. Point toes well forward. Now spread your arms out on each side of you. With a slow, swinging movement, turn your torso and make the tips of the left fingers touch your right toe. Your left hand should swing behind you. As you swing around, resist the movement internally. Now swing back to original position, and follow through until right hand touches left toe. Repeat until slightly tired.

EXERCISE 23—This will give you exercise equivalent to that obtained from bicycle riding. Lie on your back. Keep your hands stretched out naturally at your sides. Assist with hands on hips until desired position is attained. Raise both legs straight up from body, and rotate, just as if you were operating the pedals of a bicycle. Resist the movement internally and stop when tired.

EXERCISE 24—Those who suffer with constipation will find this exercise of invaluable aid—for not only does it develop your front thighs and the whole upper leg—it also massages the internal organs, like the bowels and kidneys. First stand erect, with hands at sides. Now squat down on your heels, trying not to raise them from the floor. As you come down, raise your hand shoulder-high in front. Then, push up from the floor as hard as you can.

EXERCISE 31—This simple exercise if properly performed can definitely be an aid in the correction of flat feet. Sit on a chair and place some marbles on the floor in front of you. Try to pick them up with the toes of each foot. This is not as easy as it looks and through its correct application a great benefit can result.

EXERCISE 32—Stand erect with your arms hanging naturally at your side. Clench your fists and raise your arms up at your sides. Now cross your arms, putting the right over the left, pressing as hard as you can. Apply internal resistance to the crossing movement. Then, swing your arms back to starting position, resisting the backward movement. Relax and repeat with the left over right.

EXERCISE 33—Stand erect, hands at sides. Now clench your hands and bring them together. At the same time tense all your arm muscles including the shoulder Deltoids. Roll in your hands so that the knuckles touch, and twist the entire arm and shoulder round. Try to make your elbows meet. Internally resist this twisting movement as much as is comfortably possible. Do until pleasantly tired.

EXERCISE 34—Stand erect in front of a chair and thrust your arms straight out in front of you. Now, step up on a chair with your right foot, following it with your left, until both feet are on the chair seat. Step down on the floor and reverse the process, stepping up with the left foot and following it with the right.

EXERCISE 35-36—Stand with your left hand on the back of a chair. Swing your right leg back as far as it will go. If you will bend your leg at the knee, you will feel the "pull" on the front thigh muscles. If you keep the leg stiff it becomes merely a hip exercise. Alternate and practice the same movement with the left leg. For a variation rest your right hand on the back of a chair, keeping your body erect. Raise the left foot up as high as possible in front of you and then swing it back as far as possible behind you. Do this about ten times, and then repeat with the other leg. Internally resist the forward-upward movement.

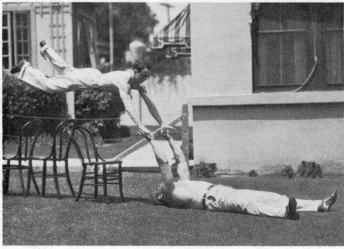

Being in top condition is a must for all stunt-men.
(Left) Some acrobatic practice.
(Above) Throwing Paul Malvern in a ditch in
PERILS OF THE WILD & holding 200 lb. Al
Baffert in the air.

Stuntmen's Association
OF MOTION PICTURES

HONORARY 🎥 MEMBER

JOE BONOMO

Dale Van Sickel
President

Fred Krone
Treasurer

One of my famous roof jumps, aided by a spring board, which helped me reach the building on the other side of the street. A circus net was spread there, instead of a regular roof top, for me to land in. In the final film a shot was cut in showing me landing on the roof from out of camera range to complete the jump.

Jumping stunts, whether on horseback or with motorcycles and cars, have always been some of the most exciting moments seen on the screen.

Chapter #36
"A CHALLENGE A DAY KEEPS AGE AWAY"

By now I'm sure you're well aware of the fact that my entire life has been devoted to the problems of the body and physical fitness. When I was young I wanted to be a doctor and this interest has stayed with me through the years. My self improvement research library (which is considered to be the most complete in the field) was built up through my determination to acquire every book and article on the subject ever written. Keeping this up to date is still an important project of mine. And, with my accompanying photo library, containing thousands of appropriate illustrations, I am always ready for immediate publication of my new books in this field.

Some years back I found myself over thirty pounds overweight, for the first time in my life. This forced me to do research on calories, and out of the necessity of the situation my "little red calorie book" was born. This constantly updated book contains all information on the subject and to my delight has been endorsed by thousands of doctors, with its sales now climbing over the ten million mark. So, losing that thirty pounds wasn't so bad after all.

Well, time keeps flying by at an amazing pace and I now find myself in the ranks of the "senior citizens". I am always asked for advice on keeping fit and staying healthy with regard to the years that all of us are adding. Today the average life expectancy is almost twenty years longer than it was half a century ago. In the past a man of sixty was considered to be an old man, while today many at eighty are just catching their second breath. Staying youthful and staying healthy are one and the same goal. The human body is a great piece of mechanism which our creator has given us. It has its own transportation system, its own construction system and its own waste disposal system—most people never giving all this a thought, as they take these complex functions for granted. If you help your body a little bit, it will help you back a lot. The right vitamin capsule in the morning, which makes up for vitamins you miss in your food, is a great aid. And, proper exercise at least once a day, to assist the body's two most important functions—**circulation** and **elimination**, also cannot be stressed strongly enough.

I learned a long time ago that there's nothing you can do for tomorrow until tomorrow comes. So, worrying about business does not keep me from getting a good night's sleep. And, sometimes if you sleep on a problem, when you get up in the morning many times it has worked its way clear in your subconscious mind.

A fighter would say that you must always

Old friends meet in later years:
(Top Row) With Hope Hampton at the opening of her night club act & swapping stories with Al Baffert.
(Bottom Row) Screen writer Jack Natteford and former Western Star Ed Cobb bring back memories of old days at Universal—Harvey Parry & Paul Malvern remind me of near fatal stunts—Harvey & Paul join Cecil Whitworth for a funny story.

"roll with the punches". This is good advice for anyone. In life I have had many disappointments, going way back to my days in Hollywood. A director might have called me to make a screen test for a part, at a casting director's suggestion.

After a few days have passed I'm told to come over to the studio to sign my contract—and then nothing happens. Something goes wrong with the picture being scheduled and there is no contract.

Well, some people might take things like this to heart very badly—I would just say it's another train I missed. Even in business I've been promised big orders which never came through. But, this doesn't get me down, for around the corner there are always two or three challenges waiting for me to sink my teeth into them.

Life is a gamble all the time, whether you're gambling with cards or with stocks on Wall Street. And, believe me, it's important to be an expert in whatever field you're in. If you're not as good or better than the next guy, drop out it doesn't pay. Competition is great when you're competing

as top man, but it takes an expert to know when to quit, or as in cards, know when to throw your hand away. As for business projects, if they're not money makers, take your loss and bow out.

One thing which I strongly believe is that life is an endless cycle. Everything tends to repeat and renew itself. And so it has been in my life. I have been very fortunate to be able to turn many reverses and disappointments into successes. Some of my darkest hours have led to my brightest triumphs.

In the course of writing this book I hope I've gotten across the fact that I'm a pretty happy and, I think, lucky guy. Everything just didn't fall in my lap. I'm the kind of person who works hard to reach a goal and there have been darn few I've missed. At the present time, although I'm now past 65, I'm busier than I ever was during my most hectic days out in Hollywood. I work more than 10 hours a day and sometimes put in 6 or 7 working days a week. But, I'm happy with what I'm doing, which I guess is one of the secrets of a well balanced life. I hope that you don't

(Above) Close to 50 years have passed and Jack Dempsey and I are still great pals.
(Below) While on a recent trip to California, Ethel, Joan and I ran a special showing of THE CHINA-TOWN MYSTERY (my only starring serial still in existence) for my grandsons Ricky and Ronnie. The boys got a great kick out of watching Grandpa track down all the villains and recover the "secret formula."

think that I neglect the social side of life with all this work—I find time to entertain friends and business associates from out of town at some of New York's leading night spots, while my still beautiful Ethel continues to draw praise for her dancing.

Little Joanie? She grew up to be an attractive and talented young woman. She became a member of the New York City Ballet Company, was a featured dancer in Olsen and Johnson's PARDON MY FRENCH, danced on television's COMEDY HOUR and was later associated with such performers as Bobby Clark, Danny Thomas, Skitch Henderson, Faye Emerson and many others. She later went on to the West Coast, got married and presented Ethel and myself with two wonderful grandchildren—Ricky (born in 1955) and Ronnie (born in 1957). We are fortunate in being able to visit them often and maintain an office and apartment in Beverly Hills.

Well, you think the old Bonomo has changed in recent years? That's not so! I have an exercise table in my office, do my "daily dozen" every day and then prepare for the day's stunts . . . **promotional** stunts, that is! My offices and sales

rooms are still in that same building at 1841 Broadway in New York City, but nobody ever falls down the richly carpeted stairs, drowns in the fancy drinking fountain or breaks their bones slipping on my highly polished floors. So, compared to Hollywood, it's pretty dull stuff, but it makes money and Ethel doesn't have to worry about me anymore.

One of my favorite projects, which I have looked forward to doing for many years, is now approaching reality. it is my FAMILY ENCYCLOPEDIA OF HEALTH AND VITAL LIVING, a complete 16 volume set which I believe can be of great aid to every member of almost every family. With the government's recent emphasis on health and physical fitness, and national interest pointing in those directions, I think we are certainly working on a worthwhile endeavor.

Life is good to me and I'm thankful for it. Whatever happiness and success has come to me, I feel did not wander my way by accident. Each person, whether young or old, can fulfill the dream or his or her life by just working at it. Perhaps that's the secret of the happy life we all search for.

• • •

WOW! Putting this book together was almost as much work as re-living half my life. But it all happened just as you see it in these pages and I hope you've enjoyed it.